"In David Helvarg's r   [tivist,] he has participated in and repo____ [   ] events of the last five decades, from the Vietnam War to Hurricane Katrina. Throughout his odyssey, Helvarg's love of the sea has provided him both a cause to fight for and a cure for his ills. In *Saved by the Sea*, the reader will discover why he cares, and why he continues to fight for the oceans—and why we all need to."

—Ted Danson, actor

"[Helvarg] possesses a narrative skill that makes his story readable and an intrepid spirit that makes his story worth reading."

—Jim Toomey, cartoonist of *Sherman's Lagoon*

"Writing is a kind of art. In telling of his life and love of the sea David Helvarg has created a narrative masterpiece. Read this book to learn about how this wild man has come to dedicate himself to our living ocean, but mostly read *Saved by the Sea* for the pure salty pleasure of it."

—Wyland, marine life artist and conservationist

"David Helvarg dives into our endangered-ocean crisis through the prism of his often endangered life. His memoir of the sea is full of compassion and concern."

—Paul R. Ehrlich,
president of Stanford's Center for Conservation Biology

"In this important yet eminently readable book, David Helvarg skillfully weaves together three narrative strands—the life in our oceans, his own colorful life, and the impact that politics, culture, and industry have had on both."

—Roz Savage, ocean rower and author of *Rowing the Atlantic*

"Ever since the publication of his wave-making book *Blue Frontier* in 2001, David Helvarg has become the premier chronicler of America's complex relationship with our oceans and coasts, our last frontier. . . . In his new book, *Saved by the Sea*, Helvarg adds a new and moving dimension to his work by exploring his own personal relationships with the ocean and the three main women in his life: his mother, girlfriend, and sister."

—*Honolulu Weekly*

Saved
by the Sea

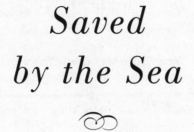

ALSO BY DAVID HELVARG

The Golden Shore: California's Love Affair with the Sea

Rescue Warriors: The U.S. Coast Guard, America's Forgotten Heroes

Blue Frontier: Dispatches from America's Ocean Wilderness

50 Ways to Save the Ocean

*The War Against the Greens: The "Wise-Use" Movement,
the New Right, and the Browning of America*

Saved
by the Sea

Hope, Heartbreak,
and Wonder
in the Blue World

David Helvarg

New World Library
Novato, California

New World Library
14 Pamaron Way
Novato, California 94949

Text design by Kathryn Parise
Photos are courtesy of the author's collection except chapter 4, courtesy of John Hoagland

Library of Congress Cataloging-in-Publication Data
Helvarg, David, date.
Saved by the sea : hope, heartbreak, and wonder in the blue world / David Helvarg. — [First trade paperback edition].
    pages   cm
Includes bibliographical references.
ISBN 978-1-60868-328-4 (paperback) — ISBN 978-1-60868-329-1 (ebook)
1. Helvarg, David, date. 2. Conservationists—United States—Biography.
3. Journalists—United States—Biography. 4. Fisheries. 5. Marine resources conservation. 6. Marine biology. I. Title.
QH91.3.H45A3 2015
333.95'16092—dc23
[B]   2014045138

First paperback printing, April 2015
ISBN 978-1-60868-328-4
Originally published in hardcover by Thomas Dunne Books/St. Martin's Press, May 2010 (ISBN 978-0-312-56706-4)
Printed in Canada on 100% postconsumer-waste recycled paper

10 9 8 7 6 5 4 3 2 1

To the Seaweed Rebels

Contents

Whatever attention this book may gain, and whatever favor it may find, I shall owe almost entirely to that interest in the sea, and those who follow it, which is so easily excited in us all.

Richard Henry Dana Jr.,
Two Years Before the Mast, 1840

Introduction

Into the Blue

The reason why I love the sea I cannot explain. It's physical. When you dive, you begin to feel like you're an angel.

JACQUES COUSTEAU

I'm free-falling past a rocky wall, gradually accelerating into the cooler, darker waters of Belize's Blue Hole when a large cavern appears below and the dive master, who's been fast drifting into the depths, stops and puts a vertical hand atop his head—the signal for shark. Though I look around and fail to see one, I know they're here. I'd just spotted a couple of fins while bobbing on the surface. I hold up at 150 feet and enter the cavern swimming around huge column-thick stalactites in what was once part of a massive cave complex before the roof fell in thousands of years ago. After eight minutes of exploring this underwater Howe Caverns, and undoing the chest strap on my buoyancy control vest so that my friend Scott can get a shot of me in my SEAWEED REBEL T-shirt, it's time to return to the surface. This is why they call it a "bounce dive." At this depth we don't have much time before the nitrogen building up in our tissues threatens us with the bends. But if we keep our bottom time short, we won't have to do a long decompression stop on the way back up.

Our small group halts at ninety feet, gathering near a sandy ledge as the dive master points up. Thirty feet above us half a dozen large Caribbean reef and bull sharks are circling. Soon I notice more cruising below me. We begin making our way toward the surface along an underwater dune as a dozen of the curious six- to eight-foot sharks slide past us, just beyond reach. But unlike the shallow-water nurse sharks that some retrograde divers like to grab on to and pet, no one attempts to harass these big fellas. Bulls are responsible for more human deaths than any other shark species, though, for prudence's sake, I'd also keep my distance from whites, makos, and tigers. Some dive charter companies in the Pacific, Mexico, and the Caribbean now promote "shark dives" where they chum the waters to draw large sharks to their boat and then place their paying customers on the bottom to feed and "interact" with the animals, with one human fatality and a number of injuries to date. This is not so different from tourists feeding jelly doughnuts and sandwiches to the bears in Yellowstone National Park, except the park rangers figured out how stupid and dangerous that was years ago and banned the practice. If you want to encounter wild animals in their natural settings it's best to do so without lures and bait. The thrill of the encounter can be just as spectacular.

I met an old local in Hawaii with a ding in the bridge of his nose where he had done a face-plant bodysurfing the Big Island's Disappearing Sands Beach. He told me how he and his brother were out surfing Hilo Bay one day, sitting on their boards between sets, and his brother said, "I don't remember there being a

sandbar here." "There isn't," he replied. "Yes, there is. I'm standing on it." Just then a big tiger shark swam out from under his
brother's feet, circled around, and bit the end off his surfboard.
It's like naturalist author Ed Abbey used to say: "If there's not
something bigger and meaner than you are out there it's not
really wilderness." Or like my fellow Californian Ken Kelton told
me after a great white lifted his kayak fifteen feet in the air,
shaking it vigorously like a chew toy with a rattle inside: "The
ocean is a dangerous place, but it's also a place you can still go
and have to yourself, a place that's clean and, yes, wild. If you go
into the ocean you're making a choice. You need to know you
can drown, you can get lost, or you can be eaten by great beasts."

I've always been drawn to the sea and its alluring dangers,
although it took me thirty years to overcome my schizophrenic
lifestyle as a journalist and private investigator. I'd go off to cover
wars, epidemics, and politics or work wrongful death and homi-
cide cases just so I could get home to the beach. My water time
was spent bodysurfing, snorkeling, sailing, kayaking, scuba diving, or just lying in the sand like some herring-besotted harbor
seal, my mind adrift and my skin slowly salt frying.

Finally, around the turn of the century, I was able to focus
my energies as an investigative reporter on the waste, fraud, and
abuse that's contributing to the ocean's unprecedented ecological decline. After writing the ocean book I'd always wanted to
write and losing the love I'd always sought, I decided to dedicate
the remaining few decades of my life to the protection, exploration, and restoration of our living seas, including those residents
of the big blue who were now checking me out as a large, awk-
ward, potential prey item.

Still, the odds are unfairly stacked. Every year some five to
eight humans are killed by sharks worldwide while we kill one

hundred million of these sleek, slow-growing apex predators, emptying the seas of sharks just as we once rid the plains of saber-toothed tigers and mammoth. Only now that we've left the savannah behind and become the planet's top predator, maybe we ought to take a deep breath and consider where it is we first came from.

Salt water covers 71 percent of Earth's surface and provides 97 percent of its livable habitat, from the shark fins I saw breaking the surface to the lowest point on earth, seven miles down in the Mariana Trench near Guam, where only three humans have ever ventured. And remember that deep breath I just mentioned? Although the tropical rain forests have been called the lungs of the planet, the oceans actually absorb far greater amounts of carbon dioxide. Microscopic phytoplankton in the top layer of the sea acts as a biological pump, extracting some 2.5 billion tons of organic carbon out of the atmosphere annually, replacing it with about half the life-giving oxygen we need to survive. The top two feet of seawater contain as much heat as the entire atmosphere. It was only in the last few years that scientists, looking at their computer models of industrial carbon dioxide emissions, were able to figure out why the atmosphere wasn't heating up at an even faster rate. The answer to that riddle, they discovered, is that the ocean has been absorbing about a third of our anthropogenic (human-generated) carbon dioxide.

While the ocean is the crucible of life on our planet, photosynthesis of carbon dioxide by marine plankton and land-based plants was thought to be the basis of all organic life in the universe—until 1977, when scientists aboard a deep-diving research submarine off the Galápagos Islands discovered sulfurous hot-water vents eight thousand feet below the surface. These vents are colonized by giant red-feathered tube worms, big white clams, crabs, and other animals that contain sulfur-burning bacteria, which provide an alternative basis for sustaining life. Now NASA scientists believe similar "chemosynthetic" life-forms may exist around volcanic deepwater ocean vents beneath the icy crust of Jupiter's moon Europa.

To date we've mapped less than 10 percent of the ocean, but we've mapped 100 percent of the moon and Mars. The funny thing is that when we send probes to Mars, other parts of the solar system, and beyond, what's the first thing we look for as a sign of life? Water! And here we have a whole blue swimming pool of a planet that we hardly connect with even though we all evolved on both an individual and evolutionary basis from salt water. We all went through a fish stage in the womb (there's even a book, *Your Inner Fish*, written about this). Our bodies, like the planet, are 71 percent salt water, our blood exactly as salty as the sea (when our ancestors emerged from it). This fact may explain why it's easier to fall asleep to the sound of the ocean. The rhythm of the waves is like our mother's heartbeat. For seven years I lived in a cliff house in San Diego that shook when the storm waves rolled in every winter. I never slept better in my life.

After the Blue Hole we dive a coral wall and some swim-through caverns where our air bubbles, rolling along the roof like silver pirate doubloons, are investigated by big-eyed orange squirrelfish and more cautious, antennae-probing lobsters before percolating through the porous stone.

We're off Half Moon Caye in the Lighthouse Reef area. I watch a ray with a six-foot wingspan feasting on a field of queen conchs.

Unfortunately, queen conchs are increasingly hard to find elsewhere in the Caribbean due to overfishing.

When I first came to Belize in 1980, escaping from Central America's nearby wars, we'd eat lobster every day on Caye Caulker, with occasional conch fritters and turtle steaks. Now the nearshore lobster and conch populations are depleted, but the sea turtles are protected, and the island, once home to a small fishing community of fewer than one hundred people, has its own airport runway, bars, restaurants, hotels, and a permanent population of 1,500 catering to laid-back twentysomething tourists who still follow the Gringo trail even though it has expanded to a freeway. Where I once saw an American crocodile sunning itself by a fast-flowing open-water mangrove cut in the coral island there's now a storm-damaged quay and scrapwood bar advertising A SUNNY PLACE FOR SHADY PEOPLE.

At our dive site there are big luminescent jade parrot fish grazing the reef, their beaks making scraping sounds as they eat coral and poot sand, a major source of replenishment for those white-sand tropical beaches we all like to visit. I also spot a field of garden eels swaying in the current like living prairie grass.

Having been on the water since dawn, including several hours bucking five-foot seas to get out here, accompanied only by chevron-tailed frigates, flying fish, and dolphins, we take a lunch break on Half Moon Caye. This wild coconut palm and white coral sand (parrot fish excreted) island is chockablock with big chunks of bleached coral and conch shells tossed up by hurricanes: one red-tinged shell has turned to limestone after being colonized by coral. Out on the lagoon's reef line a large storm-wrecked freighter has turned into a silver and rust-tinged monument to bad luck navigation.

A walk through the mangrove, past orange-blossomed ziri-cote and gumbo-limbo trees, brings me to an old metal observation tower. Shooing a large lizard off the second step of its ladder, I climb to the top and find myself alone among hundreds of croaking, whistling, blue-footed boobies who've colonized the tops of the mangroves with their penthouse views of the aqua, azure, jade, cobalt, and cerulean blues of the Caribbean Sea.

Later, after finishing a simple culinary delight of stewed chicken, plantain, coleslaw, and orange soda, we do a final dive at a site known as the Aquarium.

Along with its predictable litter of colorful fish (hundreds of grunts, wrasses, yellowtail snapper, French angels, sergeant majors, tangs, triggers, and two large groupers who accompany us throughout the dive), this site also has many big healthy corals along with gorgonians, sea whips, and barrel sponges the size of wine barrels. Swimming past the reef's outer wall at seventy feet, above a three-thousand-foot drop-off with dark branching corals the size of scrub oaks thrusting out from its narrow ledges, I feel like I'm flying with the eagles (or eagle rays), unburdened by the drag of gravity, which I am, being neutrally buoyant.

I'm feeling elated and alive and wishing my late love, Nancy Ledansky, were here with me, which she is, in a way, in my heart. I never feel sad when I'm underwater, on a boat, rushing in a curling wave, or walking by the edge of the sea. Coming back to Belize twenty-five years after covering its independence during a time of war and uncertainty and finding its outer atolls still healthy and vibrant above and below gladdens me in a way that's hard to express even for a saltwater-saturated writer. All I know is, when I encounter healthy living seas and blue frontiers—be they in Australia, Alaska, or Antarctica—it makes me feel closer to the wildness around me and to the ones I love, even those who've crossed over the bar. As Henry David Thoreau once put it, "Heaven is under our feet as well as over our heads. . . . We need the tonic of wildness." I'd just amend that to say heaven is also under our flippers.

1

Swamp Fox

I really don't know why it is that all of us are so committed to the sea, except I think it's because in addition
to the fact that the sea changes, and the light changes,
and ships change, it's because we all came from the sea.

JOHN F. KENNEDY

The sea, like death, has been a theme in my life; it has provided
rapture, joy, solitude, and solace at different points along the
journey.

I've nearly drowned in big waves off San Diego and Hawaii,
been rammed by a minke whale off Antarctica and shipwrecked

in the Sea of Cortés. I've swum with bull sharks, whale sharks, barracuda, lionfish, sea snakes, stonefish, and giant manta rays; had guns leveled at me at a guerrilla ambush near the beach in El Salvador, almost crashed in a Coast Guard helicopter off the hurricane-damaged coast of Texas; been sickened and storm tossed in the Atlantic, Pacific, and Southern Oceans. I've been sunburned and sand blasted, cut by coral, stung by jellyfish, stabbed by a sea urchin, have run out of air eighty feet below the surface, and still can't get enough of the everlasting sea.

Days after my life's love died I dreamed of Cedar Key, Florida, with its pelicans, oyster reefs, and warm Gulf waters full of mullet. The pelicans were floating at the end of a small road that dropped off into the water. *Nancy would love this place*, I think in my dream. I wake to the taste of salt water, my own tears streaming down my face. Like sea turtles, sawfish, and the people you love, waterfront communities that retain their historic maritime qualities—Cedar Key; Hilo, Hawaii; and Port Orford, Oregon— have also become endangered species.

My friends and I had a reunion in the Ocean Beach section of San Diego, one of those unspoiled surfer towns where I spent a decade one endless summer, tanning and bodysurfing by Lifeguard Tower 4. We'd fought off the developers who wanted to build beachfront high-rises and a marina that would have killed the surf break, and because we won and OB retains its early sixties Southern California beach town feel, the stucco surfer shacks we saved from the bulldozers are now going, even in a recession, for over half a million dollars each, and affordability is the new activist issue.

The other new issue is water quality. San Diego is the last major American coastal city that doesn't have secondary sewage treatment but rather dumps all its untreated effluent in deep waters at the end of a three-mile pipeline. At the same time, because San Diego is a conservative town that doesn't believe in paying taxes and almost always votes down new bond issues, the city can afford to replace only about thirty miles out of its six thousand miles of sewer lines every year. Since most of these pipes were not built to last two hundred years, the city, famed as a tourist-friendly beach town, is now experiencing periodic sewage breaks and beach closures in OB and other communities along the shore.

One of the only local politicians willing to fight for clean water is city councilwoman Donna Frye. A surfer and the wife of famed 1960s soul surfer and board shaper Skip Frye, Donna first became active in the 1990s, when she saw Skip and his friends getting sick after long sessions in the sea. She traced the problem to San Diego's stormwater runoff. A Los Angeles study found one in twenty-five people swimming near stormwater outflows got sick from pollution-related illnesses, mainly stomach flu and upper respiratory infections. The risk of getting sick was 57 percent greater for them than for those who swam farther away from the outlets.

So Donna helped craft a bill that set statewide standards for water quality, required weekly testing of recreational beaches, and ordered warning signs and hotlines to inform the public if their coastal waters were polluted. It passed into law in 1997.

A few years after that the Surfrider Foundation helped pass the federal Beaches Environmental Assessment and Coastal Health (BEACH) Act, a national version of California's law that requires coastal states to test their waters for pollutants and inform the public of the results. Surfrider is a chapter-based group of surfers and other water folk who, tired of going into the ocean for their stoke (excitement) and coming out with ear infections, banded together to fight pollution and protect standing waves. One of their early anti–oil pollution slogans was, "No Way, Dude. We Don't Want Your Crude!" Today they have over fifty thousand members in eighty chapters around the world.

In Ocean Beach the San Diego chapter holds an annual Clean Water Paddle Out around the municipal pier that draws hundreds of participants, including the Fryes.

Once I photographed it from the pier, a sinuous broken line of some five hundred surfers observed from above by scores of anglers, mostly Hispanic and Vietnamese, who were fishing for mackerel, bass, and queenfish. Gulls and big brown pelicans perched on the pier's scarred wooden rails, waiting for a handout or fumbled fish. Looking up Sunset Cliffs, I could see my old cliff house and out to sea sailboats heeling over in a freshening breeze as the sky quilted over with clouds and the air tasted of salt and iodine, the ocean at its finest, full of users and protectors.

On the fourth or fifth night of the reunion several of my friends got green OB tattoos on their arms and legs. The O was a peace sign with an up-thrust fist through its center. Although tattoos have a strong maritime tradition going back to Polynesian seafarers, I never wanted one. They have a bad association for me. A number of my parents' friends had strings of blue numbers tattooed on their forearms. My parents told me not to ask about them, saying they'd gotten the tattoos in "the camps."

My parents were both immigrants from across the sea: my father, his sister, and their widowed mother fled the civil war that engulfed the Ukraine following the Russian Revolution; my mother, Eva, her parents, and sisters were among the last German Jews to get out alive.

Having escaped to Holland after my grandfather's torture and mock execution by the Nazis, my mother's family booked passage on the SS *Rotterdam* in December 1939, on its final trip before the Nazis invaded. The night before they were to leave, another liner, the *Simon Bolivar*, headed to the West Indies, hit a mine and sank. Dozens of the girls' young schoolmates drowned. It took two weeks for the overcrowded *Rotterdam* and its seasick passengers to make it across the wide Atlantic to Hoboken, New Jersey. It was too foggy to see the Statue of Liberty in the harbor, but they could see the illuminated Wrigley's chewing gum sign on Staten Island.

My father, Max Helvarg, was already living in the United States. Years earlier, as a nine-year-old boy, he'd been among a handful of survivors who'd hidden in an attic for a week while his small town was ransacked and burned and all the other Jews living there killed by Ukrainian bandits. With his widowed mother and younger sister, Sue, he'd fled across the border and the snow-covered fields of Romania, often carrying Sue on his back. They finally made their way to the Black Sea port of Constanţa, where they sailed for the United States on the liner *King Alexander*. It took thirty days to make the passage through the Dardanelles to Constantinople (now Istanbul), past Athens, Gibraltar, and across the Atlantic to New York. There in the harbor they saw Lady Liberty with her inscribed poem "The New Colossus" by Emma Lazarus, which reads in part: "Here at our sea-washed, sunset gates shall stand/A mighty woman with a torch whose flame/Is the imprisoned lightning, and her name/Mother of Exiles."

They arrived at Ellis Island on September 22, 1922. Soon their uncle came and took them on the subway to Coney Island, where he lived. Max and Sue were certain they'd never get out of this hole in the ground they'd been taken into. Then they were out of it and riding in the light, the elevated train taking them above the buildings, the river, and to the seashore, to freedom.

My parents' stories have been repeated, with unique family variations, by millions of people over the generations. Close to 90 percent of North Americans are descendants of shipborne immigrants who came to the New World fleeing poverty and oppression, often traveling in steerage, the cheapest accommodations located by the rudder lines that "steered" their ships. Others survived the dark Middle Passage as kidnap victims in the hulls of slave ships while another million Americans can trace their roots back thousands of years to a land bridge that once spanned the Bering Sea.

Years after their arrival in the United States my mother would meet my father while tapping his phone in Allied-occupied Berlin, where they both worked for Army Intelligence. A few weeks later he approached her at a party saying, "Young ladies shouldn't be listening in on other people's conversations." She was a dark beauty. He was ruggedly handsome. A few months later they married. My sister and I followed shortly thereafter and then, after four years, they separated like a pair of wild dolphins who'd fulfilled their biological purpose.

I was born in 1951. In the blink of an eye since that time 90 percent of the large pelagic (open-ocean) creatures—including sharks, big tuna, marlin, cod, and sailfish—have disappeared. Actually, they didn't disappear. We know where they went. Onto our plates, mostly in the white linen restaurants, supermarkets, and fast-food joints of the developed world, to Japan, the United States, and Europe, where it was not hunger but appetite that drove this new war of extermination, unraveling the wonder and diversity of planetary life over three billion years in the making.

Most of the one billion people who depend on marine wildlife as their primary source of animal protein aren't even from wealthy fish-consuming countries like Japan, Canada, and Norway but rather from places such as Ghana, Liberia, Peru, Fiji, the Philippines, and India, where they work in "artisan" small-boat fishing communities that don't have the technologies to take fish faster than they can reproduce. Only when foreign factory trawlers, long-liners, and illegal fish pirates come into their waters have they seen their food source and livelihood disappear—with devastating consequences for both people and animals. One recent study of an unintended consequence, or "blowback," found that, with the loss of marine wildlife off West Africa to foreign fishing boats, there has been an increased take of "bush meat," of terrestrial African wildlife including rare and endangered species such as chimpanzees. Strangely, some people express a profound concern about the loss of top apex predators and primates on land—lions, bears, eagles, orangutans, and so on—while blithely continuing to eat their marine equivalents such as sharks, bluefin tuna, goliath grouper, and minke whales.

We also worry about the loss of wilderness habitat, complaining about the clear-cutting of ancient old-growth rain forests on land, yet we fail to appreciate that much of our wild fish catch comes from bottom-trawling gear that functions like the chain saws and bulldozers of the sea. Bottom-trawl fishing vessels use wide-mouthed nets pulled along the seabed by chains and held open by steel slabs called otter doors that can weigh several tons. Scallop and clam dredges are made of chain-mail bags and bar spreaders that drag across the bottom like heavy plows, stirring up huge sediment plumes that create a kind of oceanic smog. A number of studies and observations have shown bottom dragging causes massive damage to complex sea bottoms, plants, and animals, including sponge and coral communities. Each year trawlers scour benthic (sea floor) areas about the size of the United States and Canada combined, leaving little but rubble, cobble, and scraped mudflats in their wake. People don't seem to know or to care. Out of sight, out of mind. There's always another fish in the sea.

A 2008 study in the journal *Science* concluded that 40 percent of the world's oceans are now heavily impacted by human activities, including overfishing and varied forms of pollution (nutrient, plastic, chemical), while only 4 percent remain in a pristine state (I've heard 5). These days, sailing across the ocean, you're more likely to see a shipping container fallen off a large vessel or a tangle of abandoned fishing gear than a blue whale or a black marlin. Add to that the huge impacts of fossil fuel–fired climate change on the marine environment—including Arctic melting, coral bleaching, and ocean acidification—and you can understand my natural anxiety that my last great love is also sick unto dying.

I wish I could say my first childhood memory was of dolphins, but actually it was of bears. After my parents broke up, my mom moved to Jackson, New Hampshire, with my sister and me. When I was between two and four we lived in a small rented cottage across the road from a ski resort where she worked as a waitress. I remember one morning when she called us into the kitchen and lifted us onto the cottage's countertop next to the sink. Outside the window on a low ridge behind the house a mother bear was leading her two cubs through the snow along the edge of the woods, silhouetted against a chalk white sky. "See, they're just like us," I think my mother said.

My sister, Deborah, and I used to walk down the road beating a pan with a tin cup to ward off the bears. I remember another time Deborah pulled me out of the snow after we'd gone to see some chickens in an open coop and I'd gotten stuck in a two-foot drift.

From age four to seven we were back in a duplex in Bayside, New York, where we had previously lived with our dad. I remember the sapling out front that my dad had planted when I was born (my sister got a rosebush) and a pet dachshund that got run over on my fifth birthday.

And of course there were the family stories, like the time Deborah was eight and hanging out with these older twin sisters, Diane and Denise, up the block. One day she came home to ask our mother what *fuck* meant. Eva sat her down on the couch and patiently explained that this was a very bad word one should never use and that it meant fornicate, which is what men and women do to express love and to make babies. Deborah nodded solemnly, ran downstairs to the front of the house, and shouted up the street excitedly, "Diane, Denise. Fuck means to fornicate!"

Though I'm sure it's not related, shortly thereafter Eva moved us to a rented house in Douglaston, on the north shore of Queens, at the far eastern edge of New York City. Even though we were still technically in the city, there were fourteen acres of woods behind our house, running from Northern Boulevard all the way to the Long Island Rail Road tracks. On the other side of the tracks, behind our elementary school, PS 98, there was a big swamp edging Little Neck Bay, Long Island Sound, and the ocean beyond.

I spent my youth tromping the woods with Lady, our collie dog, playing Swamp Fox in the wetlands, jumping off the pilings at the dock on the bay, and begging for weekend trips to Jones Beach, the ten-mile-long barrier island across Long Island's Great South Bay that still draws some eight million New Yorkers to the ocean every summer.

Swamp Fox was a TV miniseries by Disney about Francis Marion, a guerrilla hero of the Revolutionary War, who would ambush the British and then retreat to his sanctuary deep in the swamps of South Carolina. My friends and I tried to re-create his adventures, heading into our own swamp every day after school, moving along well-trodden paths we had tramped down through the tall rushes and cattails to our hidden "encampments" that we built of reeds, including igloolike hutches you could climb into. We'd fight running Revolutionary War battles using stick muskets and dirt clod grenades, occasionally startling pheasants into flight and getting our sneakers and pants soaking wet in the brackish waters by the edge of the sound.

We also paid tribute to our imaginary dead by the pheasant burial ground on the railroad tracks that separated our natural retreat from Northern Boulevard and Kiddy City, our local amusement park and arcade. Here, along about ten yards of track, piles of bird bones lay as mute testament to what happens at the intersection of trains and avian flight paths. In lieu of medals we'd lay pennies on the track and wait for the trains to flatten them into small copper pans. We never laid down more than a few at a time, however, since it was an article of faith in our boys' culture that twelve or more pennies in a row would derail a train.

In the winter, against our families' stern warnings, we'd head out onto the ice that covered the swamp and the edge of the sound, skating and sliding along until one cloudy day two of my friends, Philip and Eddie, fell through into freezing waist-deep water. After helping them crawl out all three of us hid in the basement furnace room of Philip's apartment, drying our clothing and taking a self-protective pledge of silence lest our parents find out. Our waking days divided nicely into three parts, school for eight hours, off on our outdoor expeditions for three or four hours, then home for dinner.

I don't want to sound like the boomer curmudgeon I may have become, but between suburban sprawl, media hysteria about children at risk of stranger abduction, and the addictive worlds of video gaming and shopping malls most of today's youth don't get much unstructured time in nature. And being driven to adult-supervised swim practice and soccer games just doesn't provide the same calorie-burning and wonder-enhancing benefits. Rich Louv, a San Diego author I know, has written a whole book about this disturbing trend, *Last Child in the Woods*. He's also coined a term to explain kids' shortened attention spans and declining physical fitness, Nature-Deficit Disorder.

Still, one place that hasn't been entirely paved over and where I still see lots of kids running wild as their nature befits is along the edge of the sea.

Our fourth-grade teacher, Mrs. Olsen, was the daughter of a Long Island sea captain and used to bring maritime mementos into class, including the six-foot serrated bill from a giant sawfish her father had caught. Today I have a pair of crossed freshwater sawfish bills on my living room wall, given to me by a gun-smuggling Sandinista fishing boat captain back in 1980 after we spent several days netting the four- and five-hundred-pound monsters on Lake Nicaragua, which is also home to freshwater tarpon and deadly freshwater bull sharks that migrate up the San Juan River from the Atlantic. Unfortunately, many of these sharks have since been slaughtered by fishermen on the Costa Rican side of the river and their fins sold to Asian buyers for the making of shark fin soup.

Mrs. Olsen tried to instill in us a sense of what it meant to live on a large mid-Atlantic island, even one rapidly turning into a vast network of metropolitan bedroom communities.

Queens wasn't the only part of New York City that retained its connection to the sea. Manhattan still had commercial shipping piers at the time, Brooklyn had Coney Island with its aquarium and beluga whales and its historic boardwalk where we got to visit one of the last famed amusement parks, Steeplechase, and ride its tracked wooden race horses out of the great pavilion and along the shore. The borough of Staten Island, just a ferry ride from Manhattan, had more in common with eastern Long Island's duck farms and Montauk's fishing docks than with the nearby megalopolis. Its economy was based on truck farming and commercial fishing. Only with the completion, in 1964, of the Verrazano-Narrows Bridge that connected it to Brooklyn did Staten Island transform from a maritime outpost into a suburban bedroom community for city workers and the Mob.

Flying into JFK in 2009, I pass over the port of Newark, the second largest in the United States after LA/Long Beach, except that LA's port is not really a harbor but a jutting seawall designed to protect container ships and oil tankers from the Pacific's fetch. Newark, by contrast, is at the end of a serpentine network of

rivers, natural channels, and doglegs already well known to local tribes when Henry Hudson first explored them in 1609.

Looking down from ten thousand feet at today's Staten Island,
just beyond the port, is like seeing a floating piece of densely ur-
banized LA pushed up close against New Jersey. The plane then
crosses the New York Bight, passing over Sandy Hook, the narrow barrier island park that marks the top of the 127-mile-long
Jersey shore, backed onto the Shrewsbury and Navesink Rivers
and the nineteenth-century Twin Lights of the Navesink, once
the brightest lighthouse in North America. These rivers still contain large edible striped bass and healthy quahog clam beds
thanks to the work of coastal clean-water activists from citizen
groups like Clean Ocean Action and the American Littoral Society. From the other side of the aircraft, passengers can see Coney
Island's Parachute Drop. We bank into our final approach, and I
can look along the sandy south shore of Long Island as far out as
Fire Island before we pass over the empty early March parking lots
and deserted ocean strand of Jones Beach, perhaps Robert Moses's
greatest contribution to the city. We cross the Great South Bay,
and drop over Jamaica Bay, where sea-level rise is already changing the nature of the salt marsh, inundating it at a rate of 3 percent a year since at least 1994. A few seconds later we make a
smooth landing to the cheers of a California eighth-grade class
on a school trip. I'm here to talk about the ocean to some college
kids and professors at St. John's University in Queens.

Eighty percent of New York City remains disconnected from
the U.S. mainland, though its system of bridges and tunnels makes
it hard for most residents to appreciate their unique urban reality. In the immediate wake of the September 11 attacks on the
Twin Towers half a million people were evacuated from Lower
Manhattan by a fleet of ferries, tugs, and workboats in the largest

maritime rescue in world history. In 2006 I spoke to a group of fourth-graders on a field trip in Lower Manhattan. Afterward a little girl in the front of the group raised her hand.

"Is that a real island?"

"Is what a real island?" I asked.

"What you said Queens and Brooklyn is a part of."

By the time I was a fourth-grader I was determined I'd grow up to be a frogman. This was before Jacques Cousteau's underwater TV specials began airing in 1966. Back in the late 1950s and early '60s there was another TV show about a scuba diver, a half-hour black-and-white drama series with eerie theme music that my mother, sister, and I used to watch every week. It was called *Sea Hunt* and starred actor Lloyd Bridges as underwater investigator Mike Nelson. Later I'd discover a whole generation of marine biologists, oceanographers, and explorers were also inspired by Bridges's fictional exploits, which often involved underwater knife fights and cut air hoses.

My town's class divisions were defined by water, by whether you were a member of the Dock or the Club. Douglaston's classic white country club sat on a hill a few blocks from the shore and was open to the community once a year during its summer festival. Although this was a good time for pie-eating contests and carnival games, it also took much of the mystery out of the Club. Having been given a chance to look over its tennis courts, mowed lawns, and chlorinated swimming pool, those of us who were members of the Dock knew we had the better end of the deal.

The dock extended into Long Island Sound on creosoted wooden pilings from a narrow, rocky beach below a seawall. At its end was a raised platform connected to three pontoon floats.

Here we'd practice cannonballs off the pilings or play dibble, diving after Popsicle sticks that someone would release underwater, or hide under a pontoon.

Wading around the shallows was another kind of adventure, searching the muddy water with our feet for the primitive armored shapes of horseshoe crabs and then lifting them up by their spiky tails for closer inspection. Early on, our boys' culture was divided between those of us who defended the rights of horseshoe crabs to be played with and skipped across the water and those older "hoods" who liked to imprison them in rock corrals and then smash their shells with heavy stones.

I remember after one fight in which, by dint of numbers, we vanquished a group of "hoods," a gray-haired eel fisherman came over to congratulate us, explaining how sometimes you have to fight for creatures who can't fight for themselves.

Today there are thousands of grown-up kids defending horseshoe crabs, American eels, and other creatures threatened with extinction. Along the New Jersey and Delaware shores, where millions of horseshoe crabs have been harvested for eel bait and where the loss of their multitudinous eggs threatens migrating shorebirds, marine activists have won new protections for these animals that were ancient when dinosaurs were the coming thing. Before these protections were in place I watched a horseshoe crab fisherman in the small black-water fishing town of Bedford, New Jersey, a young guy with scraggly dark hair, stained jeans, and a T-shirt, pull live horseshoe crabs he'd collected out of his Boston Whaler and then cut them in half with what looked like a giant paper cutter. As he pulled the blade handle down it sounded like he was slicing through wet cardboard. He'd toss the tails back in the water and dump the crab halves in a box, earning a dollar an animal.

Other people are now trying to defend the endangered American eel, which makes its Homeric journey from the Sargasso Sea along the Gulf Stream, where it splits from its European eel cousins and drifts into the headwaters of North America's eastern rivers. Like salmon and shad, the eel spends part of its life in fresh water and part at sea, although unlike these other fish that mature at sea and spawn in rivers, the snaky-looking eel fish does the reverse. But now its eons-old voyage upriver to mature is hampered by dams, development, and a global seafood market that includes Asian demand for "glass eels," translucent two- to three-inch baby eels, and slightly larger "elvers" that in the 1990s sold for up to three hundred dollars a pound. As a result, the U.S. Fish & Wildlife Service considered adding the eel to the endangered species list, before reversing position like a startled elver in 2007. Certainly the American eel is slightly better off than the European eel, whose population is estimated to have crashed 99 percent in the last two decades.

The summer I was nine my mom worked as a framer at an art gallery in West Hampton. We stayed in a cabin next door to an eel fisherman who'd come home after work with bushel baskets full of writhing two- to four-pound adult eels that he'd then smash on his clamshell driveway. We had lots of free eel that summer. It was okay fried with fresh corn or Tater Tots, but I refused to eat it boiled.

We returned home to Douglaston in time for Hurricane Donna, which swept up the eastern seaboard like a giant freight train that September. Our mom drove Deborah and me down to a street overlooking the dock. We stood there behind the town's two police cruisers with fifty other townspeople in the whipping rain, watching the gray sound's white-capped waves smashing against the seawall, watching the dock swaying side to side until finally the slashing winds tore the wooden slats and rails off their pylons, hurling them into the sky like a runaway fence line. I thought it was the coolest thing I'd ever seen.

My dad, who lived in Manhattan and had us on the weekends, would sometimes take Deborah and me on Circle Line tour boats around Manhattan or to visit the tugboats on the Chelsea docks. During the summer he'd take us to Cleveland, on the south shore of Lake Erie, and drop us off with Aunt Sue and Uncle Al. While Cleveland was not the high point of our young lives, for a few weeks every summer it would prove to be just that. Sue and Al would drive us up to Willoughby on the Lake, a cabin resort area where we'd go swimming and fishing during the day and later catch fireflies in jars while the adults played penny-a-point gin rummy on the screened porch late into the night.

"Aunt Sue taught me girlie things like how to put on makeup but also that a woman has to bait her own hook and clean her own fish," my sister would later recall.

Out past Willoughby there was another great natural phenomenon that I considered almost as cool as hurricanes. This was the place where, as the billboards promised, you could SEE DUCKS WALK ACROSS THE FISHES' BACKS. It was a reservoir spillway on a lake full of carp, and for a quarter they'd sell you a loaf of stale Wonder bread that you could then throw at the fish. They'd swarm so thickly to suck at the bread, that squads of mallard ducks would run across their backs to snatch chunks of bread away from them. You can still visit this eighth wonder of the world today.

Our summers in Ohio also provided a shutter-snap experience of an ecosystem in collapse. Industrial dumping into the Great Lakes was an ongoing and unregulated activity at the time. We'd go out on Uncle Al's aluminum skiff and fish by the U.S. Steel plant where streams of bright orange water shot out from a big elevated pipe directly into Lake Erie. Over the years they put out warning signs that we should no longer eat the bass; next the sheephead (freshwater drum) were put off-limits. Lumps of tar started appearing on the beach, and we'd have to scrub them off our feet with turpentine. Then sudsy detergent foam and dead fish washed ashore. Then they started closing down the beach for swimming as huge clumps of green algae covered the lake's surface. First the closures were for a few days and then for a summer, and then you couldn't swim in Lake Erie anymore.

By 1969 Cleveland's Cuyahoga River, which feeds into the lake, had also started catching fire, the oil slicks and garbage on its surface setting two overhead bridges alight. The decline of Lake Erie and its burning river would become one of the powerful rallying cries and symbols of the emerging environmental movement of the 1970s. The restoration of Lake Erie and the Great Lakes over the following decades through pollution controls and habitat protection would also provide hopeful proof that environmental degradation can often be reversed when wise policies are adopted, allowing natural resiliency to kick in.

It was not pollution but ruthless development that would shake our sense of security at home and confirm an unsettling feeling we'd gotten from our parents, despite their attempts to hide it from us, that history can kick the struts out from under you at any time.

During the parts of summer we were home my mother would set up camp beds for the three of us on the wraparound screened-in back porch that was raised above a sloping hillside facing the woods.

My sister and I would share our nightly ritual before drifting off to sleep to the sound of crickets and an occasional frog.

"Good night."

"Good night."

"Sweet dreams."

"Same to you."

"Thank you."

"You're welcome."

"Good night."

"Good night."

One night around 2 A.M. we all woke to the sound of bulldozers, crunching trees, and Lady's frantic barking. Big yellow machines were pushing down and tearing away the woods behind our house. My mother went out and was told to keep away from the machinery. She began making calls to the police and town officials but to no avail. By early the next morning half of my childhood forest, seven acres, was nothing but downed trees, kindling, and mounds of tracked dirt and rock as the workers abandoned their machinery for the day.

It turned out our landlord had made a deal to build two high-rise apartments on the property but had been unable to get the zoning permits required. He figured if he started taking down the woods on his own he'd create a fait accompli. After some bureaucratic wrangling he got a permit to finish tearing down what was left of the small forest and gave my mother a thirty-day eviction notice, which she managed to get extended an extra month.

Around the same time they began leveling and paving over our Swamp Fox swamp behind PS 98 so that soon there was a network of roads and dozens of new brick houses where our hidden patriot reed encampments had been.

America has lost over 50 percent of its wetlands to agricultural and urban development since colonial times, and most of that since World War Two. In California the figure is closer to 95 percent loss. The great, wildlife-rich wetlands of California's Central Valley were filled in for industrial agriculture in the first half of the twentieth century and then, having become America's source for rice, fruit, nuts, grapes, and lettuce, began getting paved over in the latter half of the century for new housing developments, many of which, by the early twenty-first century, were in foreclosure.

For generations swamps were considered dank, dangerous, pestilent places, full of things that sting, bite, or infect; prone to flooding; thick with snakes, possums, alligators, and insects; and of no real use to adjacent human settlements.

Since then science has begun to identify wetlands and coastal salt marshes as key habitats for migratory birds and wildlife, a nursery for 75 percent of our marine fishes, a protective barrier against coastal storms and hurricanes, a pollution filtration system, a natural recharger of freshwater aquifers, and a sequesterer of carbon. At the same time, any new loss of wetlands could release massive quantities of carbon dioxide and methane, greenhouse gases that would significantly add to the problem of climate change.

Many coastal wetlands also trail off into seagrass meadows and mangroves that help secure the nearshore bottom, reduce turbidity, and also provide additional habitat for juvenile fish and shellfish.

So it was good and heartening news I found on a recent return to Douglaston. Having already talked them into a trip to Jones

Beach, I convinced my city friends Mark and Emily and their younger daughter, Sophia, to turn off Northern Boulevard so I could see how the old town now looked.

It is remarkably unchanged. After passing the two big apartments where our yellow wooden house and adjacent woods once stood we drive over the hill and Long Island Rail Road tracks out along Little Neck Bay to the country club and down to the dock, where kids are still swimming off one of the pontoons beyond the rock cobble shore. Small sailboats are moored nearby, as if waiting for a passing watercolorist to set up an easel.

On our way back we drive down one of the streets behind the impressive redbrick mass of PS 98 into the now foliage-thick neighborhood development that they built in the 1960s. It backs onto a still remarkably healthy-looking swamp running out to the bay and the sound. I get out of the car to read a city parks plaque and am thrilled to learn that most of our Swamp Fox territory has been turned into the thirty-acre Udalls Park Preserve, part of a complex of 650 protected acres of marsh and upland oak forest. The swamp is home to clapper rails, wood ducks, train-averse pheasants, woodpeckers, raccoons, turtles, and fish-hungry ospreys, big "Seahawk" raptors that were not around when I was a kid and mosquito spray trucks rolled through the neighborhood emitting white clouds of insecticide. Like bald eagles and brown pelicans, the ospreys have made a remarkable comeback since the insecticide DDT was banned in the early 1970s; it is one of a family of synthetic compounds now known as Persistent Organic Pollutants, or POPs, that kill far more than insects and continue to work their way through the food web decades after their manufacture and use.

It turns out that local citizens, tired of the filling in, dumping on, and development of Little Neck Bay, formed the Udalls Cove

Preservation Committee in 1969 and began fighting back under the leadership of a sixty-something activist and longtime Douglaston resident named Aurora Gareiss. Early on they helped defeat plans for a golf course that would have filled in fifty acres of wetlands in Great Neck, the next peninsula town over on Little Neck Bay (F. Scott Fitzgerald referred to Great Neck as "West Egg" in his novel *The Great Gatsby* and to Port Washington, the following north shore town, as "East Egg").

On the founding Earth Day in 1970 the preservation committee, having won its first victory with the golf course, gathered three hundred volunteers for a cleanup of the swamp during which seventeen abandoned cars and twenty Dumpsters of garbage and debris were removed. It would take them another two decades of work before the city park was officially dedicated in 1990. Gareiss died ten years later at the age of ninety-one, one of thousands of what I call "seaweed activists," marine grassroots heroes who fight to protect and restore our coasts and oceans.

2

Schooling Behavior

Guerrillas swim among the people as fish swim in
the sea.

MAO TSE TUNG

My father wanted to call me Seth but luckily, with her thick
German accent, my mother couldn't pronounce *th*, so rather
than call me *Set*, they named me David, David Samuel actually. I
didn't like my middle name so I started telling friends that the S
stood for Seaplane, that I'd been born on a seaplane landing on
the ocean. My mother always accused me of making stuff up,
even when I wasn't.

She had just started her own art gallery when we lost our Douglaston home to the bulldozers. Just up Northern Boulevard in the village of Thomaston, which was part of Great Neck, she found an affordable two-story wooden house, white with green trim and a big backyard for Lady.

Unfortunately, the house was a lot farther from the water, and when you got there, it was blocked off by the Merchant Marine Academy in Kings Point, the richest part of Great Neck. I'd occasionally go to academy football games to watch the Mariners play the Coast Guard Academy, but I no longer had a regular place by the water like the Dock to call my own. I joined my junior high school and high school swim teams but was never that fast or that thrilled with the warm, humid hypoxia of chlorinated competition.

After my bar mitzvah the rabbi at our temple tried to get a group of us boys to sign on for advanced study. Reluctant, we asked him a few questions, for example, how did he know there was a God? He told us about riding a transport ship back to the United States after he'd served in Korea and how one night there was a stunning sunset over the Pacific Ocean, and looking out at the orange, purple, and reds reflecting off the clouds on that warm velvet night he knew there was a God. I wasn't convinced about the God part, but it did make me want to go to sea.

I was growing up a middle-class American child, but in the shadow of unspoken horrors of mass murder and repression. My mother, who'd been interrogated by the Gestapo at the age of nine, usually switched to German whenever she and her friends began to talk of the past. From an early age I knew that the comforts and security of our lives are tenuous at best. In retrospect, it seemed inevitable that I would be caught up in the historic movements and moments of my youth. My only regret is how far they took me from the sea.

The 1960s would change the world, though not to the degree many young people hoped for. The decade would be so anti-authoritarian as to disregard its own chronology, running roughly eleven years, from the Kennedy assassination of 1963 through the Nixon resignation of 1974. It would expand the definition and reality of civil and human rights, challenge racism, empower women, and divide the nation over a murderous and misguided war in Southeast Asia.

It would also see the emergence of the modern environmental movement. This was largely inspired by marine biologist Rachel Carson's 1962 classic on chemical pollution, *Silent Spring*. She was already famous for her ocean books, *Under the Sea-Wind*, *The Sea Around Us*, and *The Edge of the Sea*. While there was a wilderness conservation movement going back to Teddy Roosevelt and John Muir, this new environmentalism with its focus on the impact of pollution broke on the scene with the force of a tsunami. Some twenty million people demonstrated on the first Earth Day, April 22, 1970, a day, right-wing critics claimed, had been chosen to secretly celebrate Lenin's birthday. At the same time, some leftists argued that Earth Day was an establishment plot to co-opt the revolutionary youth movement.

In reality, it was the beginning of a new social force, mixing the militant advocacy of the 1960s with grassroots community-organizing efforts. Direct-action outfits such as Greenpeace, which mounted maritime blockades of Russian whalers and a planned U.S. nuclear bomb test on an Alaskan island, along with neighborhood-based groups such as New York's Love Canal Homeowners Association, which rebelled against the toxic poisoning of communities where young children were being raised, soon created a powerful bottom-up demand on society to restructure its military-industrial processes and reduce waste.

Environmentalism would also, over time, transform itself from a social movement into a societal ethic, though like "love thy neighbor," an ethic often ignored in practice. Another problem was that, despite its natal connection to a marine biologist, people still tended to think of the environment as something that ended at the shoreline. Even calling it Earth Day reflects a certain air-breathing, land-based mammalian bias. Why not just call it Dirt Day?

Looking back, I can clearly see the missed opportunity, the life course not taken when I was fifteen. On February 14, 1967, my mother took my sister and me on a weeklong trip to Key West. It was two days after Deborah's eighteenth birthday and two months before my sixteenth. We flew into Miami, rented a car, and headed south.

Driving over the ocean on the old two-lane-highway bridge, looking out at the jade and aquamarine reef line, I felt strangely at peace, like I'd come home to a place I'd never seen before. We stopped at Santini's Porpoise School on Grassy Key, with its fenced-in dolphin pools blasted out of coral rock. I would later learn the CIA also kept its dolphins here for a time. During the 1960s the CIA and the navy developed a range of capabilities for their marine mammals including lethal and nonlethal anti-swimmer systems, underwater object recovery, and targeted placement of explosive mines and listening devices. The CIA even considered a plan to use a dolphin to attack Cuban leader Fidel Castro while he was scuba diving. Santini's was one of the first captive dolphin centers, and after I watched a couple of animals perform—including Misty, the Atlantic bottlenose who played Flipper in the movie that inspired the TV series—ex-fisherman turned dolphin trainer Milton Santini asked if any one of the thirty of us in the bleachers would like to take a swim with Misty. I jumped up, took off my T-shirt and sneakers, and dove into the water in my blue jeans. He instructed me how to stroke her side and to hold out my hand just until she came to me and then grab on to her fin, which I did, and she swam me around the large enclosure, dragging me in wide wake-generating circles several times till I was wearing a fixed grin not unlike Misty's own.

Today I have mixed feelings about captive dolphin swim programs. Although I know most of them have their origins in the unjustified wild capture of marine mammals and that without careful management repeated human contacts can stress the animals, I also know that swimming with a dolphin can be a life-transforming experience. Since I've also gone bodysurfing and swum around wild dolphins, I'd consider that a reasonable alternative as long as you remember that they're still wild and potentially dangerous animals and let them decide if they want to approach you or not (under the law you're supposed to keep your distance).

Next we stopped at Pigeon Key, where the University of Miami had converted an old cabin resort into a research station and where a storm had broken over the old swimming pool, smashing and filling it with live coral, big jacks, and parrot fish.

Finally we arrived in Key West, putting up at the Key Wester, out by the airport, and old Fort Taylor just across the ring road from the water. We toured the town with its small, neat Conch cottages and vivid red and orange royal poinciana trees, its shrimp boats and charter boats at the sport fishing dock where they'd hang big grouper, red snapper, dorado, and barracuda from hooks, and brown pelicans would circle around waiting for the bait fish to be dumped out. We visited Ernest Hemingway's home with its six-toed cats. By then Deborah had a lobster red sunburn that the guide cured by cutting off a hunk of aloe cactus and rubbing the sticky juice on her face, neck, arms, and legs. Within hours she was fine.

We toured the Key West Aquarium full of big jewfish (now called goliath groupers), moray eels, barracuda, sergeant majors, and queen angels. As I identified them, my mother turned to my sister and said, "Gee, I guess he doesn't just make all this stuff up."

As a young kid, I'd looked up at the stars and gotten pissed off, thinking I'd been born a generation too soon to explore other worlds. But that week in Key West, after we took a tour on a glass-bottom boat, I got hold of a mask and snorkel and went into the water on my own, swimming far off the seawall where I saw live rocks and vibrant colors, sea cucumbers and a queen conch and a small hammerhead gliding through a shallow coral canyon amid shoaling fish, and realized there was a whole other alien world right beyond the seawall. Later we ate lobster and key lime pie at the A&B Lobster House overlooking the Gulf of Mexico.

On another night my mother took us to Kraals Restaurant, which had big sea turtles in pens, and she had the turtle soup and let me order a vodka, and when I swallowed too much and grimaced she turned to my sister and said, "Does he make a face like that when he smokes pot?" We were both shocked.

I could have run off to sea right then. But there was a war dividing the nation and we had to get back home to New York, where Martin Luther King soon came to speak at our high school.

Sadly, since that first visit, the Florida Keys reef system has gone from 90 percent live coral cover to less than 10 percent, devastated by water pollution and runoff from South Florida, septic tank and cruise ship effluent, physical impacts from Jet Skis, boats, anchors, and people and from human-intensified climate change that's led to warmer seas, coral bleaching, and ocean acidification, making it harder for corals and other shell-forming critters to pull calcium carbonate out of the seawater around them to build their shell homes and limestone legacies on which new generations of coral polyps can grow.

On one of my later visits in 2005 my friends Craig and DeeVon Quirolo, founders of the activist group Reef Relief, took me snorkeling out by East Dry Rock, seven miles off Key West. The once-vibrant area was all dead coral rock, with dozens of recently added concrete wheels where people are attempting to seed and grow endangered elkhorn coral with some success. Still, the experiment looks like a small English garden planted in a clear-cut forest. One of the bumper stickers Reef Relief passes out reads, "If you're not outraged, you're not paying attention!"

I think it's vital to be able to maintain your sense of outrage as you age, particularly if you started young. When I was seventeen I ran off to protest the Vietnam War at the 1968 Democratic convention in Chicago, where the police rioted and I got my first taste of mace, gas, and blunt-force trauma.

A year later I went to Boston University as a freshman and made it three months before I was busted, beaten, and left facing a possible seven years in prison following an antiwar riot in front of the student union. I was eighteen and my ponytailed lawyer told me, "Don't worry. If it looks like you're going to prison I'll let you know and you can go underground."

In the middle of this, while I was out on bail, my mother took my sister and me to Antigua in the Caribbean's Leeward Islands, and we stayed at a converted British boatyard called Admiral's Inn, where they served tea by the water, and if you held out sugar hummingbirds would come and sip it from your teaspoon. We took a Zodiac rubber raft across the empty blue bay and climbed up a cliff to an abandoned eighteenth-century British fort (now a popular tourist site); sitting on that raft's pontoon with the saltwater spray splashing us and the vast blue sky above, I had my first experience of media déjà vu, of feeling that I was living something I'd previously seen on TV or in a movie, this time feeling as if I were on a Cousteau expedition.

Our mom had always taken us on interesting "bargain" vacations, like the time we ended up in the Dominican Republic shortly after the U.S. Marines invaded that island nation: barbed wire and artillery-shattered buildings lined the way to the beach. Now she told us she was thinking of selling her art gallery on Long Island and moving to Montserrat, the next island over from Antigua. It felt kind of surreal. I went snorkeling and saw some triggerfish, goatfish, damselfish, sweatlips, and snappers and afterward my sister told me she'd talked to a psychic in Vermont who assured her I wasn't going to jail.

I'd cut my hair short for the trial, which my dad attended. I stood five eight and weighed around 120 pounds. The three of us facing felony charges were in a separate dock from the other students.

A big cop, about six three and 200 pounds, testified that he "helped the other four officers to subdue the subject." My lawyer turned dramatically, pointing at me. "You mean the little one in the center." The courtroom burst out laughing; even the judge covered his mouth with his hand. I didn't go to jail. I did continue to protest, however.

In April 1970 Nixon sent U.S. troops into Cambodia in an attempt to destroy North Vietnamese sanctuary areas along the border, and we shut down over six hundred college campuses across the nation, including dozens around Boston, in a massive student strike that also saw the police and National Guard kill eight students around the country, four of them at Kent State in Ohio.

While we were shutting down our campuses and debating whether we could end the war and racism without a revolution, other conversations were taking place in Washington that would have a profound impact on the future of our ocean commons and how we care for it. Those decisions, like almost all made during this time, could not escape the profoundly corrosive effects of the war in Indochina and the Nixon administration's paranoid response to any perceived form of dissent.

Along with all its other innovations, inspirations, and illusions the sixties were a very hopeful time for ocean exploration, beginning with the 1960 touchdown of the fifty-foot-long bathyscaphe *Trieste* at the very bottom of the world, 36,201 feet down in the Pacific's Challenger Deep with Jacques Piccard, the son of its inventor, and U.S. Navy Lieutenant Don Walsh aboard. After a dive of almost five hours they spent twenty minutes on the bottom, where they spotted some fish. It wasn't until 2012 that film director and explorer James Cameron became the next human to go down there. While only three people have now been to the lowest point on our planet, over five hundred others have traveled into space.

For much of the 1960s the exploration of "inner space" was seen to be at least as important as work in outer space, with astronauts and aquanauts and astronaut-turned-aquanaut Scott Carpenter competing for national news coverage. Groups of saturation divers breathing various mixes of gasses were living in underwater habitats such as Jacques Cousteau's Conshelfs in the Mediterranean and Red Sea, the navy's Sealabs off Bermuda and San Diego (where a dolphin named Tuffy brought them tools from the surface), and the Tektite habitats in the Caribbean. Ocean explorer Sylvia Earle (also known as "Her Deepness") was one of these early aquanauts. Since the government couldn't imagine having mixed crews of men and women, in 1970 an all-woman crew was established, and the media labeled them "aquababes." During two weeks underwater in Tektite they studied reef ecology and performed some of the first experiments on the effects of pollution on coral reefs. Their work also inspired NASA to open its astronaut-training program to women.

Of more than sixty undersea habitats, over half were built by the United States and the Soviet Union. Major corporations—including GE, GM, Union Carbide, Lockheed, and Alcoa—competed for what they thought would be multibillion-dollar contracts if ocean exploration went the way of the space race with the Russians. In 1965 Senator Warren G. Magnuson of Washington warned, "The prevention of communist domination of the seas is perhaps our most pressing problem today. . . . This is the immediate challenge our marine scientists can and must help us meet."

"If I'd seen a Russian footprint down there instead of a fish, we'd probably still be down there," Don Walsh later told me of his descent in the *Trieste.*

Soon new submersibles, such as the navy's *Alvin,* were launched into the depths by Woods Hole Oceanographic Institution (*Alvin* was also used to help locate a missing H-bomb in the waters off Spain), and the popular imagination was fired up by salty tales ranging from Arthur Clarke's science-fiction novel *Deep Range* to John Lilly's nonfiction *The Mind of the Dolphin* to television programs like *Flipper* and *Sea Hunt.* There were Cousteau's books, films, and lyrical Undersea World specials on TV, as well as the pop sounds of the Beach Boys, Jan and Dean, the Ventures, Dick Dale, and many others who redefined the California dream as a surf safari looking for that perfect tubular wave along the golden shore of youth.

In 1966, the same year Cousteau's TV specials began airing, Vice President Hubert Humphrey helped launch the Stratton Commission, a blue-ribbon panel convened to consider America's future in the sea, chaired by Julius Stratton, chairman of the Ford Foundation.

Its 1969 report, "Our Nation and the Sea," would lead to the passage of a number of ocean protection laws, including the Coastal Zone Management Act and Marine Mammal Protection Act, and would help inspire the Clean Water Act. Its main proposal, however, was for the creation of a unified Department of the Ocean responsible for the stewardship and exploration of America's blue frontier.

But as the increasingly costly war in Southeast Asia dragged on, enthusiasm for major new government programs, including the idea of "a wet NASA," faded away.

If there was not going to be an independent Department of the Ocean, the smart money in marine science thought that an agency designed to protect the ocean and study its links to weather and climate would logically find a home in the Department of the Interior, whose mission was to manage and protect America's wilderness areas.

But then on April 30, 1970, Nixon ordered U.S. troops in Vietnam to invade neighboring Cambodia, and that set off our May student protests and killings. Nixon then called protesting students "bums." Secretary of the Interior Walter Hickel, deeply disturbed by what was happening, wrote a personal letter to the president. In it he expressed growing reservations about Nixon's refusal to listen to the antiwar sentiments of my generation.

Hickel's letter, dated May 6, 1970, read in part, "About 200 years ago there was emerging a great nation in the British Empire, and it found itself with a colony in violent protest by its youth—men such as Patrick Henry, Thomas Jefferson, Madison, and Monroe, to name a few. Their protests fell on deaf ears, and finally led to war. The outcome is history. My point is, if we read history, it clearly shows that youth in its protest must be heard."

Before reaching the White House a copy of the letter (which had been circulated at Interior) was obtained by the Associated Press and published in *The Washington Evening Star*. The president and his aides Bob Haldeman and John Ehrlichman went ballistic. Nixon told Wally Hickel that he now considered him an "adversary." Hickel was blacklisted from White House events and became the target of a well-orchestrated smear campaign in the press. Less than two months later the newly formed National Oceanic and Atmospheric Administration (NOAA) was placed in the Department of Commerce, then run by Nixon's campaign fund-raiser and future Watergate bagman Maurice Stans. On Thanksgiving eve, Secretary of the Interior Wally Hickel was fired.

Representative John Dingell of Michigan blasted the president's action, describing the newly established NOAA as the handmaiden of a Department of Commerce so dominated by industrial interests "as to be incapable of objectivity on issues of the marine environment."

Though harsh, that judgment has largely stood the test of time. For almost four decades as the main civilian agency charged with oversight of our public seas, NOAA has too often done the bidding of commercial fishing companies, the navy, and other saltwater special interests while failing to halt the rapid decline of our ocean's health, including the collapse of vital fish stocks and edible marine wildlife such as cod, wild salmon, and Pacific rockfish.

Of course, few people noticed this because, like most of the things we do in the ocean—from dumping our waste and plastic to bottom trawling and long-line fishing (with up to three thousand hooks per line) to blasting industrial and military noise in a place where sound is the light of the sea that allows many of its residents to echolocate each other, feed, and breed—the devastation we wreak on our ocean remains largely out of sight and mostly out of mind.

At the same time, in an environment that remains significantly unmapped and unexplored, we're discovering new species of life, including walking sharks and vampire squid, along with new wilderness habitats like deep-sea sponge communities and useful products such as natural medicinal compounds from sponges, sea whips, and other humble critters even as we're putting them at risk of extinction. This is not always the result of rapacious greed. Thoughtless ignorance also plays its part as we often fail to appreciate the consequences of our actions until it's too late.

As with our own species, sex can often lead to some level of confusion. One long-held tenant of "good" fishing management practice was that you catch only the big fish so that the small ones have a chance to grow up and replace them. Now scientists have found some fish species are transgender. Groupers all start out as females; as they grow older and larger they become males. But with so many big males being fished out you tend to get an abundance of females with little chance to meet new guys and make baby groupers. Evolution, not being sexist, also applies the same reproductive strategy to anemone (or Nemo) fish, only with the largest and most protective of any grouping being the alpha female. If she dies the next largest male will convert over several days to become the new alpha female. In *Finding Nemo*, Disney Pictures just wasn't prepared to show Nemo's dad become his new mom.

Conventional wisdom has also held that indiscriminate broadcast spawners such as white abalone are so fecund they could never be fished to extinction. Then it was discovered that unless there's an abalone of the opposite sex within a yard they can puff all the eggs or sperm they want into the water, but they aren't going to produce any new larvae. In 1972 commercial divers in California collected 143,000 pounds of white abalone. By the late 1990s two scientists in a research submarine were able to spot only five of the mother-of-pearl-shelled species of tasty mollusk in 150 hours of searching. Several have now been removed to a university lab, where they are being bred in tanks in the hope of one day returning a new generation of white abalone to the wild.

Even among those fish species that TV preachers might find respectful of "traditional family values," the most valued members tend to be what marine scientist Mark Hixon of Oregon State University calls "fat old females," because they're the ones that produce more eggs, and their eggs tend to be more viable. Unfortunately, because they're large, they're also more likely to be fished out by what my friend *Sherman's Lagoon* cartoonist Jim Toomey refers to as "hairless beach apes."

In the United States the overfishing of big sharks such as scalloped hammerheads led to a boom in the population of skates and cownose rays. As the number of rays exploded, they continued to feast on their favorite prey, scallops, destroying the scallop-fishing industry in North Carolina and along much of the eastern seaboard. But it's not only the removal of apex predators like sharks, dolphins, and billfish that can threaten to unravel the web of life in complex ecosystems such as coastal oceans.

Blue crabs are the unintended victims of commercial overfishing near the bottom of the food web. Around the Chesapeake Bay (and in the Gulf of Mexico) a company called Omega Protein (corporate slogan "Healthy Products for a Healthy World") is using its fleet of trawlers and spotter planes to catch some of the last great schools of menhaden, a small oily forage fish from the herring family that, like anchovies and sardine, is the essential little fish that all the big fish feed on.

But now these algae grazers are being strip-mined from the ocean. Making up one-third of all the biomass taken from the sea, forage fish are converted to fishmeal and fish oil and fed to factory chickens, swine, and industry-farmed fish or else sold as pet food or nutritional supplements in health-food stores (have you had your fish oil today?). With the rapid collapse of their favorite food source, menhaden, hungry striped bass began consuming massive numbers of baby blue crabs in Chesapeake Bay, threatening the livelihood of watermen who've already seen their once bountiful oyster harvest destroyed by poor management and disease. Plus, with the algae-grazing menhaden and filter-feeding oysters gone, the once clear bay has turned dark green and mud brown, its summer waters filled by stringy macro-algae slime mats also known as "green gunk."

In Peru the conversion of native forage fish into fishmeal has left the bay bottoms outside the processing plants covered in a white gelatinous fat—runoff from the factories. At the same time, the collapse of once bountiful offshore fishing grounds because of the ocean mining of forage fish has led thousands of desperate artisan fishermen to start killing sea turtles, undersized billfish, and dolphins for food. Neighboring Chile, which bans forage fishing in its waters, nonetheless buys huge quantities of fishmeal from Peru to feed to its farmed salmon, tons of which are then exported to North America as a cheaper, blander-tasting, and less healthy alternative to the wild salmon that many North American fishermen still depend on for their livelihoods.

Pulling on just one thread in the watery web of life can begin to unravel the entire tapestry. But forget the artful metaphors when every year we're stripping up to 90 million metric tons of life from the world's oceans and feeding it into the voracious maw of a global seafood market that now consumes anything indigenous to the sea, from barnacles and snails to illegal blue whale meat. There are only a dozen large aircraft carriers sailing our seas. Imagine if there were eight hundred crewed by four million sailors. That's how much live weight we're removing from the ocean every year, killing the world's fish faster than they can reproduce while slowly starving whales, seals, and seabirds in the process.

At the same time, we're tarring what's left with our runoff pollution from urban storm drains and sewage canals, factory farms, fertilizers, oil, and plastic. While most people are aware that we're increasing the carbon dioxide load in the atmosphere, few realize that between synthetic fertilizers developed from natural gas and the burning of fossil fuels, including auto emissions, we also doubled the global nitrogen cycle just between 1960 and the late 1990s. Natural nitrogen exists in air, soil, and lightning, but when you add about 150 pounds of nitrogen-rich chemical fertilizer per acre of corn grown in Iowa, Illinois, or Nebraska, you create a nutrient surplus. This wasteful and unneeded excess will wash off the land, following gravity down through the watershed into the Mississippi River and the Gulf of Mexico—or any of more than four hundred other coastal seas, according to the United Nations—where it will grow a second crop, fertilizing giant algal blooms that then decay and are in turn fed on by bacteria, creating oxygen-deprived (hypoxic) and depleted (anoxic) dead zones. Anything in the water that can't flee these global dead zones asphyxiates and dies on the bottom. Along with nitrogen, phosphorus from sugar production and factory-farmed chicken waste, including the droppings from more than half a billion chickens raised on the Chesapeake Bay's Eastern Shore, also contribute to these algal blooms.

Not appalled yet? How about this?

We also produce some two hundred million metric tons of new plastic stock each year. If half of that ends up reaching the sea, it means we're replacing living marine wildlife with non-biodegradable polymers at about a pound per pound basis. My guess is that most of this plastic waste is burned or land filled, we just don't know. What we do know is that half the plastic that is produced is used to make disposable single-use items.

And the significant amount of plastic that does enter the sea acts as a toxic sponge, soaking up PCBs and other persistent organic pollutants much more effectively (about one million times more effectively) than seawater, concentrating them up the food chain as microscopic bits of plastic are consumed by forage fish that are consumed by larger and larger fish until you order that seared ahi tuna or grilled swordfish steak at Red Lobster.

Some parts of the ocean have now been described as an alphabet soup of plastic, according to the Algalita Marine Research Foundation, which goes out and does the surveys. At least after we killed the buffalo we didn't leave the Plains littered six inches deep with plastic water bottles, old butane lighters, Styrofoam peanuts, toothbrushes, and Doritos bags.

Luckily, there are still parts of our global ocean—now reduced to about 5 percent—that remain in a pristine or near-pristine condition to remind us of what wild oceans are and, it is hoped, to inspire us to work for the restoration of the other 95 percent. As natural systems, living seas are impressively resilient and able to bounce back from multiple environmental insults, though you can push any natural system, just as you can push any human being, too far. I've seen the results when that happens, be it death squad body dumps or algae-covered dead reefs.

Still, there are some indicators of hope that we might yet turn the tide. These include the Obama administration's commitment to an ecosystem-based national ocean policy that got launched in 2010; the expansion of large no-take marine reserves, also known as ocean wilderness parks, in California and the Pacific in 2012 and 2014; federal fisheries reforms that have seen some edible wildlife begin to rebound; and the emergence of ocean champions both in Congress and in coastal communities across the United States and around the world.

Back when Nixon was sinking NOAA in the trade-driven Department of Commerce, however, the radical momentum of the times was about to take me to a new ocean frontier where I'd find myself needing some unusual survival equipment, including a 12-gauge shotgun and green flippers.

3

Ocean Beach

And I have loved thee, Ocean! And my joy
Of youthful sports was on thy breast to be
Borne, like thy bubbles, onward; from a boy
I wantoned with thy breakers. They to me
Were a delight; and if the freshening sea
Made them a terror, 'twas a pleasing fear.

LORD BYRON, 1818

My move to the beach in San Diego when I was twenty, discovery
of bodysurfing, and renewed interests in the mysteries of the
sea would reconnect me to the source, cementing my lifelong

connection to the ocean as solidly as any barnacle's glue cements it to a hard, slick surface. But getting there and staying there would prove as risky, scary, and challenging as a double-overhead wave on a shallow beach, or a car bomb on a crowded street.

In 1971 I dropped out of school and became a full-time antiwar organizer. A year later, while living in a fleabag apartment in Boston's Back Bay, I got a call from Pete and George, friends living by the beach in San Diego and organizing protests for the planned Republican convention that summer. Members of a right-wing terrorist group called the Secret Army Organization (SAO) had just fired a shot into their house and wounded one of their roommates, a nurse named Paula, and they asked if I'd be willing to come out and help them do security.

A few nights later we were sleeping in shifts at Pete and George's collective house in Ocean Beach. I stood watch with a 12-gauge shotgun for half the night, and when it was my turn to sleep, I snuck down to the end of the street where the sidewalk let out on a wide moonlit beach and stayed there till dawn, watching the Pacific lapping at the shore, the small breaking wavelets sparkling with silvery luminescence. I felt a core tranquility that night by the ocean, a deep connection with the source that would serve me well in the years to come.

Two days later there was a benefit concert on Sunset Cliffs for the *OB Rag*, the local underground newspaper. It was an eighty-two-degree blue-sky day. A rock band played on a cliff-top deck, and hundreds of young neighborhood residents were sitting and dancing on the beach below, drinking beer, passing joints, and frolicking in the water, including silky-haired California girls in bikinis tossing Frisbees. I waded into the green-blue water that was a bracing but not uncomfortable sixty-eight degrees and I knew that, once again, I'd come home to a place I'd never been before.

San Diego was and is a strange town. Like many other beach towns, it's a place where you can go directly from arrested adolescence to early retirement, skipping adulthood entirely. Every time I go back there my IQ drops ten points but I feel better physically. It's very conservative, with a strong military presence and history of political corruption and violence, but also has a perfect coastal desert climate, sparkling ocean, and engaging border culture. In the early twentieth century the town divided between "Smokestacks" and "Geraniums," those who favored rapid industrialization versus those who wanted to preserve the city's Mediterranean charms.

By 1972 Nixon called San Diego his "favorite city," and I felt the same way, though for different reasons. The Ocean Beach section of the city had been established in 1887 as a real-estate development of matched cottages called Mussel Beach. Later, in 1913, the Wonderland amusement park was built on the beach sand and quickly swept away by Pacific storms. After that the isolated mile-long strand attracted generations of artists and bohemians and by the 1960s a mixed bag of surfers, bikers, hippies, radicals, and welfare moms.

In 1970 radicalized surfers fought the police on the north end of the beach to stop the Army Corps of Engineers from building a seawall for a marina and hotel complex that would have destroyed the surf zone. My friend Katy Franklin recalls standing in front of a microphone at the age of twelve, crying over the pelicans who would lose their homes and no longer be able to fly along the surf, riding the updraft with their wingtips in the waves.

The surfers won their battle: Ocean Beach still faces into wind-driven Pacific swells just south of the San Diego River and the dredged Mission Bay, with its waterfront hotels, SeaWorld theme park, and Jet Ski rentals. Just over one square mile in size with over ten thousand residents, OB is located on the western side of the hilly Point Loma peninsula that terminates at a Coast Guard lighthouse and tide pools by the main harbor entry. The downtown waterfront and three major navy bases are just over the hills to the east.

OB's main drag, Newport Avenue, ends at the beach by the longest municipal pier on the West Coast, reaching almost a third of a mile offshore before terminating in a T. It was built in 1966, and surfers regularly "shoot" its cement pilings, riding waves in between its barnacle-encrusted pillars.

These swells were like nothing I'd ever seen on the East Coast. Instead of whitecaps and storm surge, these were big juicy waves, regular in shape, with frequent sets that from the hilltop you could sometimes see stretching like corduroy out to the horizon.

In the midst of working with the antiwar San Diego Convention Coalition I became an avid bodysurfer, buying my first green Churchills, short rubber flippers designed for catching waves.

When you kick your body into a wave, your velocity is slower than if you were riding on a surfboard, and so you have to wait longer, till the wave is almost on top of you to take off (kick into the wave) and then have to ride higher up on its shoulder, just underneath its crest, and try to cut across the face of the wave until you're inside a hollowed-out barrel or—more likely if you're new to the sport—until you're barrel-rolled on the sand-, rock-, and shell-strewn bottom.

My first weeks and months in the big waves were scary to me and pitiable to those around me. I was, in the vernacular of the surf culture, a complete hodad. I'd exhaust myself swimming out through the white-water shore break. Then, just when I'd get outside, into the calmer water of "the lineup," a big set would come along and I'd kick too early or too late, either way finding myself dropping over the falls or being caught below a monster breaking wave so that I was pushed hard underwater, with my limbs and head twisting in opposing directions from my body, and seeing nothing but bubbles and a few times floating black spots from lack of oxygen till I surfaced just in time for the next monster wave in the set to hammer me down again, driving me back under into the black, churning cauldron.

Until that time street rioting had been my extreme sport. After all, it involved running, throwing, ducking, and more running. Now I was getting beaten up by the waves but also catching big adrenaline rushes when I would finally catch a five- or six-foot breaker and find myself propelled toward shore by the incredibly fast force of the water, my chest and one arm thrust forward like Poseidon, hanging out on the lip for twenty or thirty seconds or maybe even a rare minute that seemed to go on forever. One time I caught a wave next to a girl I knew but felt kind of shy around, and we rode it next to each other. When we tumbled off and resurfaced she gave me a brilliant smile and said, "Isn't it great when you come together?"

After a few months I felt like the Pacific Ocean was drown-proofing me: I was now able to stay under longer, having learned to stay calm, balling myself into a fetal position if it felt like I was getting torn apart and couldn't surface right away, also learning to wait till the spinning and downward push eased and I could follow the air bubbles to the surface, even if they sometimes seemed to be going sideways.

Not knowing better, at first I'd hyperventilate before catching a wave, taking rapid gulps of air so that I could hold my breath longer. Only later did I learn that by reducing the amount of carbon dioxide in my lungs and thus reducing my urge to breathe, I might be letting my oxygen levels drop to where I could lose consciousness without warning. This is called shallow-water blackout and is the reason the Coast Guard's Rescue Swimmer School in North Carolina will kick out any student caught hyperventilating.

I don't want to suggest that thirty years of bodysurfing has left me a master of the waves, however. Even as I write this I'm nursing a cut eye and sprained neck from getting pounded at Pounders Beach on Oahu. I stopped there for some restorative ocean time after a beach cleanup on a plastic-strewn stretch of the island's northeast coast that faces into the Pacific Gyre, whence much of the plastic we dump into the ocean returns to us. After three or four good rides in the shore break a pile-driving wave slammed me into the hard sand bottom on the side of my face as an electric shock of pain jolted through my neck. For a moment I lay floating underwater, thinking that I had snapped something. Then I tried moving my arms and legs, rotating my head, and they all worked. I hadn't crippled myself or broken my neck after all. Lots of ice and Tylenol over the last few days and I'm starting to feel better. I hadn't felt anything like that since I took a surfboard to the throat some years earlier.

Obviously, every great pleasure risks its opposite. Still, just as the U.S. Secret Service stopped allowing President Barack Obama to bodysurf Sandy Beach on Oahu because of the high risk of injury at that locale (more broken necks than anywhere

else in the nation), I plan to stay out of big shore break and stick
to deeper water from now on.

The Republican convention was scheduled for August 1972,
but the venue was moved in May; it would be held in Miami,
where the Democrats were having their convention, rather than
in San Diego. One reason was the government's fear that our
antiwar demonstrations would draw hundreds of thousands of
young protesters to San Diego's late summer beaches and things
would turn violent.

Of course, we were already experiencing violence at the hands
of the Secret Army Organization, a spin-off of the Minutemen, one
of the first right-wing militias that was also involved in bank rob-
bery and extortion. After President Nixon went to China the SAO
decided he was another communist and planned to open fire on
both antiwar protestors and the convention hall. But with the Republicans leaving town, I was less concerned about being mur-
dered by the SAO (one of whose leaders later turned out to be an
FBI informant) than the thought of abandoning OB's excellent
surf to go organize a less promising protest by the flat, tepid waters
of Miami Beach. Still, having agreed to go to a meeting of antiwar
organizers, I got guilt-tripped into doing this.

When I got to Miami I felt an overwhelming sense of pity
watching my native California friends, among them antiwar
spokesman and future TV newsman Bill Ritter, trying to bodysurf the warm half-foot-high ripples of the Atlantic.

On the opening day of the Republican convention a few thousand of us hit the streets, including my affinity group (tactical
team) that we'd named Red Snapper. The riot police pushed us
off Collins Avenue and onto the white sand beach in front of the

Fontainebleau Hotel and other North Miami Beach resorts, then started firing tear gas at us that formed into billowing, choking clouds. Looking from the white gas clouds to the blue water, I felt as if my life's interests were coming together with cinematic intensity, like *The Battle of Algiers* meets *Flipper*.

Nixon was reelected and the war dragged on. At the same time, other events were shaping the future of our blue world. Foreign factory trawlers from Russia, Poland, Spain, and elsewhere were taking thousands of tons of fish off the coast of New England, but no one other than some Gloucester fishermen were paying attention. "They're fishing out there with ocean liners," they reported in amazement on returning to port. What they'd encountered were the first catcher-at-sea processor ships, equipped with fish-filleting production lines ("slime lines") and large storage freezers on board, also massive nets and stern ramps like those on whaling ships—designed to haul up not a single leviathan but rather tens of thousands of pounds of smaller fish on each sonar-guided haul. Today's huge factory trawlers are hard to miss if you're floating in the middle of the ocean. You can smell them from miles away. About seven miles out, a sheen of fish oil will appear on the ocean's surface, and you can spot clouds of seabirds hovering over the bloody source of the slick. Like pirate ghost ships, these floating piscine slaughterhouses can stay at sea fishing continuously for months or years on end, with their crews and catches being offloaded at sea while fuel, food, and other necessities are brought out to them. Some of their nets are large enough to encircle half a dozen jumbo jets. The world's largest factory trawler, the *American Monarch* (built in Norway and now working in Russia) can catch a million pounds of fish a day. Some of these fish, along with other "nontargeted species," or "bycatch," such as seabirds, dolphins, and turtles, go over the side as lifeless waste.

Patrolling the Bering Sea boundary line between the United States and Russia, Coast Guard C-130 long-range aircraft will often spot up to seventy big factory trawlers. In April 2008 the Coast Guard helped save forty-two out of the forty-seven crewmen of the factory trawler *Alaska Ranger* when the ship suddenly sank 120 miles west of Dutch Harbor in the Bering Sea. Its Japanese "fish master" had allegedly been pushing the boat and crew too hard, going into dangerous ice with a fish-or-die attitude that may have contributed to the disaster. He was not one of the survivors.

Not all the marine trends of the 1970s were negative. The U.S. Clean Water Act passed into law in 1972 (after overriding Nixon's veto), and billions of tax dollars were spent on improved sewage treatment facilities for cities, reduced industrial pollution of waterways, and protection of interior and coastal wetlands. These actions saw surprisingly rapid results in the form of improved water quality for North America's streams, rivers, great lakes, and ocean waters, reflecting nature's resiliency and a new commonsense approach to environmental management. The 1970s also saw passage of the Marine Mammal Protection Act, Coastal Zone Management Act, and other U.S. federal marine legislation.

By then I'd decided it was time to go back to school and had applied to and been accepted at Goddard, the Vermont college my sister had attended. Goddard was a progressive, self-directed pass-fail school. When my sister went there the dorms were all coed so, as a budding feminist, she'd forced them to accept their first all-women's dorm.

The school had a work-study program and allowed students

to do up to half a year of field research. Realizing there was not going to be a revolution in the United States and curious about what urban guerrilla warfare looked like, I decided to do my study covering the conflict in Northern Ireland as a reporter. I got press credentials from an alternative news service and WBCN, Boston's main rock station, flew into Dublin a week before my twenty-first birthday, and caught the train north to Belfast.

Urban warfare looked pretty mean but was also personally challenging. It made me better able to understand Hiram Johnson's axiom that in war, truth is the first casualty. I realized my sympathies didn't matter when everyone was not only willing but quite delighted to lie to me if it advanced their position. And so I quickly learned survival skills as an eyewitness and an investigator in order to try to produce accurate and analytic reports on events too often defined by the gun, the car bomb, and the disinformation campaign.

A friend in the States, a left-wing army brat, sent me a four-page letter of salutations and humorous commentary. On the back of each page were photocopied diagrams from a U.S. army manual on guerrilla warfare showing how to construct different kinds of bomb switches. Rather than pass it on to the IRA, I decided to burn the letter in my pension's fireplace. It's not so much that it was not my war, but rather that it was no longer my job. My job, I'd come to understand, was to tell the truth as best as I could uncover it, and that left no room to be an active player—or rather, that made me a different kind of player than I'd been before. My commitment was no longer to one side or the other but rather to the public's right to know. The small pages curling blue and then carbon black as they burned in that fireplace marked an important turning point in my life that I've not regretted.

While I was in Ulster reporting on "the troubles" between the IRA, Protestant militants, and the British army, the British were also carrying out a high-seas Cod War with Iceland over disputed fishing grounds. After they'd seized and fired on several Icelandic boats a mob burned the British embassy in Reykjavík. The IRA crowd in the Old House pub where I hung out went crazy watching it burn on the BBC, cheering like soccer fans. Of course, those were also the days, way back in the 1970s, when there were still enough cod in the Atlantic to fight over.

By 1992 the Canadian government had to shut down its Atlantic Cod Fishery because of the collapse of what had once been one of the most plentiful big fish in the sea (as recounted in Mark Kurlansky's excellent book *Cod*), and more than forty thousand people lost their jobs. Two years later NOAA was forced to shut down much of New England's offshore cod-fishing grounds on Georges Bank after years of ignoring its own scientists' warnings of overfishing. The British soon replaced cod in their fish and chips with dogfish, a small species of shark. As a result of this new market demand, New England's dogfish population quickly collapsed (accelerated by the fact that it was easier to catch and process the big female breeders). Still, today's New England fishermen show little sympathy for rebuilding shark stocks, seeing dogfish as competitors in the taking of small cod and herring.

At the same time, it was discovered too late that cod breed in distinct aggregations so that Arctic cod would not just swim over from Greenland to help their North American kissing cousins reproduce.

Instead, Canadian cods' ecological niche was taken over by the small lobsters that the big cod used to eat. Like their clawmates in Maine's waters that haven't seen really big predator cod in over a century, these Canadian "bugs" could now grow up and out in size, creating a new high-dollar-value fishery for the Maritime Provinces. While this makes some formerly out-of-work fishermen happy, it's also a reflection of what scientists call "fishing down the trophic levels" or "fishing down the food web." As scientist Daniel Pauly of the University of British Columbia puts it, "We are eating today what our grandparents used as bait" (or, in the case of lobster, as farm fertilizer).

I've witnessed something similar in San Diego, where the recreational fishing charter boats on Point Loma's docks now list mackerel on their daily catch boards. When I first moved there thirty years ago mackerel were what you cut up for bait. This trend is obviously well advanced when giant barnacles appear on the menus of upscale gourmet restaurants and our seafood exports to Asia include sea urchin, sea cucumber (bêche-de-mer) and skate wings. Perhaps one day soon we'll get to witness high-seas "sardine wars."

I was returning to my flat one day following a riot and shootout between IRA gunmen and the British army in the Creggan Heights neighborhood of Derry when I got a call from a reporter friend in Dublin telling me to call my aunt in Terre Haute. Aunt Renate, a family practitioner, told me my mother had contracted lung cancer (she was a pack-and-a-half-a-day smoker). I crossed the street and sat down by the ruins of the recently bombed Brooke Park public library. Someone had a radio on. It was playing Paul Simon's "Mother and Child Reunion."

Thirty-six hours later I was in Terre Haute, Indiana, where my mother had just undergone surgery. After some hugs and tears she thanked me for several days of research I'd done at Dublin's National Library. There I'd uncovered seventeenth-century settlement records and cargo manifests from sailing vessels that had voyaged to "the Emerald Isle" of Montserrat (named by Columbus in 1493) carrying Irish Catholic settlers and indentured servants to the small, hilly volcanic island. I also found a report on the first stone church on the island whose foundation she and her landskeeper, Mr. French, had uncovered while clearing brush. Eva had purchased 140 acres high up on the Soufrière, the upper slope of the verdant island's dormant volcano, where she planned to build a twenty-room inn and help establish a national park.

After she'd recovered from surgery we flew from Indiana back to New York. The stewardess asked if everything was all right and Eva said, "No, I'm dying of cancer." The lady's face went ashen and I elbowed my mother, who turned and said, "Well, I am, aren't I?"

We took a brief final trip to Montserrat, where I went snorkeling and Eva caused a sensation by claiming a wild donkey had fallen into the island's water cistern. My sister and the minister of development and tourism and several of his men had to climb up a hill at night with flashlights in search of a phantom donkey corpse.

Back home I helped my mother sort through her things and close down her art gallery. As the pain increased she decided to return to Indiana, where her sister could take better care of her. I went back to Vermont and stayed with my sister in Burlington, where I finished my undergraduate thesis on the Irish, did karate, and often stared out across the snowy shore of Lake Champlain wishing I was back on the beach in San Diego. Eva didn't want us to see her bloated by the drugs, discolored, and in pain, and so a few weeks later she died without us at the age of forty-nine.

Most of her estate was tied up in Montserrat, where her local lawyer seemed less than interested in helping us settle her out-standing accounts with the Bank of Canada. Since neither of us was prepared to move to the island and fight for her land, we eventually lost the property, which we heard then fell into the lawyer's hands. For a time the island became a popular vacation and recording spot for George Harrison and other world-famous musicians. Then, a little over twenty years later, in 1995, the Sou-frière exploded in a massive volcanic eruption that buried the capital town of Plymouth, sent an ash plume five miles into the sky, and forced two-thirds of the population of the tiny British colony to flee the island. Today volcanic activity continues on the seven-by-ten-mile Caribbean isle, though on a much dimin-ished scale.

After our mother's death I returned to San Diego, where I began editing a small weekly newspaper and building my freelance career while also finding time to bodysurf. The Pacific took me back to the salty dreams of my childhood and helped me to heal. I was living by the beach, writing stories about navy dolphins, navy nuclear weapons, and fast-attack submarines, the battle over a nude beach, white sharks, offshore oil drilling, whatever could keep me connected to the everlasting sea. I didn't know I'd also soon be bodysurfing in a place where bodies were the com-mon currency of political discourse.

4

Hooked on War

But not till the foe has gone below or turns
  his prow and runs,
Shall the voice of peace bring sweet release to
  the men behind the guns!

JOHN JEROME ROONEY,
"THE MEN BEHIND THE GUNS"

When I was thirteen and wanted to be an oceanographer I knew
there were only two places that counted, the twin Vaticans of U.S.
marine science: Woods Hole Oceanographic Institution on Cape
Cod with its stolid brick buildings, concrete pier, and big research

vessels across from the historic Eel Pond, and the Scripps Institution of Oceanography in San Diego. Scripps's low-rise labs, offices, and library sit on a scenic bluff overlooking its own pier on La Jolla Shores, just below the University of California–San Diego. Its research vessels are docked by the navy's submarine base on Point Loma.

I first visited Scripps's meandering tree-shaded campus shortly after my return to San Diego while working on a story about deep-ocean mining. The world-famous marine station quickly proved to be less than I'd imagined.

"You could grind up all the cities on earth and pour them into the ocean and it would absorb them without noticeable effect," the first Scripps scientist I ever interviewed told me. "That's why we say the solution to pollution is dilution," he went on, quoting an axiom popular among his peers.

Another outmoded theory that seemed to hold sway among the physical oceanographers who dominated Scripps was the idea that fish populations were too abundant and fecund to be significantly impacted by human harvesting (fishing) except in localized areas and for limited periods. Nutrient upwellings, larval dispersion by currents, winds, and tides, along with changing ocean temperature and chemistry, all played far more significant roles in the appearance and disappearance of species like the California sardine, which was why a better understanding of the physical aspects of the ocean was so essential, they claimed.

This struck me as slightly odd and certainly at odds with what I'd been reading about the ocean's living ecosystems in popular works by Rachel Carson, Jacques Cousteau, and marine biologist Ed Ricketts of Monterey, whose friend, the author John Steinbeck, lightly fictionalized him as Doc in *Cannery Row*.

It was while working on stories about Scripps that I began to unravel the hidden history of postwar ocean science in the United States.

While doing a feature piece about the development of the atomic bomb for *San Diego* magazine I interviewed Scripps director Bill Nierenberg, a gruff bald physicist with a fringe of gray hair who favored khaki work clothes and whose major qualification as an ocean scientist seemed to be that he was a former assistant secretary general of NATO and anti-mine expert who'd also worked on the Manhattan Project building the bomb. At the same time, I discovered that the director of Woods Hole was a former navy admiral whose specialty was antisubmarine warfare.

Scripps was founded as a marine biological station by Berkeley zoologist William Ritter in 1903 with the support of the Scripps newspaper family. Its early work helped secure a place for oceanography in the mainstream of American science. Ritter believed in looking at whole organisms and their relationship to their habitat and environment, a field of study later known as ecology.

For the next few decades marine science remained a largely shore-based biological enterprise involving the study of fish, invertebrates, plant life, and the land/ocean interface, with few deepwater vessels available for research and exploration beyond the continental shelf. Then on December 7, 1941, Japanese forces attacked the United States naval base at Pearl Harbor in Hawaii and the world changed forever.

Scripps, Woods Hole, and other marine stations quickly joined the war effort. Scripps's Roger Revelle, the tall, personable, and always curious father of modern oceanography, became the first Oceanographer of the Navy shortly after setting up a university war lab at the Point Loma submarine base. Among his colleagues was an Austrian-born graduate student named Walter Munk.

"Now physical oceanography, the study of acoustics, water temperature, currents, the bottom structure, visibility, all things that might affect submarine or ship operations came into their own," Munk recalled in an interview with me years later.

By helping in the development of sonar and sound location to track enemy subs, the physical oceanographers at Scripps and Woods Hole helped the navy win the war at sea. They also developed underwater cameras and explosives, anti-fouling paints, diving technology, and surf predictions for Allied amphibious landings, including D-Day.

But the end of World War Two quickly segued into a cold war with the Soviet Union, and the testing of U.S. atomic weapons in the Pacific. In the winter of 1945 Revelle was put in charge of studying the ocean impact of nuclear bomb tests at Bikini atoll. "We had most of the oceanographers in the country out there. There weren't so many in those days," he recalled with a wistful smile when I interviewed him at his lovely oceanfront home in La Jolla.

Appreciating the good thing it had in marine science, the navy provided war-surplus deepwater vessels to its oceanographer friends and, in 1946, established the Office of Naval Research (ONR), which became the major funder of U.S. ocean science for much of the cold war. By 1949 ONR was providing 40 percent of all science funding in the United States. Along with supporting Scripps and Woods Hole, ONR also created or greatly expanded marine science programs at universities in Washington, Oregon, Texas, Florida, New York, and Rhode Island.

"The physical oceanographers became the directors of all the stations, and the marine biologists felt like they were now second-class citizens," explains Deborah Day, Scripps's senior archivist.

In 1955 Roger Revelle helped choose a deepwater site 450 miles southwest of San Diego for Operation Wigwam, the navy's test-firing of a nuclear depth charge. The blast was not supposed to break the surface, but it did, showering his observer ship with radiation. Two days later, on May 16, 1955, a spike of radiation passed over San Diego. Revelle told me that a number of the scientists he'd recruited for Wigwam later died of bone cancer and leukemia, radiation-related illnesses. "Those bomb tests made an antiweapons man out of me," he said. "I feel very strongly about it. I don't think anybody should be developing nuclear weapons."

Still, a year later, in 1956, Woods Hole hosted Project Nobska, a summer-long retreat of leading oceanographers and weapons scientists that led to the concept and development of submarine-launched, nuclear-tipped Polaris missiles. This marked a major turning point for two cold war adversaries: the navy had broken the air force's monopoly on offensive nuclear weapons. From that time on, there would be a nuclear "triad" of land-based, airborne, and sea-launched nuclear weapons. For the next thirty years the navy would dedicate itself to protecting its boomers (missile submarines) while going after Soviet subs using satellites, helicopters, surface ships, and attack submarines along with the best available science.

The civilian marine stations became top-heavy with physical oceanographers and physicists with high-level security clearances working not only for the navy but the air force, CIA, and DARPA (Defense Advanced Research Projects Agency), the Pentagon's R & D center. They were also blessed with a growing fleet of navy-funded blue-water research vessels, including the deep-submersible *Alvin* and its mother ship, *Atlantis*.

The growing field of physical oceanography made several significant contributions to earth science. It proved the theory of plate tectonics (continental drift) and, with the support of Roger

Revelle, helped identify the link between rising levels of carbon dioxide in the atmosphere and industrial greenhouse gas emissions. Revelle also lectured about the human impact on climate change at Harvard University to, among others, a young student named Al Gore.

Unfortunately, oceanographic biology, marine ecology, and work in the nearshore environment were badly neglected in the latter half of the twentieth century. Despite a huge expansion of American oceanographic power during the cold war, as measured in terms of people, ships, and dollars, the public interest was not well served. The civilian marine stations became so much a part of the navy's deepwater world that they failed to identify and alert the public to the blue frontier's near shore and other living resources at risk. They failed to let us know that watersheds, estuaries, salt marshes, mangrove swamps, wild beaches, sea grass meadows, barrier islands, seamounts, coral reefs, and the 90 percent of marine wildlife that depend on them were in a state of rapid decline as a result of cascading environmental insults. While the responsibility for this awful neglect may be limited, we are all sharing in its consequences.

By the late 1970s I'd settled into what we called Cliff House, a brown clapboard three-bedroom rental sixty feet above the sea. It had a sandy garden on an alleyway entry and floor-to-ceiling plate-glass living room windows (lined with abalone shells) that looked out onto a wooden deck, ice-plant-covered cliff, ocean vista, and open air where once a residential street had passed in front of it. Sunset Cliffs, like much of the California coastline, was slowly eroding and had formed a cave below us that would make the house shake on stormy winter nights when the waves would crash into it. One block south a condemned pink stucco three-story apartment hung half suspended over the edge; its demise finally came several years later with a loud clattering collapse.

For myself and my roommates—Manny Ramos, a bodysurfing Cuban American lawyer, and Charlie Landon, a California-bred surfer and TV cameraman for the local CBS affiliate—it was the perfect retreat and party house. More than once we spent "the morning after" collecting empty Corona bottles off the ice-plant-covered cliff while shaking people awake. Luckily, none of them ever rolled over the edge. That would be the edge of a vast and mysterious wilderness, and we never forgot it was just beyond the glass reflections of our living room fireplace.

Every evening brown pelicans would fly in V formations past our deck on their way to roost along the cliffs. In winter we could look out and see gray whales migrating south, returning from feeding off Alaska to begin breeding in the warm waters of Mexico's Baja lagoons. With some twenty thousand protected grays, the restoration of this once endangered cetacean tribe stood as a tribute to whale and marine mammal conservation. I'd often keep an eye out across the slate-colored water for the spray clouds of their breaths and then try to count their tail flips or breaches when they'd rise full-bodied out of the sea before crashing down again with a great splash. Some say they do this to remove parasites from their skin; others think it's for the pure joy of it.

In the spring and summer, when hollowed-out aquamarine waves left rooster tails of spray in the diamond-dappled sea, I'd clamber down the sandstone cliff with Charlie or Manny, Churchill flippers in hand, and dive off the rocks to catch the breaking wave off Crab Island, a small outcrop just to our north. Sometimes we'd encounter a hauled-up sea lion or tide pool octopus along the slick marine shelf on our way home.

Ours was also a dangerous wilderness. Once I asked Charlie to show me how to board-surf, and he took me out in a storm surge and then paddled off. I spent the next hour with my ankle strapped to what felt like an elongated cement barge as I worked my way back through tumultuous eight-foot shore break into the narrow beach at Santa Cruz Cove, motivated only by my desire to kill my roommate.

Once I had to throw one of Charlie's longboards down to a pair of lifeguards trying to rescue a young girl who had fallen off the narrow sandstone path that ran below our deck, while a Coast Guard helicopter hovered nearby. She died on the way to the hospital. Another time we saw a cabin cruiser breaking up in the surf. Charlie grabbed his video camera while I took the sound deck. By the time we joined the paramedics on the beach below Pescadero Avenue it was getting dark. We provided illumination from the camera's portable light as they applied their shock paddles to the chest of the victim, a heavyset man in swimming trunks and a white T-shirt. Again, it was too late. Three of the six people on that boat drowned.

Around this time I did a year's work for the People's Bicentennial Commission (PBC), founded by my iconoclastic friend Jeremy Rifkin. PBC promoted a wry alternative vision to the staid corporate-sponsored celebrations of the American Revolution. In 1973, for example, we led a march of twenty thousand young people through the snow on the two hundredth anniversary of the Boston Tea Party and dumped empty fifty-five-gallon drums into Boston Harbor to protest offshore oil drilling and the power of the big oil companies.

My father worried I was neglecting my journalism, and I

agreed but explained it was just a short break from freelancing, which was proving financially difficult, in order to have some paid fun.

As I matured my dad and I had stopped fighting and began to enjoy each other's company. He was both emotionally support-ive and respectful after my mother died. Although Max was a bald, roguish, charming guy, I don't think he ever got over Eva. I liked to bring my friends by his place when I was in New York. He'd cook us steaks and fries and offer some vodka and salted black bread. Once when I was there with my sister we asked him if he'd really supported the Vietnam War.

"Of course not," he said with some emotion. "How could I support a war that was turning my children against the country that gave me refuge?" I was twenty-three and it was the first time it really struck me what it meant that my father was an im-migrant and a refugee.

A year later, on a hot summer day in New York City, he suf-fered a massive stroke and heart attack. In the hospital it became clear that, along with partial paralysis, he'd also lost much of his intellectual strength and sense of presence. After a few weeks we had to move him to a nursing home in Fort Smith, Arkansas, where Aunt Sue and Uncle Al had retired. His sister would take care of him over the next three years, and I would fly in from California every few months. I'd sit with my dad and we'd talk about his past growing up in Coney Island and shared memories, like the first time he took me fishing off Sheepshead Bay in Brooklyn and I caught a conger eel.

One of the nursing home's male attendants, Ken, turned out to be an ex–Navy SEAL who'd worked with military dolphins carrying out top-secret missions in which the animals would swim into North Vietnamese waters and attach limpet mines to enemy wharves and piers before returning to their pickup boats. "The thing that still sticks with me after all these years is the intelligence of those water mammals," he recalled. "You'd listen to them in their pens or working together in the water and swear they were talking to each other." I interviewed Ken and a number of other ex-trainers, scientists, and military personnel for an exposé I was doing at the time on the navy's (still active) decades-old marine mammal program, which has involved dolphins, sea lions, beluga whales, even a pair of orcas. You just never know where you'll find a source.

Meanwhile, my dad got a pacemaker installed and slowly faded. At our last Passover seder he sat in a wheelchair with a crooked smile and lopsided yarmulke, which I straightened out before kissing him on the forehead.

He was unconscious during his final days, but when I arrived in his hospital room and took his hand, he squeezed back to let me know he knew I was there. I was at his bedside reading John Steinbeck's *In Dubious Battle* when he passed away.

"He's gone," the nurse said. I looked over at him and there was only a corpse where he had been breathing a moment before. I understood what she meant. Aunt Sue came into the room, and I went into the hall to call Deborah, who'd moved to Boston. I couldn't speak when she answered the phone. "I know," she said, and began to cry.

A month later, on my twenty-eighth birthday, I broke up with the first woman to break my heart. I couldn't get much work done. I spent a lot of time alone in my room so people wouldn't see me crying. I stopped going to the beach. I began feeling like I was wasting my time in the water, that I was being self-indulgent. I finally escaped my grief when I decided to cover the Sandinista revolution in Nicaragua with my good friend John Hoagland, a former navy brat and surfer turned San Francisco ironworker and photographer who'd moved to the Mojave Desert. I made some contacts, got us press credentials, and in the spring of 1979 headed back to war.

It was during the five years I covered the civil and highly un-civil conflicts in Central America, amid the bombs, bullets, mu-tilated death-squad victims, coffee fincas, DDT-scented cotton fields, crowded barrios, and burned-over forests, that I came to appreciate the close connections between issues of war, develop-ment, population, poverty, and natural resource management, including management of the greater part of our blue world that's salt water.

I was traveling through Guatemala's Alto Plano in the bloody winter of 1980. We had just hitched a ride on a truck out of the town of Nebaj, where three days earlier the army had killed eight Mayan Indians, shooting into a crowd of demonstrators in the town square. "What did they want?" I asked one of the soldiers who'd opened fire on them. "Who knows?" he said in Spanish. "They don't even speak our language."

As we drove along the dark switchback of the steep, unpaved road we came upon a convoy of open trucks full of Indian cam-pesinos guarded by army troops carrying Israeli Galil assault rifles and wearing black woolen balaclavas to hide their identi-ties. Their "recruits" were the Mayan army of labor who would be used as seasonal pickers in the cotton fields of the Atlantic lowlands. There they would have a month-long reprieve from the brutal repression in the mountains, only to face pesticide poisoning and backbreaking wage slavery as they harvested an agro-export crop that was eroding and drying out what had recently been lush coastal rain forest.

Crossing the lines into the guerrilla-controlled mountain regions of El Salvador, I often heard gunfire but never a wild bird song. Hungry people had eaten them all. In Honduras I lived for a time on the second floor of a two-story hotel with rats that would scratch inside the wall behind my headboard and a tarantula that periodically visited my wrought-iron balcony. When we went out for steak they'd tell us to cut away the fat because that's where the DDT concentrated. The river running through town was little more than a sewage latrine, not unlike the muddy, parasite-infected lakefront in Nicaragua's capital of Managua, where I watched the Red Cross burning bodies during the insurrection to stop the spread of infection.

Tegucigalpa, like most of the region's refugee-swollen cities, smelled of dust, diesel, and dung. "Ecology in the Third World," a Brazilian expert later pointed out, "begins with water, garbage, and sewage."

At the edge of town there was a huge dump where children dug through mounds of burning garbage for anything of value, recycling at its worst.

Central America's conflicts were at their heart about land, food, water, and inequality exacerbated by an exploding population. The infant mortality rate was around sixty per thousand live births. One out of ten children didn't make it past the age of five. Hunger and malnutrition were the common facts of life in the countryside and many urban barrios. For many, little has changed in the last thirty years.

I remember covering a U.S. military war game on the Honduran coast close to Nicaragua in 1983 with thousands of U.S. paratroopers dropping out of big C-141 jets and a photojournalist taking a picture of a bare-chested Miskito Indian man with a spear and a fish passing in front of a then state-of-the-art Black Hawk helicopter.

By the turn of the twenty-first century most of the adult Miskito Indian men along the coast of Honduras and Nicaragua were, despite the end of their region's horrendous crimson-stained wars, still struggling to survive, diving for lobster that was then exported to the United States. "Red Gold" had grown into a fifty-million-dollar seafood business, by far the biggest on the region's isolated Mosquito Coast. As the lobster were stripped out of the shallows, the divers began hunting their quarry in deeper waters of up to 150 feet, working five or six hours a day with little or no safety training and piss-poor equipment. When they stayed down too long and came up too quickly, the nitrogen from the compressed air they breathed built up in their fatty tissue, forming bubbles in their bloodstream that could lodge in joints and other parts of their bodies, including their lungs and brains, resulting in excruciating pain, maiming, or death. The traditional treatment for decompression sickness, or the bends, is to put the victim in a recompression chamber, taking him back to the pressure he was under sixty feet below the surface so the nitrogen goes back into stasis and then slowly decompressing him again, having him breathe oxygen to help purge the nitrogen. It's kind of like opening a beer bottle that's been shaken up. If you just crack a corner of the cap, the fizz escapes and equalizes slowly. Pop the top and you get a foamy mess.

Unfortunately, there were only two recompression chambers for the entire coast, and they were too far away and too expensive for most of the men to get to. Plus, many of them believed that decompression sickness was a punishment by protective ocean spirits (not unlike mermaids) aimed at those who took too many lobsters, which included almost everyone trying to feed his family or get ahead quickly. As a result, over four thousand of the roughly nine thousand divers suffered serious injuries, including crippling paralysis, deafness, and damaged limbs that had to be amputated.

Horror stories like these keep multiplying as more than half the world's population is now living within fifty miles of its coastlines, and the impact of this demographic shift puts both the ocean and those who live too close to it at risk, not only from the exploitation and depletion of its natural resources but also from disasters, both natural and unnatural.

Without good potable water and sewage systems, without controls on industrial dumping, pathogens and bacteria float out to sea and return with the tides, as do industrial solvents, toxic chemicals, oily wastes, heavy metals, and Harmful Algal Blooms (HABs). Harmful Algal Blooms are naturally occurring phenomena sometimes called red tides (they can also appear to be brown, green, or even black) and are made up of dense concentrations of certain algae, including dinoflagellates and diatoms, which produce potent neurotoxins. Fed by human-generated nutrient pollution from agriculture and cities, they are reportedly on the increase worldwide. HABs taint seafood, kill marine fish and mammals, and cause human respiratory and skin irritations that have hospitalized people from coastal China to south Florida. Other HAB-related illnesses include ciguatera fish poisoning, sometimes lethal neurotoxic and paralytic shellfish poisoning, always unpleasant diarrheic shellfish poisoning, and amnesic shellfish poisoning that can cause permanent short-term memory loss.

Not surprisingly, polls have found that citizens of the poorest cities of Latin America and Africa express the same opinions as those living in the richest parts of North America and Europe—that we have to do better by the environment, even if it means sacrificing short-term economic advantage. Most people I've met in my travels have the same commonsense understanding that clean air, clean water, productive soil, bountiful seas, and wild places—including untrammeled beaches and coral reefs—are not luxuries to be deferred by the poor during a process of rapid integration into the world market, but rather the essentials of a decent life.

John Hoagland had brought his surfboard down to El Salvador, and the beach became our escape from the daily horrors and emotional deadening of war in which we'd no longer find ourselves flinching at the sound of bombs and automatic-weapons fire or reacting to the sight of mutilated bodies left behind by the death squads. It also filled the need for some kind of action in between the military operations and rebel offensives.

One time I had a dream about my father. He was in his wheelchair talking to me in my old house in Douglaston and then suddenly the meat on his face and chest started falling off, exposing his skull and ribs like on the fresh corpses we found dumped each morning after the military curfew lifted. My aunt Sue, who was there in the dream, said, "You know he was lying to you. You know he's already dead, don't you?" After I woke up I called

John on my pension's tapped telephone and asked if he wanted to go to La Libertad.

John liked surfing the break off the town of La Libertad, forty-five minutes south of San Salvador. I preferred the long body-friendly barrels along the Costa del Oro. North of La Libertad a modern highway twisted for miles along a rocky coastline not unlike northern California's, marked by small sandy coves and abandoned beach clubs up to the border with Guatemala. There was a Japanese-owned beach club about an hour north, completed just as the war was beginning in 1979. It remained open but empty. For five dollars they'd serve you lunch and let you use their wave-splashed sandy-bottomed pool cut out of a tidal shelf or their crescent-shaped surfing beach with its powerful rip current.

To the south of La Libertad lay endless expanses of curving white and gray sand beaches, tropical estuaries, and mangrove swamps leading to the island-speckled Gulf of Fonseca. The gulf was a shallow seven-hundred-square-mile inlet shared with Honduras and Nicaragua, a natural shrimp factory with mangrove nurseries and river-fed nutrients for their fast growth. El Salvador's small navy was based out of the mosquito-ridden gulf port town of La Unión.

The first time I went to La Unión I was told the guerrillas had staged an attack, but when photographer Stuart Zitin and I arrived, it turned out the army and navy had actually had a Wild West shoot-out with the National Guard over control of the shrimp and gun smuggling rackets. A short time later we saw a drunken machete-wielding *guardia* attack and kill an unarmed sailor. His gun-toting buddies discouraged any intervention.

My first Salvador surf safari was a Sunday excursion south of

La Libertad to the beach at La Zunganera. On the way in we passed an army patrol that had stopped a busload of campesinos. About fifty men, women, and children were grouped by the side of the road, the adults with their hands behind their heads, while troops armed with G3 rifles frisked them and searched their belongings.

We turned onto a rocky dirt road, bouncing through the densely populated countryside past planted fields of corn, sugar, and cotton where a crop duster plane was spraying insecticide, oblivious to the campesinos walking along the road that fronted the fields. We finally arrived at the "beach town," a small grouping of thatch and tin huts built alongside two cinder-block cantinas. Pigs, scrawny dogs, and chickens wandered freely in the sandy street that opened onto the beach. We headed down onto the hot sand and laid out our towels. The beach stretched as far as the eye could see into distant ground mists. It was backed by scrub pines and coconut palms. Three blue and white fishing boats lay belly up in the sand. A hot tropical sun shone overhead as six-foot jade-colored breakers rolled just offshore. The water was around seventy-eight degrees. After getting munched in a couple of large waves I caught some good long rides with clean faces. There was a strong rip in the water and, after about an hour, it brought me to shore a mile down from where I'd started.

On the walk back I collected some bright pink coral and yellow shells, passing the empty pools and locked beach villas of some of the country's wealthier families, who'd fled to Miami.

That afternoon we had a couple of pilsner beers in front of one of the cinder-block cantinas, saying no to the kids who offered to sell us turtle eggs on banana leaves. Sitting around our table listening as someone played Ronstadt's "Blue Bayou" on the open-air jukebox, we could almost believe we were in a place of peace. I spotted a large animal break the surface of the waves where I'd earlier entered the ocean, then dive below again. I thought it was a seal, but the locals insisted it wasn't a *foca* but a shark, *el tiburón.* "Never swim at night," an old fisherman warned. "The sharks feed at night."

"And if the sharks don't get you, the ORDEN (a right-wing paramilitary group) will," one of the younger guys said.

We were driving back toward the city, the sun setting blood orange over tall fields of green sugarcane, when we ran into a large group of campesinos and displaced travelers. They told us their bus had been hijacked by the guerrillas and was being held down the road. There was a middle-class-looking girl of about sixteen, with shiny dark hair and wearing jeans and a halter top; she was standing off with two boys and crying hysterically. We asked her what happened. "I borrowed my father's truck . . . to go to the beach . . . with my boyfriends," she sobbed. "And I didn't tell him and . . . the guerrillas stole it and . . ."

"She's grounded for life," I told my colleagues Stuart, Renato, and Peter, who gravely nodded their agreement. We parked and, with damp shorts and salty wet hair, grabbed our cameras, note-books, and my tape recorder and began walking down the road. It was getting dark and we could just make out the bus pulled across the road in the distance. We could see a small fire in front of it and goods and packages scattered on the ground. There were four standing figures and a fifth, possibly the bus driver, lying facedown on the ground. *"Periodistas! Prensa!"* (Reporters! Press!) we yelled as we approached.

"Go back. We can't talk with you now," one of the guerrillas with a rifle yelled.

"Which group are you with?" we shouted. "FPL? [Popular Liberation Forces] Are you sure we can't come over there? We'd like to talk with you."

One of them dropped to one knee, aiming his assault rifle at us.

"Okay, I think we'll probably be heading back now. See you around."

It was only when I looked back years later that I considered my personal motivations for being there. I'd lost both my parents and was deeply depressed when I took off with John for Nicaragua. He'd broken up with his longtime live-in girlfriend and had been mining turquoise in the Mojave Desert. Our good friend and brother-under-fire Richard Cross, a landscape photographer, had walked into his fiancée's apartment in Bogotá, Colombia, to find her in the arms of another man. Two days later he was in the war zone. We were all close to thirty, single, and with little to lose.

"Hey, Dave. I heard they caught you hanging out with the Gs [guerrillas]," Al Schaufelberger noted with wry humor when we spoke after my arrest by the Salvadoran army in 1983.

Al was a Navy SEAL, an elite Sea, Air, and Land commando from the Coronado base in San Diego, and I was writing for the hometown paper, the *San Diego Union*, so that was a good start for our casual friendship. Plus, we both loved the ocean, though our approach was a little different. SEALs tend to be great watermen but also highly focused warriors. A commercial diver who worked in the offshore oil industry once griped to me, "A SEAL knows sixty-nine ways to kill you underwater but hand him a wrench and he's lost." I think Al was a little jealous that, as a reporter, I could cross the lines and interview the guerrillas, the

"Gs," whom he respected much more than our shrimp-stealing "allies" he was training.

Thirty-three, blond, and stocky, Al ran the U.S. Navy Military Group out of a cluttered office in the fortresslike U.S. embassy in San Salvador, traveling every week by air to La Unión, where he and three SEAL teammates were training a seventy-man Salvadoran navy commando unit known as the Piranhas. They'd equipped them with Zodiac rubber assault boats, sea search radar, high-frequency communications gear, and other maritime toys. They'd even gotten them to stop hijacking shrimp boats and instead head up through the mangrove swamps south of Usulután to challenge the guerrillas in some direct combat.

I told him I still thought the FMLN (Farabundo Martí National Liberation Front) guerrillas could take the navy base at La Unión any time they wanted. "That's why we sleep in a barracks near the water," he explained with a grin. "If they come over the wall we'll head out to sea. Nobody can take on a SEAL in the water."

The rebels knew that, too. Al was waiting to pick up his girlfriend outside the university in San Salvador when an assassin walked up to his car window and shot him in the head. His was the first U.S. military death in El Salvador acknowledged by Washington.

A few weeks later, on June 21, 1983, my friend Richard Cross and Dial Torgerson, a reporter with the *Los Angeles Times*, were killed when their car ran over a land mine on the Honduras–Nicaragua border.

Nine months after that, on March 16, 1984, John Hoagland was shot and killed in a crossfire during an army-rebel shoot-out near Suchitoto, El Salvador. He was taking pictures for *Newsweek* at the time of his death.

A few months before his death Richard had stayed with me at Cliff House in Ocean Beach while John was visiting his family in nearby Lemon Grove. We'd all gone to the beach and then to a party out on Black Mountain Road east of I-5, which was dry coastal desert at the time. There was lots of pot and beer and te-quila and dancing with friends and girlfriends, and the people who owned the place had a wolf dog that would growl softly to let you know he was there when you'd go out back to piss on a cactus. If I tried to find that place today I'd be driving through the middle of a sprawling upscale suburban development. There are over twenty scientific papers indicating that if more than 10 percent of a watershed becomes impervious (is cemented over, for instance) its water quality will inevitably decline. Sprawl is the method by which we love our coasts to death. Still, it's hard to have empathy for the death of nature—for whales, watersheds, and wild beaches—when we as a species are still so willing to kill our own kind.

"John didn't go looking for trouble, trouble just seemed to find its way to him," I claimed, speaking at his funeral. It was an open casket, and I remember being surprised at how soft his hair felt. Of course we'd both gone looking for trouble, and we'd found it in spades. Richard was thirty-three years old when he died. John was thirty-six.

I produced a documentary, "John Hoagland—Frontline Photo-grapher," with help from my Cliff House roommate Charlie. In the documentary I interviewed John's son, Eros, who was four-teen at the time. He talked about a little yellow submarine that John had carved for him; he'd toss it in the ocean in San Francisco and it would always come back. "That little yellow submarine," he said with a sigh. He also said he'd like to be a photographer like his dad someday; I just felt sorry for the kid.

In 2008 I had dinner with Eros on his return from Baghdad, where he'd been shooting pictures for the *New York Times*. He'd become a professional photographer like his dad, starting with visual profiles of postwar street gangs in El Salvador. When I invited him to a party a short time later, he called from the airport to say he couldn't make it. He was off to New Zealand to chill and go surfing with a buddy who lives there. "Does he have [surf]boards for you?" I asked.

"I'm bringing my own sticks. I mean, just to be safe," he said, and for a moment I could have sworn it was John on the phone.

In 1984, along with the documentary that aired on PBS and the Discovery Channel, I curated a photo exhibition of John's work, then expanded it to include Richard's work, calling the finished product "Two Faces of War."

"Just one thing, a request from a friend of theirs," I wrote in the brochure for its opening. "The next time you see a picture in a newspaper or magazine from Nicaragua, El Salvador, Beirut, or some other Third World trouble spot, a picture that gives you pause or makes you think, look closely.

"Down there at the bottom or along the side in tiny print will be a name. Read that name. It's the name of a person like John Hoagland or Richard Cross who, for whatever personal reasons, is out there risking his or her life to show you another face of humanity."

Over the next months I spent a lot of time lying in the sand pretending I was dead or else floating in the ocean waiting for the next set of waves to roll in. Back then the ocean was still clean enough to heal most wounds.

5

Private Eye to Scuba Guy

I'm just a guy working underwater, working not playing games.

MIKE NELSON, *SEA HUNT*

In my early thirties I would take new directions in my life,
changing what I did for work, where I lived, and how I inter-
acted with the sea. I missed my lost friends and colleagues from
the wars and life under fire. I was like a junkie or tobacco fiend

having to kick a habit that would otherwise kill me. Three times a week my kenpō karate class would run for three or four miles down the beach, out to the end of the Ocean Beach pier, and into the hills overlooking the sea before heading back up Newport Avenue to our dojo to begin class: we'd do sixty to ninety minutes of jumping jacks, leg lifts, practice kicks, punches, blocks, and katas before free sparring with each other. Then Ray Leal, our instructor, or sensei, would turn off the lights and have us lie on the floor, close our eyes, and slow our breathing. That allowed me to get centered and find my *ki*.

Charlie also bought a Hobie Cat, a sixteen-foot green catamaran that we'd take out into the ocean and sail on one hull. We'd be "trapped out" (standing) on the edge of the trampoline above the upper free-flying hull, wearing hip harnesses clipped to a trapeze line so we could lean back and push the wind until, flexing with the swells like a living beast, it might flip over on us and we'd have to jump off the craft and then use a long rope while standing on one hull to try to right it again, pulling with all our strength and leverage to lift up the soaking wet sail.

One time Charlie got us going so fast the bottom hull dropped below the waterline and we purled, pitchpoling (cartwheeling) forward as the Hobie tried to become a submarine, and I found myself underwater with the mast and sail, trying to unclip various harness connections while clearing bungee cord from around my neck without panic.

More controlled thrills occurred when we'd surf the Cat onto the beach at Pescadero near Cliff House, climb up top for a quick snack break at home, then relaunch into the surf. That and body-surfing kept me sane. But I also needed work to keep me engaged and pay the rent.

My favorite TV show as a kid had been *Sea Hunt* in which

Lloyd Bridges played diver/investigator Mike Nelson. I also liked *The Rockford Files* in the 1970s. Jim Rockford lived in a trailer by the beach near his dad (these scenes were shot at Emerald Cove in Laguna Beach, California). He could hardly make ends meet and often got beat up working his cases. Not surprisingly, he's been a longtime favorite of real PIs. I'd thought of becoming a private investigator even before I became a reporter, and now, disillusioned with my chosen vocation after too many years at war putting lives—my own and others—at risk, without seeing our reporting have any noticeable impact, I returned to this earlier idea.

I used my background as an investigative journalist for the six thousand hours required to get a California private investigator's license, then studied for six weeks before taking a half-day exam in LA. Although I would have liked to do maritime investigations like Mike Nelson, mostly I ended up doing criminal and civil cases, including homicides, drug charges, and wrongful deaths, starting with a 1984 attempted murder case at a San Diego bar named the Aztec Inn.

Just after I became a PI, my sister married and moved to the San Francisco Bay Area with her husband, Patrick. Deborah came down to visit me and said that if I was ready to pull up stakes, I was welcome to move in with them for a time. Professionally frustrated and ready for a change, I packed my clothes, my wet suit and flippers, my boogie board, artwork, books, and guns and headed north up the coast through Los Angeles, Santa Barbara, Big Sur, Monterey, and Santa Cruz to the famed and foggy City by the Bay.

Actually, Deborah and Pat lived on the sunnier east side of the bay, in the Alameda County neighborhood of Fruitvale. It was named back when the area was full of fruit-packing warehouses, just as Jingletown on the Oakland waterfront was named for the money those warehouse workers would spend in its waterfront bars. That was during the early twentieth century, when oyster pirate turned marine enforcement agent Jack London was sailing up and down the bay, living adventures he'd later recount in one of his books, *Tales of the Fish Patrol*.

Initially I did contract work for a well-known San Francisco detective agency. At the same time, the local PBS station, KQED, aired the John Hoagland documentary and offered me additional work, starting with a half-hour documentary on offshore oil drilling, which we titled "Troubled Waters."

Fellow producer Steve Talbot and I visited fishermen, kelp harvesters, and innkeepers in northern California who were opposed to the new offshore oil drilling proposed by the Reagan administration. We also helicoptered out to offshore drilling rigs off Santa Barbara, the site of the infamous 1969 Union Oil platform blowout and spill that helped launch the environmental movement of the 1970s and turned most Californians against offshore drilling. We also shot video at a new onshore refinery under construction by Chevron just north of Santa Barbara.

After the show aired a Chevron vice president complained we'd been unfair to them, though they refused to go on air with us to debate the show, explaining that, as a California-based corporation, they couldn't risk the backlash. We sent them a letter pointing out that there'd been six pro- and six anti-drilling interviews in the program, but I knew what was really going on. They'd been killed by the visuals in a highly visceral medium. Against the anti-drilling voices coming from Mendocino's pine- and redwood-covered bluffs, one of the most scenic stretches of coastline in the world, the Chevron spokesman had chosen to have his interview filmed in front of the company's new refinery, then under construction. "Some people think their ocean views are beautiful. Some of us think an oil rig is beautiful," he'd said to the background sights and sounds of a construction site and a jackhammer. If they'd asked, we would have told them they were killing themselves, but they didn't.

Of course, today the oil drilling debate is no longer about energy versus marine pollution. It's become a larger product-liability issue. This product, used as directed, overheats your planet.

In April 2009 the Department of the Interior held a series of public hearings on the future of offshore energy in New Jersey; New Orleans; Anchorage, Alaska; and San Francisco, California. In San Francisco I was one of more than five hundred people— including Senator Barbara Boxer, Governor Ted Kulongoski of Oregon, the lieutenant governor of California, and four House members of Congress—who testified and rallied for clean energy and against any new oil drilling. Boxer noted that the coast was a treasure and a huge economic asset, "just as is," generating twenty-four billion dollars in annual value and 390,000 jobs. Surfers, dockworkers, wind-energy entrepreneurs, and fishermen all agreed with her. The only two people advocating for more oil drilling were a guy from the Western States Petroleum Association (people held dollar bills up as he spoke) and the operator of a Super 8 motel.

In the late 1980s I was working as both a private investigator and a TV producer, reporting on the navy, on high-seas drift-net fishing vessels that were devastating the North Pacific ecosystem, and on nuclear waste that had been dumped in a national marine sanctuary. I also reported (for the Group W TV network) on the

AIDS epidemic that was devastating the gay population of the Bay Area and, with the rapid spread of HIV to different at-risk communities, impacting the lives of millions of gay and straight people across the United States. I produced a national documentary on AIDS and the U.S. healthcare system titled "Critical Condition" narrated by Richard Dreyfuss.

At the time, epidemiologists and other scientists were tracking HIV to the rain forests of Africa, where they discovered a form of the virus had existed in chimpanzees and the indigenous people who ate them for at least sixty years and possibly for centuries. It was only with the industrial logging of the forests and the road building that accompanied it, with truckers driving timber out of the forest and having assignations with the prostitutes in the boomtowns that sprang up along the roads, that the sexually transmitted and blood-borne virus suddenly emerged in the global village. The rapid spread of HIV showed how the disruption of rain forests and other intact ecosystems, including marine ecosystems such as coral reefs and coastal mangrove forests, could unleash life-threatening epidemics and global pandemics.

The increased introduction of human viruses and pathogens into the ocean environment also created public health concerns around the globe. In the early 1990s cholera was discovered in the ballast water of several ships from Latin America that docked in Mobile, Alabama. The Food and Drug Administration then discovered the same strain of cholera in oyster samples taken from the bay. More common today are gastrointestinal diseases that result from sewage discharges and pulmonary and neurological impacts from harmful algal blooms. Recently there have also been reports of bacterial staph infections from swimming in polluted coastal waters, including the death of a man who was shoved into Honolulu's Ala Wai harbor following a sewage spill in 2006.

In 1985 my sister and Pat moved back to Boston, and I moved into San Francisco with my writer friend Steve Chapple and his eighty-pound Alaskan malamute, Ed. It was a perfect town for a PI. More than once, driving around doing casework in my 1967 Malibu, I felt as if I were living in a Dashiell Hammett novel.

I loved San Francisco but hated the weather, which, like all weather and most rain, is a product of the ocean. Evaporation from the ocean generates clouds and rain, which runs down from our mountaintops in streams and rivers, following gravity through watersheds into bays, estuaries, salt marshes, mangrove swamps, sea grass meadows, kelp forests, coral reefs, seamounts (submerged mountains), submarine canyons, and, ultimately, to the deep black plains of the abyss where slime eels feed on whale falls and where marine worms burrow through the mud. From here, the waters begin their slow ascent back to the surface and into our atmosphere, continuing the circulation of vapor that feeds the circle of life.

In San Francisco it was the marine layer I had a problem with, the vapor known as fog, as in bone-chilling. I understood where the summer fog came from but didn't blame the ocean. I blamed the valley. The sun heats the Sacramento and San Joaquin valleys, creating low atmospheric pressure. Meanwhile, productive offshore ocean upwellings bring cold, nutrient-rich water to the surface, where it forms into a mist of fog. Out on the ocean there's a high-pressure area known as the Pacific High which, because air masses like to equalize pressure, is drawn toward the hot low-pressure area inland. This generates wind that sucks the fog through the Golden Gate, a major gap in California's coastal mountain range, and smothers the city in a romantic, fast-moving blanket of white—assuming you find hypothermia romantic. "The coldest winter I ever spent was a summer in San Francisco," wrote Mark Twain. If nothing else, the fog helps the vendors down by Fisherman's Wharf and Pier 39 sell overpriced SF hoodies and sweatshirts to tourists in T-shirts and shorts who come to the city believing California's eleven hundred miles of spectacular coastline is all just a sandy extension of Malibu Barbie's beach house. Personally, I didn't like living among the only urban people in North America wearing wool and leather in July and August.

To get away from it, I began taking trips to Hawaii, the most isolated archipelago in the world, thousands of miles from anywhere, though as lush as Eden, even if most of its plants are now imports. My initial trip took me to the Big Island, where I snorkeled South Point, saw large green sea turtles, and dove through cold, blurry upwellings of fresh water from undersea springs. When I got back to the black sand beach I met a spear fisherman who told me he'd moved there from Ocean Beach. The Big Island, even following the decades of development that have taken place since I made that first visit, is still my favorite place on the planet to chill out in the heat.

I met up with Charlie Landon on Oahu, and we stayed with a mutual friend and former Cliff House neighbor, Ted Woerner, who was living the life, working as an anchor for the local ABC affiliate while renting a Quonset hut with an outdoor shower on Sunset Beach. Here and on the Big Island was where the Hawaiians first perfected *he'e nalu*, wave sliding, and where the royals forbid the commoners from practicing it for fear they'd abandon their taro fields and go surfing. It was on the north shore of Oahu that I would experience both the best and the most terrifying surf of my life.

Inside Waimea Bay I bodysurfed eight-foot faces so smooth you couldn't seem to fall off them. Then, on Sunset Beach, I took Charlie's warning as a dare and went into fifteen-foot waves breaking on a shallow reef. As soon as I felt the surge sucking me up and out, I knew I'd made a mistake. Charlie said he could see my entire body in the face of the wave as I fought to punch through it and out the back side of the shoulder before it sucked me headfirst over the falls. It took me close to an hour to get back into shore without getting mangled on the reef. I had to wait until several sets of waves bridged up and over each other into a churning cauldron of white water that I could swim and tumble back through. It was the first time since El Salvador I'd had that jangly adrenaline rush you get when there's the imminent chance of bone-crushing death.

Sleeping by the beach, I dreamed I was back in El Salvador. It was the tropical heat and lush foliage, the sugarcane fields and third-world feel of the 1980s, when Japanese investors were buying up agricultural lands and turning them into high-end golf resorts whose fertilizer runoff was poisoning the reefs and promoting ciguatera fish poisoning. Native Hawaiians talked of living in an occupied land that once had been their own. More than Texas with its brief republic, Hawaii really was an independent nation until 1893 when, with the backing of U.S. Marines off the heavy cruiser *Boston*, American planters staged an armed coup, overthrowing Queen Liliuokalani and her government.

. . .

In 1985 I also exhibited the "Two Faces of War" photo show at the Eye Gallery in San Francisco. I was at gallery codirector Andrew Ritchie's house in Berkeley that September, planning the exhibit, when a volunteer from the gallery dropped by to pick up a kitten. She was five three with long, straight dark hair; a lithe, athletic body; a feisty, slightly mocking attitude; full lips; bright, lively eyes; and a funny name, Nancy Ledansky. She later claimed I kept blinking my "big brown war reporter eyes" at her, but she had eyes only for the Poose, a little fur ball that mewled in her hand as she stroked it with two fingers. The kitten was (like Nancy) terminally cute and the runt of her litter, a tiny gray and black tabby with yellow-green eyes and a white spot around her nose leather. Before taking the kitten home Nancy looked over the Hoagland and Cross prints I had with me and discussed what she could do to help the exhibition.

After she left I asked Ritchie about her. He told me to forget it, everyone was interested but she wasn't available—she was living with someone in Oakland. Still, Nancy came through on her promise, helping put together a well-attended video presentation to complement the photo exhibit. I found her wry, funny, and flirtatious, although she later insisted that she was only being friendly, not flirtatious, that she just preferred the company of men despite their "perviness."

Two years later I went back to the Eye Gallery to meet up with my war photographer buddy Bill Gentile. I missed him but Nancy was there, and she let me know she was now available. We began to go out together.

I took her down to the tide pools at Fitzgerald Marine Reserve by Moss Beach, south of the city. The rocky intertidal zone where land and ocean meet can be a mesmerizing window into the sea, and at Fitzgerald, it was a wide, flat picture window stretching out a hundred yards to where the sloshed-over rocky reef with its rushing surge channels met a sandbar on which gray wet-eyed harbor seals hauled up at low tide. During low tide, pools of trapped water also formed in its rocky depressions, creating natural aquariums. In these pools you'd find flowery anemones, limpets, big sea stars (or starfish) in orange, red, brown, pink, and purple, also small blenny fish, spiky sea urchins, and sometimes an elusive flounder or other larger critter that had missed the last tidal train home.

Few animals in this dynamic tide-driven ecosystem can harm humans, but many are sensitive and can be harmed by us. The tide pools of California, for example, used to contain large abalones clinging to the rocks along the surf zone—until they were stripped away for sale and consumption. The same problem's now occurring where people collect mussels, sea palms, turban snails, and owl limpets for food even in places such as Fitzgerald, where this kind of foraging is strictly prohibited.

Nancy and I explored until the afternoon tide turned, getting wet to our knees, separating ropy strands of seaweed to reveal living dioramas and dramas no more than a yard or two across. I tickled some anemones till they pulled their purple-and-white-tipped tentacles back into their bulbous green bodies, and let a periwinkle snail crawl across the palm of her hand. She carefully placed it back in the water, telling me the ocean was her favorite place to come.

We walked around on the cypress pine–covered bluffs after the tide covered over the pools. Late in the afternoon we went back down onto the beach and into a sandstone cave where we had our first lingering kiss. She said my kisses made her back tingle. Hers made me spike a fever.

Nancy would prove an enduring partner in love and adventure. During ten years living together we'd dive Australia's Great Barrier Reef, also Hawaii, Florida, Monterey, Mexico, and the Caribbean. We'd climb the Rocky, Sierra, Cascade, and Adirondack Mountains, visit Big Sur, the Oregon dunes, and Alaska's Kenai Peninsula. She took great pictures along the way, attracted many people with her dry wit, fierce independence, and natural beauty, established herself as a respected computer graphics designer in the San Francisco Bay Area while keeping this reporter engaged and grounded.

One day Nancy and I took a trip down to Monterey Bay to visit its famous aquarium and stare out at the sea otters, seals, and seabirds floating in its extensive kelp beds. For decades the kelp had gone missing. After the sea otters (also known as sea beavers because of the value of their pelts) were hunted to near extinction, sea urchin had proliferated, eating away at the kelp's roots until the bottom turned into vast, spiky urchin barrens. Then in 1938 a surviving colony of sea otters was discovered below the steep wilderness cliffs of Big Sur, just south of Monterey. When the otters were reintroduced to Monterey Bay they began eating the urchins with the voracious appetite that only a marine weasel can express. This reopened the ecological space needed for the kelp to return, just as the reintroduction of wolves in Yellowstone has kept the elk from overgrazing the young aspens, giving the trees a chance to grow back along the park's riverbanks, which in turn has helped restore the beaver, martin, and other small fur-bearing mammals that depend on riparian forest growth.

Giant kelp and bull kelp are no aspens, however. They are the redwoods and sequoias of the sea, able to grow up to two feet a day from their "holdfasts" on the bottom, creating complex underwater structure and habitat for whole populations of marine wildlife.

Later, as divers, we would visit the sixty-foot-tall kelp forests from below, watching cathedral shafts of sunlight playing through their tendrils and translucent leaves where kelp bass, bug-eyed rockfish, flounder, leopard sharks, and wolf eel hang out, also seals and sea otters above seafloors littered with anemones, starfish, urchins, and abalone.

I'd been thinking about taking a scuba diving course for a long time when I went to visit my reporter friends Carl and Kathy Hersh in Florida. Carl, a TV cameraman, had an assignment to shoot an underwater hotel in a marina in Key Largo for a Japanese game show called *How Much Does It Cost to Buy the World?* This was back before Japan's financial bubble burst. On a long hookah air hose from the surface I accompanied Carl thirty-five feet down to the former science habitat, entering through the hotel's underside moon pool. Inside the habitat, we unpacked his TV gear from a couple of waterproof Pelican boxes. Along with three bedroom suites, a head, and a shower there was a central living/ dining area with a video player and selection of tapes, including *20,000 Leagues Under the Sea* and *Beneath the 12-Mile Reef.* It reminded me of the Futurama II exhibit at the 1964 World's Fair. We filmed the owner's bikinied safety assistant showing off the different spaces and taking a freshwater shower, as any newly arrived diver would. When the Japanese producer on the surface used the com line to ask Carl to ask her to please remove her top, Carl told him that wasn't going to happen.

When I got home to the Bay Area I signed myself up for a six-week course from PADI, the Professional Association of Diving

Instructors. Most of it took place in a classroom and a heated, Olympic-sized swimming pool near the San Francisco Zoo. I still use most of the equipment I purchased at that time. Instead of using dive computers, we memorized dive tables designed to keep us out of trouble by not staying down too long or too deep or coming up too quickly. Sometimes when I go out on dives today I'm challenged by dive masters who want to know where my octopus, my spare regulator, and air hose are. I explain that what you see is what you get. "So what happens if you or your dive partner run out of air?" I was recently asked.

"We buddy-breathe," I explained. Of course, that assumes that the panicked person you give your regulator to will give it back. If not, you can punch him in the stomach and send him to the surface (though if he surfaces without exhaling he could rupture his lungs).

I first learned to buddy-breathe in that pool where I got certified. I was partnered with an attractive blond classmate in a blue bikini, and once underwater, we took turns sharing our life's breath off her regulator's mouthpiece. It was probably the sexiest thing I've ever done with someone whose name I don't know.

A week later my class got certified in the bracingly cold green waters of Monterey Bay. After removing and replacing our masks underwater, adjusting our vests to stay neutrally buoyant, dropping and recovering our weight belts, and meeting other test requirements, we were set free to explore. I buddied up with our dive master and swam along the Monterey pier, staring in fascination at boulders covered in berry bright strawberry anemones and sea stars and staring back at big blue rockfish hanging out without concern in the twisting stalks, floats, and translucent aqua green leaves of the giant kelp. A couple of sea lions darted in and out of our peripheral vision.

Some people get nervous underwater or have trouble clearing their sinus cavities as depth and pressure increase, one atmosphere's worth for every thirty-three feet. I found diving one of the most relaxing yet engaging endeavors of my life, a kind of natural sedative for the harried reporter.

I use up very little air when I'm down under, though I do give an occasional muffled shout-out to some curious seal, sea lion, turtle, or grouper as my way of saying, "You're one awesome critter, dude." I also like to do drift dives in which you float along in the current, the most relaxing thing you can do that's still called a sport.

Off the coast of Kona, Hawaii, there's a popular night dive I've been on where up to thirty divers will sit in a circle on the bottom. The dive masters set up plastic milk cartons full of dive lights pointing toward the surface. The lights attract krill, which in turn attract small goatfish and giant manta rays with wingspans of eight, twelve, and sixteen feet who do acrobatic feeding loops in the water. The tips of their wings will occasionally brush your hair. That seemed less like sport than a performance of Cirque du Soleil, a classic example of nature as spectacle. A few days later in Hilo, on the other side of the Big Island, I went into the town's only dive shop, where I rented a patched and faded wet suit and some other well-worn gear from an old salt who explained that he had to dive at least thirty days a month, " 'cause I'm an addict is why." I took my friend Susan, a local flower grower, on a shore dive outside Hilo: we were the only humans in the water hanging out with a bunch of big green sea turtles whose contented feeding on underwater grasses, though less acrobatic than giant mantas doing backflips, was equally charming.

Of course, there are basic precautions you have to take whenever you go diving, such as making sure that your airflow is working before heading down, something I once left to someone else and then had to correct eighty feet below the surface. Breathing underwater does not come naturally to our species.

Two years after I got certified I moved in with Nancy in the Noe Valley neighborhood of San Francisco. Then, for her thirtieth birthday, I enrolled her in a dive course, telling her it was the first part of her present.

She got through the six-week course without a hitch, then got certified off Monterey's Monastery Beach on a freezing cold day in January 1990, when you could look up and see snow frosting the Santa Cruz mountain peaks. "That was really cold and miserable," she complained, drying off. "But I did it," she added with a proud, purple-lipped grin.

I was now entering one of the most satisfying periods of my life. Through my TV documentary work I had reconciled with my chosen vocation as a journalist while finding ways to maintain what newspaper editor H. L. Mencken had insisted was the job of the press, to "comfort the afflicted and afflict the comfortable." I was also finding both social utility and job satisfaction in my second career as a private investigator.

More important, with Nancy I had found a true love to share my experiences while I was enriched by hers—and by her often wry perspective. We didn't complete each other. We were each complete unto ourselves. We just enjoyed our time together.

Three weeks after she got certified I gave her the second part of her present, which was also a present to myself: a trip to Australia's Great Barrier Reef, one of the great wonders of the world, the only living object that can be seen from space and the coral heart of our blue planet.

6

Coral Gardens

In the multicolored sea gardens seen from a boat as
one drifts above them, there is a tropical lushness and
mystery, a throbbing sense of the pressure of life.

RACHEL CARSON, *THE EDGE OF THE SEA*

Coral reefs are like rain forests in that they thrive in low-nutrient
environments yet produce a mind-boggling abundance of unique
and specialized life-forms. Twenty-five percent of all known
ocean fish are reef residents, also thousands of species of mol-
lusks if you're into brightly colored sea snails. Endangered monk
seals, sea turtles, and seabirds—including frigates and albatross—

nest and breed on coral islands, cays, and atolls, which also, historically, have been a favorite site for pirates to bury their treasure. Coral reefs, along with submarine volcanoes, create the tropical island paradises of our imaginations and of other people's daily lives. Tropical reefs also act as storm barriers and protected anchorages, sources of food, sand, recreation, tourist dollars, and local pride for many coastal and island nations.

Australia's Great Barrier Reef is the largest living thing you can see from space. About 350,000 square kilometers in size, it covers only one-tenth of 1 percent of the world's ocean surface. Yet it supports 8 percent of the world's known fish species, some fifteen hundred, plus more than five hundred species of living coral, including elkhorn and staghorn, branching species listed as threatened in U.S. waters. I figured if she'd never seen a reef before this was the right place for Nancy to start.

"Giant Cod Linked to Diver's Death" blares the headline of the *Cairns Post*, the voice of tropical north Queensland and the Cape York Peninsula, that jutting finger of reef and rain forest that points like an Aussie bush knife at the soft underbelly of Papua New Guinea.

"A heavy blow to the forehead by a giant potato cod is believed to have led to the death of a twenty-four-year-old Innisfail man who was found drowned in the Cod Hole, near Lizard island," reads the lead. It goes on to describe the "freak accident" as similar to past occurrences in which divers were knocked out cold by the big fish and had to be rescued by their dive buddies. Friends of the dead man on the *Explorer 11* said the cod were acting "extremely frisky" at the time of the accident.

I show the article to Nancy to get her mind off sharks. We've just signed up for a three-day trip on the *Explorer 11* live-aboard dive boat.

After buying the newspaper and loading up on film, snacks, and sunblock at the Port Douglas newsagents, we retire to the Hibiscus Inn, where we settle behind a couple of Victoria Bitters on the porch with the proprietor and a few other blokes and sheilas. The proprietor, a bluff fellow with an ample gut, starts expounding on all the great things that can either eat, sting, or poison you to death in Australia's last frontier.

"Crocodiles, of course, they've taken nine people in the last two years, then you have your sharks and snakes. Reckon we've got about seven kinds of snakes in the bush, including the death adder. Then there's your box jellyfish, your poison tree, and your venomous spider. Is there anything in America that can kill you?" he asks, cracking another tinny.

"Only the people," Nancy replies, to a hearty round of laughter. Even the frogs around the pool seem to trill their appreciation.

The next day we head out of port on the *Explorer 11*, a sixty-foot diesel catamaran. We're twelve to dive and a crew of seven: Aussies, Yanks, a Japanese businessman, a BBC cameraman, and a Canadian dive master from British Columbia anxious to swim with blue starfish rather than blue lips.

Personally, I've been waiting on this trip since the age of eleven, when I first read a *National Geographic* article about the Great Barrier Reef, describing how this 1,200-mile-long living maze grew from the limestone skeletons of millions of tiny coral polyps. Actually, it was the picture of a sea snake, whose venom is said to be ten times more deadly than a cobra's, that had captured my youthful imagination. So here we are cruising north into the night under an equatorial sky bright with constellations and star clusters unseen in northern climes, watching the Southern Cross rise and fall, rise and fall. The seas are beginning to build. The first mate, in pirate head rag and earring, is banging away belowdecks to keep the diesels turning while the rest of us retire to our cabins. Hanging on to our rack, Nancy sings us to sleep with the theme song from *Gilligan's Island*: "The weather started getting rough, the tiny ship was tossed. . . ."

Dawn lights up the pink underside of scattered clouds over the calm blue shallows of the outer reef. A full rainbow arches across our open fantail, the only sign of the storm that's passed, as a seaplane drops down to rendezvous with us. We eat a hearty breakfast of eggs, toast, and fresh pineapple as a Japanese TV crew waits on the seaplane's pontoons for our Zodiac raft to pick them up.

Nine A.M., ninety degrees, and ninety miles from shore, it's time to dive the Cod Hole. We pull on our gear, check our buddy's gear (Nancy tugs on the shoulder straps of my buoyancy control vest, makes sure my air's on), and take a giant stride off the rear platform, splashing into the water.

The water temperature is a wonderfully bathlike eighty-five degrees, visibility eighty feet or better. Looking down the anchor chain we can see a dozen big fish lazing around a rock and coral garden. Schools of yellowtail snappers and bright green parrot fish drift by. One of the crew touches bottom with a bucket of defrosted mullet. The big-lipped groupers, spotted blokes with huge sloping heads, gather round like swine for the slopping. These fish are no prissy multihued reef dwellers like triggers and harlequin tusks, aquarium heartthrobs in luminescent colors of red, blue, black, and yellow acting as shills for Kodak and Agfa. No, these brutes are of the Vance Packard school of fish, so ugly they're attractive, ranging in size from 200 to 350 pounds, five and six feet long.

I sidle up to one and stroke his side. He looks at me with a flat, bored fish eye. No food to offer, he isn't interested. Another one is getting greedy by the slop bucket. The dive master bangs his snout with the lid, and he takes off like a scaly offensive linesman. Not a fish you want to be blindsided by.

A real-estate fella from Sydney is wrapping himself around another big cod, riding, stroking, and petting it. I wonder if the local judiciary has any moral statutes covering fish molestation.

Keeping a bit more distance are four or five equally large Napoleon wrasses, blunt-headed, short-tailed creatures colored bright aqua green and blue. Although they can grow to over four hundred pounds, you won't see many in today's unprotected waters. Chinese in Hong Kong and elsewhere will pay ninety dollars a pound or more for their flesh and lips, which are considered a delicacy by the rich and ostentatious.

A large green moray eel comes out of his crevice for a hand-fed fish and a pat on the head. Several large shadows pass overhead. We look up. Media sharks, the Japanese video crew circling above us, twisting their underwater camera this way and that. I look over at the Gal, who's grinning behind her mask and regulator, also snapping away with the Nikonos underwater camera I bought her.

We climb the ladder back onto the boat happy and hungry. Snacks are waiting. As the TV crew members transfer back to their seaplane and fly off we get into our boat routine: dive and eat, catch some sun on the top deck while moving on to the next spot, then dive, eat, dive, eat, dive.

Our second dive takes us to Shark Alley. Unfortunately, most of the sharks are out with the tide. Still, we do get to see our first giant clams. Beautiful, soft mantles of purple, green, and red algae-covered mollusk skin open like fat lips to the sea, getting their nutrients both from the algae and from what they can suck out of the water. Touch them and they withdraw inside their great fluted shells, a second tickle and the shells snap shut with an impatient click.

Some burrowing clams are embedded deep within the hard coral, others rest fully exposed on the sandy bottom, monster bivalves weighing five hundred pounds or more; they could easily absorb ten gallons of tartar sauce. Protected on the Barrier Reef, they appear to have calmed down considerably since the days of my early TV viewing, when they were constantly grabbing Lloyd Bridges by the leg and trying to drown him, forcing him to use his dive knife. I drop down next to one of the four-foot-tall boulder-sized clams, pull my regulator from my mouth, and smile for Nancy's underwater camera.

Our next dive is at Pixie Pinnacle, a coral peak growing along the outer ribbon reefs that drop off into the deep sea. Here, we see shoals of fish playing in and out of the varied corals: soft and hard, fan and mushroom, brain and staghorn, in shades of yellow, green, and pink. Orange-and-white-striped clown fish peek shyly out from the protective embrace of soft stinging anemones. We're not fooled. Anyone who's picked up a dive magazine knows they're the biggest photo hogs on the reef (and that was before *Finding Nemo* made them into top celebrities).

After each dive Nancy and I fill out our logbooks, calculate our depth and time under, and pore over the fish charts. So far, among the critters we've seen are white-tipped reef sharks, rays, angelfish, sea turtles, squirrel, parrot, trigger, unicorn, trumpet, batfish, pullers, groupers, barracuda, pipefish, red emperor, razor, wrasse, box, and long-snouted coral fish.

Later we do our first night dive. Nancy is nervous but pumped, as am I (though less willing to show it). Before we step off the fantail one of the crew throws out a bucket on a rope to see what it is that's curling on the surface at the edge of the light. He hauls it in and they turn out to be red centipedelike sea creatures. No one's quite sure what they are, but at least they're not sea snakes. We take our giant strides into the black water and begin to make our way down the anchor chain.

For me, the dive quickly becomes a scene from *Star Wars*: we're neutrally buoyant, weightless as we would be in space. All we can hear is our own breathing and air bubbles. Our lantern beams cut through the darkness like laser swords, turning green before being lost in infinite space. Then we reach the bottom. There's another big potato cod directly under the boat. Here the bommie, or flat-topped coral head, takes about half an hour to swim around. If we stay together and don't get lost we'll be fine. You don't want to lose your sense of direction fifty feet down and one hundred miles from shore. If you do, you're instructed to go to the surface and look around. That distant light should be your dive boat. Just be sure you're not swimming toward the moon on the horizon. Years later a dive boat out of Port Douglas will miscount its returning divers and leave a couple behind on the reef. Some of their dive gear will be found six months later, though no bodies are ever recovered.

We begin to swim along the outer edge of the bommie. My light finds half a dozen large Napoleon wrasses, grazing like buffalo up a side canyon. My mind now leaves space and slips into an imagined past. I feel like an outrider in the Old West, checking the open range for predators. I shine my beacon up at the coral and out into the open sea. Other divers' lights become green glow sticks in the distance. I reach down to pick up a blue starfish, and the sand explodes beneath it. I've disturbed a sleeping ray that streaks off into the night. I look up into the face of an amused Aussie, who beckons me with his light. I spot Nancy nearby and wave her over. The Aussie points his light at a brilliant aquamarine parrot fish sleeping in the rocks. During the day you can hear them munching on the coral with their hard little beaks. It takes us a moment to see what he's showing us. The two-foot-long fish is asleep inside a clear bubble egg composed of spit that the parrot spews out around itself every night. If a predator breaks the shell, the parrot fish has a fraction of a second to fight or flee.

Around the bend we find a handsome coral trout, red with blue spots. It's a truly fine fish, beautiful to look at, delicious to eat. As a general rule, I'll eat any fish that's able to outbreed human hunger, though that list is shrinking.

Back on the boat we do our logs and listen to the Aussie rock band Midnight Oil playing "Beds Are Burning" on the boom box. (Years later its lead singer, Peter Garrett, will become Australia's environment minister.) Nancy is soon involved in the ongoing card game around the galley table. I grab a Coke and go out on the fantail to trade war stories with the man from the BBC, who once spent six weeks living in a tree in order to get pictures of an African leopard feeding.

Next day it's more of the same—eating, reading, and tanning as we motor to our last dive sight. We've done eight dives in three days. The sharks have been small but sleek, like jet fighters swooping in formation around the edges of the bommies. Once they harass a crew member to the point that he has to stand atop a shallow coral shelf and get picked up by the Zodiac.

Our last dive is pure magic, a special bommie with a shallow top and steep ledges. Doing back rolls off the Zodiac, we enter gin-clear waters littered with fish. It's a vast garden of coral guarded by lionfish. These majestic fellows wear cloaks of feathery fins, striped in cream, yellow, and brown. They move like Japanese geisha fans, fluttering across their territorial bits of coral. Their dorsal fins contain a venom that can produce excruciating pain and lead to respiratory failure. The CIA used to keep an aquarium full of them.

I follow a blowfish over the edge, where a pair of blue and red harlequin tusks are preening. Looking back up, I see a shoal of blue and yellow sea perch part like a curtain. Behind them a crew member is snorkeling after a seven-foot-long sea snake. This one clearly wants no part of big clumsy humans. It swims past me, heading toward the bottom. I follow it down to sixty feet, but it's headed to ninety and beyond, sliding away into the depths.

"And what would you have done if you'd caught up with it?" Nancy wonders when we're back aboard.

We while away our last hours running along a coastline of uninterrupted green. Late that afternoon we pull into Cooktown, the last dot on the map before you hit the Aboriginal reserves on the top end of Queensland. This is where Captain Cook fixed his ship and named the kangaroo. One of our favorite spots in the world is Kealakekua Bay, below the town of Captain Cook on the Big Island of Hawaii. This is where Cook was killed on his return voyage from Australia; his heart was eaten by local warriors as a sign of respect, another reason I've never sought respectability.

Things don't seem to have changed much in Cooktown in the last few centuries. The road's been paved to the edge of town, the ceiling fans work in two of the three pubs, which attract both lizards and frogmen, and big white cockatiels squawk at you from the treetops, uninterested in English as a second language.

After a high-speed ferry ride back to Port Douglas, we'll continue our adventures with visits to a crocodile farm, Mossman Gorge, and the Daintree rain forest, where we'll spot a rare six-foot-tall flightless blue-headed cassowary.

We snorkel with bat rays and sharks at an offshore sandbar near Cape Tribulation, where warning signs tell us not to swim near the estuarine crocodiles or the box jellies.

On our last night in Australia we head south along the two-lane Bruce Highway. After driving for some time we put up at a holiday lodge that reminds us of the Bates Motel from *Psycho*. Actually, it's a very nice two-story place with a pool and bluff overlooking Dunk Island. It's just that we're the only guests there. We take the second-floor terrace suite with the ocean view. Once we've settled in we go to nearby Mission Beach for an Italian dinner. When we return invasive cane toads are sitting by the pool and on the stairway to our room, making deep thrumping sounds. Nancy's amused by the fact that I don't like toads the size of house cats that also contain a lethal toxin (what doesn't in Australia?). Cane toads were introduced in the 1930s to get rid of sugarcane insects but have now become a much greater threat themselves. By the first decade of the new century Cape York's major predators, including death adders and monitor lizards, have all but disappeared, probably as a result of the spread of cane toads, which will poison anything that bites them. One scientist calls it "the great silence up north."

At 5 A.M. I wake to howling winds, thrumping toads, and the electrical flash-crack of lightning bolts. I shake Nancy awake and point outside. The sky is bloodred, the sea black, and the tops of the palm trees are bending over, their fronds whipping like kite tails in a gale-force wind. It's awe-inspiring.

We drive back to the Cairns airport under darkening thunderclouds, with fronds and foliage blowing across the tarmac of the two-lane "highway." The airline's not sure if it's going to cancel our flight but finally decides to let the plane take off into the wind. We leave the runway, lifting up through a world of green and gray as the first fat drops of the monsoon season fall on Australia's "deep north." It's at once a beautiful and ominous sight.

It's a sight I'll return to more than a decade later as an environmental journalist. I'm on assignment for *E* magazine for a special "Feeling the Heat" issue that will then be expanded into a book. Ten journalists cover the world, looking at the state of human-enhanced climate change. My assignments include climate-linked coral bleaching in Florida, Fiji, and Australia. More than 20 percent of the world's tropical coral reefs have died in recent decades as a result of pollution, overfishing, physical damage from boats and storms, and the growing impact of climate change, including bleaching and ocean acidification. Another 25 percent are likely to be extinct within a decade.

Thirty hours into my trip from Washington, D.C., to LA to Sydney to Cairns and on south through the verdant valleys and sugar fields of Queensland I decide to pull over in Mission Beach. This time I put up at the Horizon, another lovely inn with a wooden pool deck overlooking Dunk Island. I have a drink at the outdoor bar, trying to ignore Georgina, the mean-looking pheasant sitting on the chair next to me. I drive down to the beach for dinner and spot a three-foot wallaby hopping through my headlight beams on the way back. That night I finally get some sleep, despite the surrounding jungle sounds, including the scuttle of large lizards and a loud white cockatoo screeching in the tree next to my bungalow. In the morning I hike down to an eroded beach with a river outlet and a familiar wooden sign: WARNING: ESTUARINE CROCODILES INHABIT THIS RIVER.

A few hours later, I pull into Townsville, a waterfront city of 120,000 that bills itself as the Capital of the Great Barrier Reef (even though Cairns took away most of the tourists years ago when it opened its international airport). Townsville is trying to make a comeback with a new IMAX theater, reef aquarium, and casino, but also hedging its bet with a zinc processing plant, army base, and government offices, including the Great Barrier Reef Marine Park Authority and the Australian Institute of Marine Science (AIMS). I call Jeremy Tager, of the North Queensland Conservation Council, who invites me over to his island home, a half-hour ferry ride from Townsville.

He greets me at the dock and proceeds to fulfill his duties as a professional activist, briefing me on some of the environmental threats to the world's greatest marine park.

"There's bottom trawling by commercial fishing boats still allowed in [parts of] the park, also nutrient [nitrogen and phosphate] runoff from the sugar industry, forest clearing for cattle and new developments along the coast, plus the oil industry keeps pushing to open up offshore drilling just beyond the eastern boundary of the park in the Coral Sea."

Magnetic Island is like Catalina Island off LA, only with death adders. "They like to lie under piles of leaves," Ann Tager advises as she shows me the family's woodsy, leafy backyard. The most visited of the Great Barrier Reef islands, Magnetic is rich in tropical birds and wildlife. It is home to adders, pythons, rock wallabies, sea eagles, flying foxes, curlews, koalas, and equally cute marsupial possums. It also has its own living coral reefs, but no longer in Nelly Bay.

Nineteen ninety-eight, the fourth-hottest year in history (after 2014, 2010, and 2005), saw a global outbreak of coral bleaching as corals' thermal tolerances were exceeded by a combination of gradually warming ocean temperatures spiked by that year's El Niño phenomenon. The idea that climate change is accelerating El Niño warming and the ensuing La Niña ocean cooling has become a subject of growing scientific concern. The United States Coral Reef Task Force reported that the extensive 1998 global bleaching was a direct result of climate change caused by the burning of fossil fuel.

"When we saw one-thousand-year-old coral colonies bleaching and dying, that's something new, at least in recorded human history," agreed Paul Hough, a friendly, sun-reddened Magnetic Island resident and research scientist with the Great Barrier Reef Marine Park Authority.

Hough specializes in coral reproduction. "I was looking at the corals that didn't die, and found their reproduction was down to 40 percent of normal the first year after the bleaching and was at 80 percent the second year. Now they're experiencing 1.5-degree-below-normal water temperature from La Niña so we've had a four-degree swing in four years and with greater frequency and severity of El Niño/La Niña events that's going to make it more difficult for corals to recover from these kinds of impacts."

In addition, as the ocean absorbs more human-generated carbon dioxide, it becomes more acidic. The carbonic acid that's created is corrosive to the shells and skeletons of corals, clams, and other creatures that have to extract calcium carbonate out of seawater to build their hard-shelled homes. A spring 2008 study in the journal *Science* found that, like the loss of Arctic sea ice, the acidification of the ocean is happening at a much faster rate than the world's leading climatologists had previously predicted. Other scientists believe the ocean may soon become so saturated with anthropogenic (human-generated) carbon dioxide that it won't be able to absorb any more, and as a result we'll see a more rapid heating of the atmosphere.

"I think we're seeing not a crash, but a slow decline of the [coral reef] system," Paul Hough warns, in what has by now become a scientifically conservative point of view.

He and other observers believe nearshore fringing reefs are at most immediate risk because they already face other stresses from human development, polluted runoff, and cyclones (Pacific hurricanes).

I'm visiting Magnetic Island following the two wettest months in North Queensland's history. Big gum trees and foliage are still down from Cyclone Tessa, which struck two weeks earlier.

My second evening in town I'm invited to the Magnetic Island Film Festival where the friendly, beery crowd of more than one hundred is mostly costumed—in bathing suits and in drag. Here I learn that the island's two thousand residents are divided over a proposal to revive a failed harbor project. The real-estate development would add six hundred new housing units to the community and its overstressed septic systems. To date, Queensland, like Florida, has not let climate-enhanced storms, increased rainfall, sea level rise, or dying reefs stand in the way of its beachfront development schemes.

The island's once healthy Nelly Bay, a kind of neighborhood reef where kids used to learn to snorkel, is one of Paul Hough's seven study sites. "Unfortunately, the cyclone following repeated bleachings was the final nail in its coffin," he tells me. I decide to visit it anyway, to see for myself.

I head down to the beach, past stately banyan trees, hoop pines, coconut palms, and a sign reading WARNING: MARINE STINGERS ARE DANGEROUS . . . EMERGENCY TREATMENT FOR SEVERE BOX JELLY STING: FLOOD STING WITH VINEGAR. IF BREATHING STOPS GIVE ARTIFICIAL RESPIRATION.

Luckily, I've borrowed a stinger suit (what we Yanks call a rash guard) from Jeremy Tager.

I swim out to the black buoy that marks Paul Hough's research site and begin free diving. The bottom is a rubble field of broken branch corals, dead, bleached and gray-silt-covered hard corals, and a few small fish. A burrowing clam is encased in the limestone skeleton of a dead rock coral. Its blubbery mantle is striped and spotted with the blue, purple, and green colors of healthy symbiotic algae, giving it the look of a fashion model posing in a cemetery.

The Australian Institute of Marine Science is located forty minutes south of Townsville. To get to it, you drive out Cape Cleveland, a wetland and wilderness peninsula full of storks, egrets, cattle, and the occasional wallaby bouncing off into the bush. Eventually you arrive at a metal gate with a speakerphone in the middle of nowhere. The remote gate opens. On the other side of a grassy hill is AIMS's low-rise glass-and-concrete research complex, like something out of a James Bond movie, and just beyond it, down a brushy path, five miles of wilderness beach facing out onto the world's largest living reef.

"Climate impact has happened. The four most serious bleaching events were in 1987–88, '92, '94, and 1998, which was the biggest," explains Katharina Fabricius, a bright, vivacious AIMS research scientist, also a refugee from Germany's harsh winters.

Our interview took place before 2005, when the Caribbean's corals were badly hit by the same warm pool of water that super-charged Hurricanes Katrina and Rita. "Corals can take a fair amount of disturbance—they're not fragile," she told me in an office filled with soft coral samples as varied and unique as snowflakes. "If these disturbances become more frequent, how-ever, weedy species will take over. You already see branching species replacing massive slow-growing brain corals. We lost a thousand-year-old coral head off Pandora reef in '98. These reefs are really the canaries in the coal mine, where you now see a whole ecosystem being impacted."

I tell her I know an Antarctic scientist, Bill Fraser, who thinks his penguins are the canaries for climate change.

"Ten years ago people were blasé about this being a pristine area," she continues, ignoring my comment. "Now with climate change even the most conservative projections are pretty bleak. And if your [Australian] government wants to sell brown coal they may not be likely to consider alternative fuels or solar or other changes that need to take place." Still, not everyone is convinced.

"In many ways the jury's still out on the global climate effect on coral bleaching," claims Virginia Chadwick, a former re-gional tourism minister and the political appointee who chairs the Great Barrier Reef Marine Park Authority. "Not to say this apparent correlation between bleaching and temperature isn't a worrying trend," she adds. "From a local management agency point of view we're wondering about adaptability, about corals' ability to adapt to temperature changes."

"We've no evidence corals can adjust to rapid temperature changes," counters Fabricius. "Maybe they can over hundreds of thousands of years, but that's not the scale we're now dealing with."

Having seen dead coral, I decide to take a dive trip to Kelso, one of the outer reefs that's recovered from the little bleaching it did suffer. It's nice to be in a living aquarium again, with big coral walls and bommies and canyons littered with fish: luminescent coral trout, batfish, coral-munching parrots, and anemone fish who inoculate themselves with the toxins generated by the anemones they hide among, still waiting for someone to take their picture. There are sea stars and cushionlike sea cucumbers, unicorn fish, and lots of bright juvenile fry hugging the reef for protection. A six-foot black-tip reef shark cruises past, adding a dash of predatory grace to the mystery and magic of a healthy reef.

"Ours is a large reef region, more robust than the Florida Keys or the Caribbean, with more than four hundred twenty species of corals, six to seven times as diverse as your Atlantic reefs," Paul Hough explains to me.

"What does that mean in terms of long-term projections?" I wonder.

"Larger diverse [coral] communities [like those in the Great Barrier Reef, New Guinea, Indonesia, and Palau] will last longer," he says, "but North America's gonna get hammered."

After Australia I spend a week in Fiji, where I learn about climate change impacts being felt on the 322 islands of this Pacific nation of 750,000 people. I drink kava with the locals. It's a pepper-plant-based brew that's like muddy water with a mild Novocain aftertaste. Diving in the Somosomo Strait off Taveuni, I see my first bleached reef that looks like a snowstorm has passed over it. About one-third of the corals have turned wedding cake white.

"Did you see that bleaching?" I ask one of the other divers, a travel agent from Minnesota, after climbing back onto our boat. She looks at me curiously.

"When the water heats up the coral polyps expel the zooxanthella algae that give them their color. Unfortunately, the algae also provide them 70 percent of their food, so they begin to slowly starve to death," I explain to her.

"Really, I thought they were supposed to be white like that," she replies and then turns to watch a fruit bat flying overhead.

I'm reminded of a cartoon I saw in a marine journal: it showed a diner and a waiter in a restaurant. "I'll have the Chilean sea bass," the diner says.

"I'm sorry but they've gone extinct."

"Oh. Well, how's the veal?"

On the next dive several of us struggle against a ripping current. We have to crawl hand over hand, retreating behind a protective reef to avoid being swept away. Later I have to get another diver to open the valve on my tank when my air cuts off, and I also cut my hand on some sharp coral. This will require hand surgery when a small piece of the coral calcium gets embedded in my palm. It really wasn't my fault. I got distracted by a big parrot fish that appeared to be eating a smaller fish, something you don't normally find on this herbivore's diet. By the time I realized this was a cleaning station and the fish had opened its beak to allow a cleaner wrasse to remove parasites from the inside of its mouth, the current had driven me into the razor-sharp coral.

On the way to the surface I watched what appeared to be gushing black blood coming from my hand until the red end of the color spectrum reappeared closer to the surface and I could see it was actually a mild stream of crimson. That night I had a bad headache and dizziness that lasted more than twelve hours but only later considered I might have bent myself despite what the dive tables told me. Not my best dive to date.

While in Fiji I hang out with a guy named Steve after we share a night flight from Nadi across the main island of Viti Levu to Suva. Steve's here to advise the U.S. ambassador; he says he's from the State Department and reminds me of CIA types I knew in Central America. There's an expanding ethnic crisis following the election of the first Indo-Fijian prime minister whom the native Fijian nationalists strongly oppose. Suva, the capital, is a typical ramshackle third-world backwater, with a central market and bus depot, a university, Japanese and Taiwanese fishing vessels tied up at its docks, and foreign-owned clothing plants on its outskirts. It has little charm and few of the amenities that attract tourists to Nadi and the outer islands. The day I arrive the prime minister overrules his secretary of home affairs and decides to allow a protest march by the nationalists. Steve tells me the U.S. ambassador helped convince him this was the right and democratic thing to do.

Four days after I leave, the protest march takes place, and an armed gang leaves the march and takes the prime minister and his cabinet hostage, which sets off a military coup. As a journalist, I'm naturally disappointed to have missed it, arriving home with pictures of eroding seawalls instead of Fijians burning Indian shops in Suva. On the other hand, I know that while ethnic conflicts can be resolved, there's little the Fijians can do to protect their kids from a future of rising seas and dying reefs.

. . .

Nine years later, in 2009, I return to Fiji to find that while the corals have recovered from major bleaching events in 2000 and 2002, most of the marine wildlife, including almost all the mid-sized and large fish, have disappeared, at least where my friend Scott Fielder and I dive the ghost reefs of Kadavu, Fiji's fourth-largest island.

There are healthy and extensive hard and soft coral communities on the Matanuku and Astrolabe reefs that are also home to small nursery fish but few if any sea stars, sea cucumber, urchins, eels, parrot fish, snapper, grouper, trevally, sharks, or turtles. By our third dive we begin wondering what's going on. "I've dived all through the Indo-Pacific for thirty years and have never seen anything like this," Scott notes. Amid spectacular nine- and ten-story-high underwater pinnacles, swim-through caverns, and deep canyons, mesas and vertical walls dropping into the abyss, we also find the first indicators of algal disease: corals cannot maintain themselves without schools of large parrot fish and other grazers to control the algae growth.

In dive sites with names like Canyons and the Aquarium we see only a handful of large critters, a single large bronze whaler shark that leaves as soon as we arrive, a single lionfish, two manta rays, one good-sized eel, a deadly stonefish. It's kind of eerie. With these types of diverse corals and big structures we should be overwhelmed by the living abundance, by a huge biomass of marine wildlife that's gone missing, leaving the reef feeling hollowed out.

In an example of shifting baselines (in which we judge reality based on our own lifetime experiences) our dive companions, mostly from Texas, seem to be having a great time tweaking their equipment, taking pictures of anemone and clown fish amid colorful corals and squeezing through the swim-throughs.

Our Fijian dive masters—Cerrella, forty-seven, and Saula, twenty-four—are from the small tin-and-scrap-wood villages of Navuatu and Drue, adjacent to the fading Matana dive and fishing resort that provides them employment and electric power from its generator. They seem reluctant to talk about changes in the water they've seen during their lives, and I can understand why. Later, after talking with other locals, we learn that the villagers have to travel farther in their boats to catch reef fish that used to be found just offshore. On some nights they see lights out on the reef that are almost certainly poachers. "Fish used to circle in the water here, but you don't see that anymore. Twenty years ago there were lots of turtles that are not here now," says a Fijian who doesn't want to be named for fear that criticism of the status quo might anger the latest military strongmen in the capital.

Outside the reef line, big longline fishing trawlers from Asia are taking thousands of tons of tuna, shark, and other open-water species, having paid small licensing fees to deplete Fiji's EEZ (Exclusive Economic Zone) ocean waters. The Fiji Hotel Association has written a letter of protest to the military government but gotten no response.

Our best dives leave me both exhilarated and saddened. One night, waves crash and rain and wind lash our *bure* (small guest cottage), inciting birdcalls from the forest canopy. The next morning breaks clear as we load our gear and extra tanks onto the pontoon dive boat and run down the coast to Vunisea, the island's main town, where the airstrip, hospital, and post office are located. From there, we load the tanks onto a canvas-covered truck for the short run across a narrow, hilly isthmus to the south side of the island, where we reload our gear into three long, narrow Panga boats with forty-horsepower outboards and head out to the Astrolabe reef guided by Joseua Bilo, a big mustached local dive master. Soon, after back rolls off the boats, we're again below the surface, drifting over bottoms and bommies that have 95 to 100 percent live coral cover in green, brown, red, yellow, and purple colors, including large elkhorn corals with brown stems as thick as my wrist. We soon encounter and admire the elegant grace of a gliding pair of manta rays. One, with perhaps an eight-foot wingspan, flies a few feet over my head while I hold my breath (they don't like our bubbles).

After our second dive Joseua takes us to the Solabe Settlement, his family compound where they catch fish, grow kava and casaba, and occasionally lead dives. His daughter serves us lunch in front of their tin shacks where nylon netting and dive gear are drying. The kids have a rope swing over the beach; they launch from a high tree branch, swinging out in a big arc above the canopy. When we return to the seawall at Namalata Bay the tide has dropped six feet, revealing the roots of the surrounding mangroves.

On another day we head to the reef's outer wall by Kong Mountain, an ancient cloud-shrouded volcano where locals insist B-roll for the 1933 *King Kong* was shot. There's an island beyond the point, a coral beach and a small surfing resort close to where double overhead waves are breaking on the razor-sharp reef. We drop down into a spur-and-groove landscape not unlike the canyon land mesas of the American West, except we're able to fly weightless between them and hang out over the cliffs, where we can see not only coral and small fish but a migrating school of good-sized pompanos and trevally emerging from the pelagic blue followed by first one and then a second large gray reef shark. The sharks move toward and then away from us with their usual predatory grace. Soon a school of one hundred barracuda with chevron markings cruise by. We move on as a group, drifting with the current. I spot Saula dropping down into a box canyon and follow him to where he's pointing with his knife. We're now at 110 feet. Twenty feet below us an eight-foot banded sea snake writhes across the bottom in hunting mode, searching for small fish before swimming vertically up the cliff toward us and then into a crevice ten feet below us, which is fine by me. It's a fun anticipatory dive with about seventy feet visibility. We see a large green turtle and small endangered hawksbill but no more large schools of fish or sharks, except for a single sleeping nurse shark. On our second dive I try to stay above eighty feet. After eleven dives in five days the nitrogen building up in my tissue is pushing my decompression times. I'll have to wait fifteen feet below the surface for the gas bubbles to dissolve out of my blood.

After days of diving mostly ghost reefs I convince Scott that we ought to cut out of our dive trip early and head over to the capital, Suva, on the "mainland" island so I can do some interviews and see if our suspicions bear out.

We fly from the Vunisea airstrip into Nadi on a Twin Otter prop plane, crossing a string of offshore atolls and reefs. There we rent a car to drive across the big island of Viti Levu to Suva. On the way the radio announces that the military has banned this year's Methodist conference because the gathering "threatens to promote instability in the country . . . by planned discussions of the present political situation" (that is, the military's repression of journalists, students, and judges). Usually thousands gather for the annual church meeting and singing competition. Two years ago the locals on the island of Vanua Levu threw a conference feast that included eighty-two sea turtles. I joke to Scott that what's bad for democracy might prove good for endangered marine reptiles.

Despite the latest tensions, there are few troops visible in the capital. In fact, Suva has hardly changed in the years I've been away. The Centra Hotel on Victoria Parade is now a Holiday Inn, and the big rusty Japanese and Taiwanese longline fishing vessels in the harbor have now been joined by others from mainland China, Korea, and Indonesia. We count over fifteen that among them can put more than fifty thousand hooks in the water on any given day.

I set up interviews at the Department of Fisheries and the University of the South Pacific but first stop at the Greenpeace office, located in the old municipal building above a Chinese restaurant. There, we're told about international efforts to reduce the take of tuna, sharks, and other targeted victims of the Pacific's long-liner and purse-seiner fishing fleets. At a recent international meeting in South Korea scientists proposed an immediate 30 percent reduction in the Pacific tuna catch. Greenpeace proposed a 50 percent cut. The final agreement was for a 30 percent reduction over three years, considered a major victory given another recent international agreement (in Morocco in September 2008) that will allow the continued unsustainable killing of endangered Atlantic bluefin tuna.

Greenpeace's Steve Shallhorn and Seni Nabou tell us that the local Suva chapter has a harbor watch program that often spots ships whose identification numbers have been painted over or whose numbers don't match the vessel's registered name, sure signs of illegal pirate fishing. Nabou says there are also reports of sea cucumbers being stolen in the isolated Lao Island group, where her family is from.

Between Fiji's coups, the Australian government gave the country three patrol boats to help with fisheries enforcement, but since Commodore Frank Bainimarama, head of Fiji's four-hundred-man navy, is also head of the military junta, I figure he has bigger fish to fry.

At the fisheries office in the village of Lami, a few miles outside of town, we meet and talk with Sunia Waqainabete, the senior research officer in the Fisheries Department of the Ministry of Primary Industries (fishing, farming, and logging). Waqainabete is a brown-eyed, gray-haired Fijian man, about five ten, with a friendly, informed manner, faded blue Aloha shirt, blue sulu skirt, and flip-flops. Even as a leader of FLMMA, the Fiji Locally Managed Marine Area program, a bottom-up effort to merge customary village claims on fishing areas with an ecosystem-based approach to protection, he's still deeply worried about the future of his people and the ocean wildlife they depend on for food and barter.

He tells us our suspicions are correct, that unregulated poaching is widespread inside the reef lines, with urban fishermen from Suva raiding customary (traditional) fishing areas in Kadavu, where we've been diving. "But it's now everywhere in Fiji. Our local [appointed] fish wardens don't have the boats and engines to catch them. They [the poachers] have powerful sixty-horsepower engines that they'll sometimes paint over to say forty. These people have big networks with funding and boat operators.

"The two major issues are poaching and depletion of resources where most communities are telling us it's taking them longer to catch fish and they're seeing a decline in catches, and the trend just keeps going down. We had a big drop in inshore fishing data between 1998 and 2004. In some areas you had

10,000 tons (of fish caught) drop to 2,400 tons in one year," he continues.

I ask if the poaching is mostly for the export market. "Both the commercial aspect and local," he says. "I've seen them show up on Saturday morning at the [Suva Municipal] market with these really huge parrot fish and groupers."

He thinks unscrupulous businessmen could be funding up to one thousand night divers with spears (Fiji's population has grown to just over 800,000). The fisheries department has only 116 employees.

He tells us how his uncle was killed on his home island in the Lao Island group after stopping one of the poacher's boats. "He tried to seize it, but the outboard had been rigged where, when he went to turn it off, it went into forward drive and he was thrown overboard and killed by the propellers. But the Indian businessman who'd hired these people was well connected and brought all the island grog (kava) from a local connection who was directing them where they could go to steal the fish, and with these connections no one was ever punished."

Later Scott suggests that while conservation groups, academics, and government agencies are working on the locally managed marine area program, he'd be willing to help my Blue Frontier Campaign raise money for more powerful Honda four-stroke outboards to help the guys in Waqainabete's department do more effective law enforcement on the water. I begin researching the idea on my return to the United States. But our efforts are stymied by Fiji's "Present Political Situation."

A few days earlier the recreational dive group we were with had brought school supplies to the Drue village primary school at the end of a long afternoon. There, we were serenaded by twenty students who sang, in beautiful two-part harmony, hymns and songs both in English and Fijian about "waves on the ocean" and "paradise good-bye to you," and as the fading light turned their blue-and-white school uniforms into a shadowy gray, Kamala, the dive tour leader, told them, "We think you children are the best ambassadors of the islands and hope you grow up to become divers so you can enjoy what you have in your front yard."

And as she says this, I can't help but think how much of their front yard ocean paradise has already been stolen from them.

But I'm getting ahead of my story here. After Nancy and I returned from our trip to Australia we moved from the city to a Sausalito hillside duplex where we looked down on Richardson Bay through redwood trees, across blackberry brambles, over the top of a neighbor's homemade chicken coop.

What we lacked in roots Nancy and I made up for in restless adventuring over the years we were together. We spent much of our thirties, and part of my forties, doing things many people would have liked to have done in their twenties. Arrested adolescence, you say? Guilty as charged. We worked hard and we played hard and often managed to eliminate the line between the one and the other.

We fly into Cabo San Lucas during a window of steamy calm between two storm fronts. The power lines are down, which means the construction cranes and work crews transforming this tail-end spit of Baja desert into a major resort complex have been forced to take a break. Progress called on account of nature. Basic services are still being met, however, and the Amigos Dive Shop has spare tanks of air, filled up and ready to go.

We head out from the jetty on a thirty-foot pontoon boat. Our first dive is about half a mile off the docks, along a spine of rock that separates the Sea of Cortés from the Pacific. The water is warm and littered with the usual tropical blend of soft corals, yellowtail snappers, clown fish, parrots, and puffers. At thirty feet there is a wide, steep slope of sand, like a beach dune that forgot to stop at the water's edge. Beto, our dive master, signals us to follow as he swims a descending spiral down the narrowing slope.

At ninety feet it funnels into a fine crystal sand falls dropping over a rock lip. We float suspended, watching the sand drift through our fingers and down into a 3,500-foot-deep abyss. The continental shelf is like a wall here. These depths invite a variety of deep-sea visitors. I flip over, floating head down, waiting for some giant tentacle to rise up out of the depths and grab me. Sure enough, something cold and clammy begins to contract around my lungs. It's my weight belt, which has slid up my ribs.

Storm surge becomes more noticeable as we round the cliffs to our second dive site, a one-hundred-foot rock that juts out of the water marking land's end, where the Pacific Ocean and Sea of Cortés merge.

Franco, an older diver from Milan, checks his camera rig. Leslie from the dive shop, whose fridge is out on account of the power failure, has plastic bags filled with thawed turkey. Beto suggests we make it a drift dive because of the strong surface current. Nancy is the first one out the stern gate.

We settle to the bottom, a wide sandy area fifty feet down, where we're greeted by shoals of sleek silver jacks, some parrot fish, and a few hardy groupers. Leslie is trying to feed her turkey to a large green moray eel who keeps shaking his head as if to say, "No, but your fingers look tasty." She swims off to catch up with a zebra eel in the hope that its natural prey might include defrosted leftovers.

I'm exploring a small wreck that looks suspiciously like a dive boat. Some orange-red anemones have taken up residence inside the hull. As I'm watching their pinky-thick tips wave in the current I catch my dive buddy signaling in my peripheral vision.

I turn to see Nancy gesturing excitedly out toward the big blue. And then I see it, swimming out of the pelagic depths, white spots on blue, the biggest, handsomest whale shark I've ever seen, actually the only one I've ever seen where I couldn't turn the channel.

It's probably just a teenager, about twenty feet long with a collection of remoras (suckerfish) hanging off its belly and head. Beto and I swim toward it, awed.

As Beto takes hold of its dorsal fin, it turns in my direction. Its huge catfishlike face with a wide-lipped baleen mouth moves toward me like the grille of a '52 Chevy about to run me over.

Small black fish eyes hold no interest in the bubbling bipod that's frantically churning its flippers to avoid this. As I swim around its huge head I notice it has three side gills, each about the size of my arm. Rising across its back, I grab onto its dorsal fin alongside Beto. It doesn't seem to mind us any more than the suckerfish. It tows us on a smooth, gliding journey back out to sea. Its dorsal fin and back have more of the smooth-skinned feel of a dolphin than the rough silk or sandpapery texture of other sharks.

In the blue-green distance we can just make out the ghostly shape of a second, even larger whale shark swimming in the open sea. I pull on the tail of a remora in front of me and he lifts off his host, swims forward a foot, and resettles, like a disturbed pigeon. Our host is now carrying us back out to the ocean depths at around five knots, much faster than we can swim. I look at my depth gauge and realize he's also taken us from fifty to seventy-five feet. After a few minutes we reluctantly let go of our shark friend. It swims on, unconcerned, a monarch of its realm.

Whale sharks like this animal have today won limited protection from slaughter under CITES, the Convention on International Trade in Endangered Species, signed by 173 nations. Unfortunately, with Asian markets offering up to ten thousand dollars per whale shark fin, pirate fishermen continue to slaughter these largest of all fish in the sea. Personally, I think it's time for an international ban on all shark fishing. But that's not what we were thinking about at that moment.

Back up on the pontoon boat we're euphoric, stripping off our gear. Franco says he thinks he's gotten some good photos of us (I now have one hanging on my living room wall).

"I can't believe I was staring at this huge shark and the next thing I know you're swimming toward it," Nancy says.

"That's because I knew it was a vegetarian."

"Lucky it didn't mistake you for a kelp burger." She grins.

Leslie is the last one on board, wondering what all the excitement is about. When we tell her she goes ballistic. "I can't believe it! I've been diving this point for two years and I've never seen a whale shark," she moans. Tragic proof, I think—never swim without a dive buddy.

"Rode whale shark—20 foot—possible pix. Wild," I write under REMARKS/OBSERVATIONS in my logbook.

"I saw it first—NML!!" And "It's True!" the Gal adds, signing the line marked DIVE BUDDY VERIFICATION.

Just as we start to motor in, she lets out a shout, "Over there!"

The bigger whale shark is basking near the surface, then glides beneath us like a speckled shadow, larger than our thirty-foot boat. We grab our masks and fins and jump back into the water, but by the time we get below the surface and look around he's gone, vanished back into the infinite blue like a ghost. We're left feeling both honored and humbled.

"How could I have known it wasn't going to eat us?" Nancy frets over her margarita that evening, wishing she'd gotten to pet and ride it too.

"You just have to watch more Cousteau reruns," I suggest.

"I do." She nods solemnly.

I don't want to suggest that Nancy and I had some kind of idealized romantic relationship. We often fought, during our travels and in between.

I remember on the Big Island of Hawaii one evening we'd had a major fight over who knows what, and she stomped off through the hotel garden. I thought, I don't need this shit anymore.

Over by the night-lit tennis courts I spotted an attractive long-haired woman in a tank top and cutoffs and thought, I could get out of this stupid relationship and find someone like that. Then she came into the light and I realized it was Nancy. Damn . . .

Unlike most women I'd gone out with, Nancy was a serious adventurer. She was the ringleader and organizer of many of her college crowd's hairier escapades; she'd hiked around Europe and Guatemala with her sister when they were in their twenties; even chased after a large mugger who hit her and stole her purse in Oakland ("What were you going to do if you caught up with him?" I asked).

.   .   .

Her fearlessness makes it difficult to impress her, though I keep trying. She buys me a lovely textured gray shirt as a gift. I'm producing short segments called "Green Means" for PBS at the time. One of my stories involves the U.S. Fish & Wildlife crime lab in Ashland, Oregon, where they use forensic technologies like DNA matching to track poachers and smugglers of endangered species.

"Humans cheat," lab director Ken Goddard explains to me. "They violate laws: they try to take more than their fair share. It's good old human greed, and that's what our laboratory is here to fight."

Along with the lab he has a large warehouse full of confiscated ivory tusks, leopard-skin coats, tiger bone remedies, sea turtle shells, and walrus heads.

When his work gets too depressing, Goddard (a former SWAT team member in LA) likes to visit a nearby wildlife rehabilitation center and get in a fenced enclosure with "Griz," a five-hundred-pound grizzly bear that cannot be returned to the wild because he's blind in one eye. Still, Griz has all his claws and teeth and, being an adolescent, likes to roughhouse. We videotape them wrestling, which consists of Ken grabbing the bear around the neck and Griz playfully swatting him, sending his glasses flying, then pulling him to the ground and stomping on him. When we've gotten enough footage, I get permission to go up to Griz and rub his furry back, making sure my crew takes some pictures with my still camera. I'm wearing tan chinos and my new shirt. Griz is wearing dark brown fur. Back home I get the pictures developed. They come out nicely. I show them to Nancy.

"Look," I say, "I'm wrestling a grizzly bear," exaggerating for effect. She looks at the first photo, scowls.

"You're wrestling a grizzly bear in your best shirt!" she complains. Like I said, a hard woman to impress. Still, I continue to try. One day, knowing that she'll never say no to an ocean adventure, I invite her to sail the Sea of Cortés in a homemade eighteen-foot sailboat.

7

Shipwrecks

They make glorious shipwreck who are lost in seeking worlds.

GOTTHOLD EPHRAIM LESSING

By the early 1990s reporting on the environment was providing me with new and challenging work opportunities while the ocean environment kept Nancy and me enthralled, never certain where our next travels might take us.

Every weekend sailor has a recurring fantasy that goes something like this: you design and build your own boat, take it to an exotic locale, and sail off to where civilization has no hold.

My friend Jon Christensen was a friendly bear of a man and inveterate blue-water sailor who owned a succession of boats, even living on one for a time, a thirty-two-foot ketch named *Annie* that we once surfed into Mission Bay while seeking shelter from a major storm. Now he was organizing an expedition to the Sea of Cortés to test out the eighteen-foot folding trimaran he'd designed and built during the four years since the birth of his son, Eric.

"You realize the mast fell down and almost killed me, and that was in Mission Bay!" Nancy complains as we pack for Jon's Baja expedition.

The previous weekend we'd test-sailed his boat on Mission Bay, the placid, polluted water park that separates Mission Beach from Ocean Beach in San Diego. Nancy and I had flown down for the shakedown cruise, and she'd been aboard for the raising of the sails and collapse of the mainmast. Jon had assured us that once he redrilled the stay lines and added a little more fiberglass, the boat would be totally seaworthy.

Now we will see if he's right. Confident in his ability as a sailor, if not a shipwright, I want to know what logistical support he plans and why we're going in winter, with its rougher seas. He says there will be a land support crew in several four-wheel-drive vehicles and a shallow-draft chase boat. He hopes that by sailing in winter we'll be able to take advantage of the prevailing northerly winds to do up to thirty miles a day, starting from Bahía de los Ángeles, four hundred miles south of the border, and—if all goes well—sailing round land's end at Cabo San Lucas by mid-January.

Nancy, though dubious, helps me organize our supplies, laying everything out on our bed: tent, sleeping bags, ground cloth, rain gear, dive gear, and my newest toy, a high-eight video camera with water housing to document the journey. She calls the cat sitter before we catch the shuttle flight to San Diego.

The night after Christmas, a baker's dozen of us gather on the cement drive in front of Jon's house to load our supplies and check the trailer rigs for the trimaran and fourteen-foot rigid-hull inflatable chase boat. Rodney, a swarthy red-bearded Alaskan, is the designated chase-boat handler. Our friend Scott Fielder, who's just purchased a new four-by-four Jeep, will be running with the land crew. After a champagne toast and Jon's battle cry of "Banzai!" we all retire for three hours of sleep.

The following morning we cross the border in three vehicles towing two boats and enough high-tech communications and recreational gear to seriously impact the level of development of lower Baja. As we take the exit for Playa Tijuana I get some nice shots of the corrugated-metal border fence with a few Mexican migrants climbing over its top. Ten hours later, after we have traveled through the cactus forests south of Cataviña, the potholes turn to tank traps and the trailer hitch on the trimaran explodes off Jon's truck. It smashes onto the rear bumper before swinging free on its safety chains, threatening to drag boat, trailer, and truck over the edge of the unpaved mountain road leading down to Bahía de los Ángeles. After stopping to inspect the damage and reconnect the rig, we pull into town without further incident.

By dawn Bahía de los Ángeles shows itself as a wide, island-studded harbor backed up against steep ocher-colored mountains spotted with cardón cacti tall as giraffes. The town has little more to offer than sun-bleached whalebones since the silver mines shut down in 1900 and the Federales banned turtle fishing in 1990. After a breakfast of huevos rancheros, Nancy, Jon's friend

Al, and I track down Antonio Resendiz at his stone-and-thatch research station off a sandy path two miles outside town.

A passionate, dark-haired man, Resendiz is one of Mexico's leading sea turtle scientists. Originally sent to the area to draw up a harvest plan for turtle fishermen, which he refused to do, he now studies, raises, and releases the big turtles as part of a government-sponsored restoration program. He admits to some pessimism about the prospects for the recovery of marine wildlife in the Sea of Cortés.

"The big problem, now that the killing has been banned, is plastic pollution, also shrimp boats with their indiscriminate nets, and tourism. We need the tourists, but at the same time you have all these people coming here with their garbage and their trucks, running on the beach at low tide when a lot of animals, like egrets and crabs, eat: and also pristine beaches being built up for hotels that disturb the nesting habitat of these guys." He points to his turtles in their concrete tubs.

Today all seven species of sea turtle, air-breathing marine reptiles from the age of the dinosaur, are threatened or endangered by human activities, with three species—the hawksbill, Kemp's ridley, and giant leatherback (which can grow to ten feet and two thousand pounds)—listed as critically endangered.

The next morning we launch early, the bay's waters calm and glassy under a brilliant white sun. We motor past noisy pelican rocks and a sea lion with his flippers and nose floating above the surface so that at first he looks like a sailfish and then just looks strange.

"What's wrong with him? Is he sick?" Nancy wonders. Hearing her, he pops his head up, stares at us for an instant, gives a surprised grunt, and dives below the surface.

"Just asleep," Jon concludes.

We pass between looming wind-sculpted pinnacle islands topped by spindly cactus, where blue-footed boobies nest, and we soon emerge onto the vast widening sea between Baja and the Mexican mainland. Frigate birds, shearwaters, and vultures ride the thermals in an otherwise empty azure sky. The only other traffic our first day out is a group of sea kayakers near a white crescent beach and a large spotted whale shark that escorts us for a time.

Within hours of taking to the water, our boats have been christened. The trimaran, with its sleek, low-riding black-and-white hulls below a multihued mainsail, becomes *Orca*, while the chase boat, using its forty-horsepower outboard to leap and skip around, becomes *Blue Dolphin*.

By late afternoon the *Orca* has fallen too far behind the four of us in the *Dolphin* to make our planned rendezvous and so beaches itself on a wide strip of sand ten miles back. At dusk we're in radio contact with the land crew, which has suffered the first of four flat tires and a broken trailer axle. They've managed to push and drag their way through a series of arroyos, washouts, and washboard trails which, at this stage of the trip, they still regard as fun and challenging. We try to locate them in relationship to a long, flat mesa to the west, but the landscape is too vast and undifferentiated to make the visual connection until they turn on their headlights. Suddenly, bright beams like lighthouse beacons mark their position on the coast. There is no other source or indication of man-made light, not even a reflection off a broken bottle.

We set up our camp on the white powder beach at San Rafael, near two other tents established by backcountry travelers with four-by-fours. Just after dark, one of them approaches to ask if we have any antihistamines for his son, who's been bitten by a scorpion while collecting firewood. We do.

The local coyote population howls and yips late into the star-spangled night while Nancy and I shiver under a blanket, doubled up with Rodney and his girlfriend, Rosemary, in their tent. The *Orca*, with its dry centerboard locker, is carrying our camping gear.

In the morning we explore the dunes behind the beach, which overlooks a well-protected blue lagoon and miles of high chaparral scrubland ranging out to the Sierra de La Libertad. We find a number of bleached bones along with the elongated skulls and skeletal remains of triggerfish, dolphins, and sea lions. Coyote tracks suggest how their remains got so high off the beach.

Around 10 A.M. the *Orca* sails past us on its way south. An hour later we pack our gear into the chase boat while the land crew heads off in a cloud of dust. Nancy wants to bring a dolphin skull along, pointing out how attractive it would be as a decorative figurehead, but Rodney refuses, claiming it's bad luck. So we leave it on the beach, raise the inflatable's Bimini top for shade, and head back out into the vast reflective spaces of a seemingly empty green sea. Early in the afternoon we spot and then lose track of a whale after its dark back breaks the shimmering surface sixty feet from us.

We set up our tents that night in the protected cove at San Francisquito, an abandoned but still pungent fishing camp littered with clamshells, rotting nets, brush huts, and metal packing crates. Among the broken Tecate beer bottles and plastic bags I find something more disturbing, a pile of desiccated sea lion flippers that appear to have been hacked off the animals, probably after they were killed by Mexican fishermen, who view them as competitors.

Jon had once been outsmarted by a pair of sea lions while spearfishing off San Diego, carrying a string of fish he'd just caught. As the two approached him underwater he pulled the fish behind his back and waved his Hawaiian sling spear at them so they went away. A moment later, after catching his breath at the surface, he saw the larger eight-hundred-pound sea lion charging straight at him like a torpedo. As he again pulled the fish behind his back it did a graceful flip away from him. At the same moment, the second sea lion, which had snuck up behind him, grabbed his fish and took off.

The following morning the wind is up and there is a sense of excitement as we reduce the sea crew to six: Jon, Al, and I on the *Orca*, Rodney, Rosemary, and Nancy on the *Dolphin*. With good breezes we should have three or four days of wilderness sailing ahead of us before reuniting with the land crew ninety miles to the south at Santa Rosalía.

Once we round the first point out of the harbor, the seas become rougher, creating a washing-machine effect of sharply peaked, disorganized waves; I have to climb out on the center bow to set the jib without falling in. We're soon cruising along at a brisk pace as the seas settle.

Late in the day we land on a small, wind-protected beach near Cabo San Miguel, making camp on a narrow shelf above the high-water mark. We collect the dead, wicker-hollow branches of cholla cacti—they burn like torches and light our campfire with a single match.

We have a 1991–92 New Year's Eve supper of fresh-picked tide-pool mussels on a bed of noodles before Nancy and I depart for a short stroll. The night sky is cold and brilliant, with cloud nebulas of stars and a brief meteor shower that brightens our spirits: "Hey, guy, make a wish." The only visible light beyond our campfire is a distant glowing dome across the water, which we guess is the mainland town of Guaymas.

The next morning Jon and I take a brisk snorkel with our sling spears, but the goatfish and grouper lurking around the submerged tide-pool rocks are far too wary of predators to let us get close.

The winds have picked up overnight, and the seas are running around three feet when we push off. Nancy and I have changed places so she can get a turn on *Orca*. We sail south past red volcanic cliff formations with odd striations of darker rock. Al catches a small barracuda and throws it back. The winds and seas keep picking up—to four feet, then five, later swelling to eight-foot following seas with sudden crosscurrents and wind shifts. We later learn that the fishing fleet in Santa Rosalía has holed up in the harbor, afraid to go out in the growing winter storm, known locally as a *chubasco*.

Our little boats handle themselves well. The *Dolphin* rises and falls like a cork, with Rodney (at the helm) surfing high across the shoulders of the waves, only occasionally shipping water over the bow. The *Orca* has let out its mainsail and is sliding gracefully across the waves and through the spray. I take some video of Nancy shooting back with her orange and black Nikonos.

Suddenly their outer starboard hull begins taking on water, spilling its excess into the centerboard well. Jon, Nancy, and Al begin bailing, donning their life vests, and calling us on the marine radio, anxious to know where we are. We're four hundred yards directly behind them, but they can't see us since our boat rides low in the rolling seas. We close the distance as their outer hull fills with one thousand pounds of excess water weight and they begin dropping deeper into the troughs, their mast disappearing from view behind the wave peaks around us. They can hear the connecting hinges creaking ominously, threatening to break loose and sink them quickly. We come alongside and stand by as Jon begins looking for a beaching location.

For the next three hours the only thing we can see are the crests of whitecaps and dangerously rocky, boulder-littered shores. Jon considers running the *Orca* up onto the rocks to save our gear and water, but disembarking would prove a hazardous operation with the shore break slamming against the slick rocks. We decide to keep offshore and try to get the boat around the next point, where there might be some protection from the wind and cold rain that's begun falling.

The seas prove marginally better around the point, showing a broad exposed beach with a rough but navigable shore break about a mile and a half in. I figure if the *Orca* founders at this point we can avoid having anyone drown if Jon, Al, and I get in the water and hold on to the inflatable's pontoon ropes while Rodney, Rosemary, and Nancy ride inside it.

Rodney suggests trying for another point two or three miles on, but Jon decides the *Orca* isn't up to it and takes her in. We watch as Jon threads a dangerous rock pile and, flapping his mainsail against the crosswinds, rides the sailboat over a four-foot beach break and up onto the sand. We come in fast behind them, with Rodney at the centerboard console, Rosemary bailing at the stern, and me pulling anchor rope from the wet locker between bouts of seasick vomiting over the side.

Once ashore we drag the boats up as high as we can (the water-heavy Orca barely moves), hug and backslap and congratulate each other on a job well done. We begin moving our supplies inland behind some low bushes that provide a modicum of protection from the wind and rain. I set up my Hi-8 tripod and do a wide-tracking panoramic shot of our boats set against a long crescent beach framed by endless mesas and serpentine hills. The *Orca*'s fate does not look good, as she lies there, half buried and listing in the tidal sands.

That evening, after we review our supply situation (five gallons of water, twenty-four of fuel, plenty of food, including oranges, Cokes, and trail mix), Rodney checks our position on a Magellan Global Positioning System. Handheld GPS is a pretty high-tech toy for New Year's 1992. A few minutes after receiving four satellite signals it tells us we're near Punta Trinidad, 27 degrees, 47 feet north; 112 degrees, 43 feet west; just over 36 nautical miles north of Santa Rosalía.

"Great, now we know exactly where we're lost," Nancy points out.

We set up three dome tents and go to sleep. In the morning, after Nancy and Rosemary deny us a hearty breakfast ("If we don't ration, you guys will eat everything in half an hour"), we hike two miles to the next point. According to our topographic maps, there should be a four-wheel access road somewhere nearby. The rocky hillsides and high chaparral are green with scrub grass and budding cirio trees, giving the landscape an almost tropical sheen under threatening skies. This is Baja's wettest winter in living memory. Jon and I search for the alleged access road, following an animal path north. After an hour of hardscrabble hiking, we climb a ridgeline filled with loose red volcanic stones to gain another stunning vista of our beach and miles of uninhabited coastline. Las Tres Vírgenes, a 6,800-foot mountain, dominates the interior landscape, capping the southern spine of the Sierra de San Francisco. A dry arroyo leading back into the mountains is as close to a "dirt road" as we can find.

Our beach, we realize, is the only one at Trinidad. Had we rounded the next point, we might have faced a genuine disaster.

Once the seas begin to calm, Rodney and Rosemary load the *Dolphin* with fuel and take off for Santa Rosalía to notify the authorities of our stranding.

After a lunch of oatmeal, raisins, and Cokes, Al, Nancy, and I decide to help Jon refloat his boat. Al begins digging in the rain, excavating channels in the sucking sand that has built up around the hulls. We bail out the boat, clear the drain plug on the outer starboard hull, and wait for the evening tide. Nancy prepares us an early dinner using macaroni and cheese, three jalapeño peppers, four garlic cloves, and an onion. Well heated for our night's work, we set a large beach fire and dig deep channels into the sand.

Nancy and I again sing choruses from *Gilligan's Island*: "The weather started getting rough, the tiny ship was tossed . . ." Jon and Al join in. With water draining well from the compromised hull we begin rocking and muscling the boat around 8 P.M. as the tide rises.

It's an overcast, intermittently rainy night, pitch-black except for our camp and beach fires and the marine phosphorescence that lights up the wave crests and runs over our bare arms and wet suits like hallucinatory green fireflies. Just before midnight Jon, Al, and I push and shove the *Orca* free of the sucking sand. It rides up on the cool, dark water.

Jon and I motor it out one thousand feet, guided away from the rocks by Nancy and Al's fading flashlight beams. We argue over loose ropes, a sputtering outboard, and the best way to judge distance in pitch black, but still manage to set a sea anchor twelve feet down on a seventy-foot scope. We then slip on our flippers and dive into the water, swimming back through the blackness toward the distant firelight, not stopping to tread water, admire the green phosphorescent wakes we're leaving, or listen to the mysterious night sounds of the ocean. We come ashore shivering with cold, drying ourselves by the beach fire and then the campfire before climbing into our tents. After a body-warming snuggle Nancy and I fall into an exhausted sleep. Later in the night I wake to the sounds of heavy rain and howling coyotes.

The next morning a Mexican navy C-123 Search and Rescue plane out of La Paz buzzes our camp. Al swims out to the boat and gets on the radio with them. They tell him a patrol boat left Guaymas last night to pick us up but turned back because of high seas. It departed again this morning and will be here in a few hours.

Two hours later we've packed our gear onto the beach and are standing around a smoldering campfire, considering raising a tarp, when the one-hundred-foot Aztec-class patrol boat appears on the horizon.

Within a few minutes we've made radio contact and are motoring the *Orca* out to the P-14 *Felix Romero*. Casually dressed Mexican sailors watch our approach from the bridge of the rusty gray gunboat. *"Gilligan's Island* meets *McHale's Navy,"* I tell the Gal. We tie on to the stern and load our personal gear aboard before putting the *Orca* on a towline. I notice the muzzle guard on their 20-millimeter deck gun consists of a plastic grocery bag secured with rubber bands. We're served hot soup, stringy meat, and warm tortillas with sea salt in the pilothouse as the morning rain turns into a downpour. It's one of the finest meals we've ever had.

Lt. Fernando Torres, the boat's captain, explains that the rescue is free but the tow will cost. He suggests a price of five hundred dollars. Jon and he are negotiating when one of the crewmen comes inside to report a problem. The *Orca*'s outer hull has again begun taking on water and is now threatening to take her down. We pull her in and remove the rest of our gear. We're still two hours from port. The captain suggests speeding up to try to keep her high in the water. The *Romero* increases speed. After about twenty minutes, it appears the *Orca* is foundering. The *Romero* cuts engines, and we pull the trimaran alongside. Ensign Luis Pirron suggests using their boom winch to lift up the outer hull, drop some tires for cushioning, and try to float her off the port side. Jon scrambles down onto the *Orca* to tie a rope around her mast. He's waist-deep in water as waves wash across the canvas decking. As I help haul Jon back aboard, Al and a group of sailors begin yanking on the pulley rope. Within seconds the ten-foot metal winch boom collapses, glancing off Al's wrist and shoulder as it falls to the deck with a sickening clang.

The captain now sends a man onto the sinking sailboat to cut away the last entangling ropes. He climbs down in socks without a safety line or life vest. He begins sawing away with a pocket-knife as the *Orca* starts to flip onto its side. He just manages to grab on to the front end of the center hull and gets lifted back onto the navy boat as the *Orca* floats free and slowly turns turtle all the way over. It's 4:05 P.M. Jon has a stricken look on his face. "It's like losing a child," he says.

No sailor likes to see a ship go down, so I have no problem accepting Ensign Pirron's explanation for the failure of the boom. "We just don't have the resources." Nancy goes over and hugs Jon. "Arrogance," he mutters. "Just plain arrogance."

A mustachioed officer in a black woolen turtleneck brings a pair of .45 pistols onto the deck.

"Why has he got those guns?" Nancy asks me.

He pulls the slide back on one and solemnly offers it to Jon.

"What's going on? Why is he giving a gun to Jon?"

"Shh . . . ," I say. "It's a guy thing."

Jon fires to hole the *Orca*, which now poses a hazard to navigation. On the third booming shot Jon's gun jams. The officer fires the second gun three times before it too jams. Apparently gun-cleaning kits are another resource the Mexican navy lacks.

Floating upside down, the *Orca*'s mast is pointed toward the bottom, over one thousand feet below us, as we stand by, several miles off the wild and barren coast of Cabo Tres Vírgenes.

"At least no one was hurt," Ensign Pirron says, and tries to cheer us up with tales of recent boating fatalities in these waters, including a sinking in which twenty-six of twenty-eight ferry-boat passengers drowned.

With her curved black bottom above the white trim at her waterline, the *Orca* now looks even more like her namesake, so I'm startled when one of the crew ties an iron spike onto an oar, creating a harpoon to try to finish her off. But after a few futile tosses Captain Torres decides the capsized boat does not in fact pose a threat to navigation and, for better or worse, turns the *Felix Romero* toward port.

"At least they didn't use the deck gun to finish it off," I note.

"It would've blown up and we'd all be in the water," Nancy completes my thought.

A few minutes later an exuberant school of two hundred dolphins passes between the *Orca* and us, leaping and rolling through the seas. It feels a bit like a tribute.

We're a somber group in our green, blue, and yellow slickers, arriving at the Santa Rosalía marine facility that evening in a steady downpour. Rodney, Rosemary, and the land crew are waiting for us on the unlit dock. We hug, go to dry off in a leaky motel, eat dinner, and get drunk.

The next day we drive out to Punta Chivato, a remote coastal resort on the far end of a flooded dirt track. I sit Jon down in front of the camera and ask him to explain what he thinks happened.

"It was the wildness of Baja that defeated us," he says, his voice strained from a mild fever, regret, and a lingering hangover. He thinks he lost his boat on land, that the starboard hull's integrity was compromised when the trailer broke loose outside Bahía de los Ángeles so that it couldn't handle the *chubasco*. Of course, he can't know for sure.

"Think you'll build a new boat?"

"I don't know." He smiles uncertainly, tears welling up in his eyes.

"But you'll continue sailing?"

"Of course. It's in my blood."

"Will you take your son sailing with you?"

"Of course. But not until he learns to swim."

Nancy gives me a half-cross look as I pack my gear and take it back to our room.

"What?"

"You made him cry for the camera."

"No. He was going to cry anyway, I just got some good interview footage."

We walk to a nearby beach made entirely of shells, broken and whole. Nancy stops to collect some, puts them back as she finds better ones, fills up a bucket, and makes me hold out my T-shirt to carry some more shells. This, to her, is like a day at Neiman Marcus for some other women. There are laughing gulls strutting along the edge of the water, and pretty soon we're imitating their *arrh, arrh, arrh, arrh* mating conversations. We return to our room to wash her shells in the big tile shower. She's still making gull sounds.

From Punta Chivato we caravan to Loreto and then back-track to Concepción Bay, where we camp, go scuba diving, and watch a big rusting shrimp trawler trailed by a cloud of gulls. It's emptying out the Sea of Cortés's waters, its crew netting up to ten pounds of bycatch—finfish, shellfish, and sea turtles—that they'll throw back dead for every pound of shrimp they capture. Later the United States will ban shrimp imports from Mexico and other fishing nations whose boats fail to use turtle excluder devices. The World Trade Organization (WTO) will then rule this is an infringement on free trade.

That decision will inspire a "turtle-Teamster alliance" during protests by tens of thousands of environmental, labor, and human rights activists at the 1999 WTO meeting in Seattle. Hundreds of the demonstrators will dress up as sea turtles with cardboard shells and green head caps to voice their dissatisfaction with the WTO's ruling. While the media will focus on window-smashing black-clad anarchists, and police attacks on demonstrators and bystanders, one of the most impressive parts of the "Battle of Se-attle" will be when the International Longshore and Warehouse Union (ILWU) shuts down all the West Coast ports for a day in solidarity with the protesters. Today the ILWU has also become an ally of the ocean conservation community, protesting port pol-lution and offshore oil drilling, a blue–blue collar alliance.

From Concepción Bay we drive north to see the whales at Scammon's Lagoon. Stopping in a market, we spot a missing-persons poster for a couple who disappeared with their sailboat off Cabo Tres Vírgenes three months earlier. No one says anything. After visiting with the gray whales, one of whom comes up to our Panga boat and lets us rub her huge head, we head back to San

Diego. From there we catch a Sunday ride home to Sausalito with Scott, whose new Jeep just got a good shakedown cruise.

"You know, I really feel bad for Jon," the Gal says on Monday as we're cleaning our gear.

"Me too."

"I mean what happened to his boat was really fucked, but what an adventure." She grins.

Producing a TV documentary at the Rio Earth Summit several months later will prove a different kind of adventure and disaster, one that will help me figure out the evolving role of environmentalism on the world stage.

With the end of the cold war and the collapse of the Soviet Union in 1991, there was a moment when Senator Al Gore's prediction that the environment would be the next defining global issue seemed not unreasonable. In June 1992, 107 world leaders, more than had ever come together at one time, would meet for the United Nations Conference on Environment and Development (UNCED), also known as the Earth Summit, in Rio de Janeiro.

Unfortunately, the international treaties and agreements signed in Rio by the gathered heads of state would prove to be worth less than the pulped trees they were written on.

- The Rio climate agreement was supposed to reduce greenhouse gas emissions to 1990 levels by the year 2000. Its failure led to the 1997 Kyoto treaty agreement, which set far weaker standards but was nevertheless sabotaged and rejected by the United States so that a new international agreement had to be delayed until 2010.

- A biodiversity treaty that was supposed to protect the world's declining wilderness, including marine wilderness, also went nowhere fast as the sixth great extinction pulse in planetary history continues apace. In 2008 the International Union for the Conservation of Nature reported that 25 to 35 percent of wild mammals now on earth, more than one out of four, including polar bears and beluga whales, are at risk of extinction as a result of human activities. Some marine scientists estimate the extinction rate in the ocean is five times that of the land.

- Forestry and marine agreements in Rio also failed to slow global deforestation and the devastation of our ocean commons from industrial overfishing, pollution, and climate impacts.

- A voluntary agreement among the developed nations to help poorer countries obtain renewable energy and other sustainable technologies by upping their aid programs to 0.7 percent of their GDP also proved an empty promise. Within five years aid had actually declined on average from 0.32 to 0.27 percent of GDP.

- Proposals dealing with human population, nuclear weapons, and women's empowerment weren't even addressed in Rio in deference to the fragile sensibilities of the Vatican, France, Saudi Arabia, and other interested parties, both pre- and post-enlightenment.

My best memory of the summit was not of the official sessions but of the night fifteen thousand Brazilians and fifteen thousand international activists marched together through the streets, under the lights of army helicopters and behind a group of Buddhist monks with cell phones and a banner that read, WHEN THE PEOPLE LEAD, THE LEADERS WILL FOLLOW.

The linkage between that kind of bottom-up democratic perspective and environmental protection is both critical and dynamic if we're to save our living blue planet.

In Seoul, South Korea, I met with and did a video profile of Yul Choi, founder of the Korean Federation for Environmental Movement and winner of the prestigious Goldman Environmental Prize. It was a hard road Yul Choi had traveled to become his nation's leading environmentalist. As a student activist he'd been arrested, tortured, and jailed for five years by the military regime that ruled his country. The other student prisoners talked about organizing workers and peasants when they got out of jail, but Choi was a bit of a science nerd who had studied to be a chemist while in school. So, while in solitary confinement, he got Amnesty International to send him hundreds of environmental books, which the military jail authorities let through because they figured they weren't communist tracts. What harm could they do?

Released in the early 1980s Yul Choi led massive anti-pollution protests that helped spark successful student-led pro-democracy battles in 1987–88. By the time I visited in the mid-1990s he had strong support among newly elected members of a democratic parliament but also many still-powerful opponents, including the Korean CIA, which tried to interfere with my video shoot.

We still managed to pull it off, including a trip with Yul Choi to Dik-juk Island in the Yellow Sea, where the local fishing

community was fighting plans for a nuclear waste dump on a
nearby island. After we filmed their protest, half the population,
about 350 people, boarded our ferry for the return trip to the
mainland. The next day, in the thick yellow-white smog of downtown Seoul, they protested outside the Ministry of Science and
Technology. Squads of body-shielded riot police appeared, and
there was some spirited pushing and shoving and fisticuffs. After
two hours the protesters and the cops all boarded their respec-
tive buses and left the scene.

I asked my Korean cameraman, Charlie Lee, why the police
hadn't beaten up or arrested the demonstrators.

"If these were students rioting for ideology the police would
beat them very badly," he assured me. "But the policemen understand, these fishermen are rioting from their heart."

In 1994 I produced a book on how violent environmental back-
lashes are not limited to authoritarian regimes. *The War Against
the Greens* had its origins at a 1990 Redwood Summer protest in
the coastal mill town of Fort Bragg, California, where we saw a
crowd of 1,500 anti-logging protesters and hundreds of pro-
logging hecklers kept apart by 425 riot police in an angry scene
that reminded me of Marching Days in Northern Ireland, when
Protestants and Catholics clashed over conflicts almost as ancient as California redwoods.

What piqued my curiosity was that only two years earlier
Fort Bragg had been the scene of a larger protest by some two
thousand residents—including fishermen, loggers, shopkeepers,
homeowners, and environmentalists—unified in their opposition to a federal plan to lease salmon-rich offshore waters for oil
drilling.

Now the loggers, mill workers, their families, and their white-collar bosses were part of a new industry-backed "grassroots initiative" that called itself either the Wise Use movement or the Property Rights movement and supported not only unrestricted timber cutting and mineral mining on public lands but also off-shore drilling and federal compensation whenever a law or regulation restricted a developer's ability to build on a coastal wetland or required an oil company to double-hull its ships. It also had a nastier edge, trying to scapegoat local environmentalists for job losses in rural resource-dependent communities. As the Wise Use movement failed to gain traction in the West, this tendency expanded into a national campaign of violence, harassment, and intimidation—including death threats, shootings, beatings, and arson—targeting both rural environmentalists and federal resource agents.

Down in the Gulf of Mexico region, it was a right-wing shrimper opposed to turtle excluder devices who led the local Wise Use group even as Diane Wilson, a Texas shrimper who opposed a chemical plant that was polluting her bay, became the target of Wise Use gunfire and sabotage.

Wise Use's links to armed right-wing militias, which I and other journalists documented before and after the deadly 1995 bombing of the Alfred P. Murrah Federal Building in Oklahoma City, contributed to the decline of the movement as its industry sponsors from mining, timber, and agribusiness withdrew their financial and logistical support.

One of Wise Use's last visible victories came in 2002 on the Klamath River, which flows through Oregon and California on its way to the sea. With loud street protests and behind-the-scenes pressure from Vice President Dick Cheney and Bush strategist Karl Rove, Secretary of the Interior Gale Norton, herself a veteran of the Mountain States Legal Foundation that billed itself as "the litigation arm of Wise Use," announced that water supposed to be kept in the river for endangered salmon and suckerfish would instead be diverted to farmers in eastern (Republican) Oregon. Right-wing radio commentators like Rush Limbaugh had a field day talking about "farmers versus suckerfish," even as a U.S. Geological Survey report showed that keeping water in the river would generate thirty times more economic benefit for fishermen and other downstream river users in (Democratic) California.

Six months later tens of thousands of salmon died in the partially drained river. California congressman Mike Thompson and his constituents, including Indian tribes and commercial fishermen whose livelihoods and treaty rights depended on the fish, then dumped five hundred pounds of dead, rotting Klamath salmon on the front steps of the Department of the Interior in Washington, D.C., as a protest. The decline of the Klamath salmon led to wide-ranging restrictions on offshore salmon fishing in 2007 out of fear that the last threatened Klamath fish would be caught and killed.

Shortly thereafter California's entire fall chinook salmon run collapsed: an estimated 1.5 million fish in 2005 had dwindled to an estimated 60,000 in 2008. Agricultural water diversions in the Sacramento delta, combined with changing oceanographic effects from climate change, seemed to be the main culprits.

Today, recognizing how dependent we all are on healthy rivers, watersheds, and the ocean, farmers, fishermen, environmentalists, government officials, and PacifiCorp, a private power company, have reached an agreement to remove four marginally productive dams on the Klamath River in the hope this will help restore historic water flows and fish runs along more than three hundred miles of the river that will be opened up for the first time in decades. Similar dam removals have worked elsewhere.

In 1999 the 160-year-old Edwards Dam was removed from the Kennebec River in Maine. By the tenth anniversary of its demolition, the river had gone through an environmental and economic transformation. With the restoration of its uninterrupted connection to the sea, over two million alewives now return to the river, one of the largest river-based herring runs in the United States. Eagles, osprey, and big sturgeon also returned, as seals were chasing striped bass far up the river. Newly created river parks, boat launches, kayak concessions, and waterfront development were providing financial benefits to the state capital of Augusta and other riverfront towns in economic hard times.

The long-sought removal of four dams on the lower Snake River in Washington State that could prove key to the recovery of endangered salmon in the Pacific Northwest, a plan blocked during the Bush years, is now being seriously considered, partly as a result of citizen lawsuits brought by environmentalists, salmon fishermen, and Northwest Indian tribes.

It's these kinds of collaborative efforts, combined with bottom-up pressure, that may lead not only to the restoration and sustainable use of the heroic, Homeric, and iconic ocean-spanning salmon but to the preservation of countless other natural and shared resources on our ocean planet.

The Wise Use/Property Rights backlash of the late twentieth century sought to maintain the fallacy that environmental protection is the enemy of resource-based economies and development. A twenty-first-century perspective recognizes the truth of what former Colorado senator Tim Wirth has said, that our economy is a fully owned subsidiary of our environment. Trillions of dollars' worth of irreplaceable natural services are provided by oxygen-generating algae in our ocean and trees in our forests, also from wetlands, mangroves, prairies, savannahs, coral reefs, Arctic ice, and other life-generating habitats.

When *The War Against the Greens* first came out, things were going extraordinarily well in my life. Nancy and I were continuing to travel, snorkel, and dive as well as hike the California coast every weekend. My sister's marriage hadn't lasted, but it had lasting value in that it produced my nephews, Adam and Ethan. When they came to visit as young boys we took them out to the beach, where they picked blackberries and collected sea glass.

Any time the cold waters of northern California began to chill my bones Nancy and I would find an excuse to take a trip to San Diego, Hawaii, Florida, or to the island of St. John in the U.S. Virgins, where Nancy's sister, Deb, was schoolteacher. We'd snorkel the drier east side of the island, swimming with the nurse sharks. I wrote a story for *Audubon* magazine on marine sanctuaries and another for *Smithsonian* on NOAA's "fish cops," and began outlining my idea for a book on the state of the ocean.

Unfortunately, as every son of a Holocaust survivor knows, there is no such thing as a steady state. My life was about to take a series of emotionally shattering turns that, oddly, would also lead me deeper into the sea.

8

Polar Opposites

> Away with the superficial and selfish phil-*anthropy* of
> men; who knows what admirable virtue of fishes may
> be below low-water-mark, bearing up against a hard
> destiny, not admired by that fellow-creature who alone
> can appreciate it! Who hears the fishes when they cry?
>
> HENRY DAVID THOREAU

I was moving to Washington, D.C., where I'd live for almost a
decade, working as an environmental journalist covering the
world and later as an ocean advocate trying to save it. But the
eastern seaboard no longer felt like home. It felt more like exile

from the Pacific's wide, wild beaches, cold sparkling waters, and from the woman I loved.

I left Nancy on August 14, 1997, after ten years of living together. I thought it was time to raise a family. She didn't feel ready to marry or make that commitment.

"I can't believe you're leaving us," she says. She means her and the cat, now twelve years old.

I'm brushing my teeth in the bathroom. She's standing behind me, doing a running commentary in a squeaky cartoon voice she'll sometimes use in play. I watch her in the mirror, checking herself to see if her long hair is "winging" at the temples. She stops.

"Who am I going to make silly voices to if you leave?" She begins to cry.

She doesn't think I could support her if we had a child. "You'd be watching TV and not hear the baby crying," she charges. "You'd never change the diaper." She doesn't really want a child, I think. She wants to go to Paris. She doesn't believe you can have adventure and a family. I don't think she had many adventures growing up with her working-class family in Kenosha, Wisconsin.

A few days before I'm to leave one of the trees behind the house cracks and breaks, falling down from fungus rot. I'd call it an omen, but it's the second time in two years. The other tree's crown ended up on our second-floor porch during a wild winter storm. Night herons from the bay took refuge in the branches of the redwoods behind our deck. The downpours were torrential, tropical in their intensity.

I go down the street and pick blackberries from the bushes. She says I'm like a bear, obsessed with the berries. Later I'm kneeling in my office wrestling with the Poose, and start to cry, thinking, I'm crying over leaving a cat.

My last day in Sausalito the Ryder truck is packed. There are robins, hummingbirds, and chickens flitting about behind the house, mocking me. I've been dragging this out for months, she claims. It's true. "Nothing's ever resolved," she says at the end of all our arguments.

She suggests lunch by the docks. It's one of our regular places. We sit down with our tuna sandwiches, looking across the marina at all the sailboats and yachts on Richardson Bay, sparkling in the warmth. It's been one of the nicest summers in years. I'd been out bodysurfing with my friend Tim three weeks ago. I caught a surfboard to the throat and had to have a CT scan (after Nancy made me go to the hospital). Last Friday we rode waves again till sunset at Stinson Beach, a harbor seal in the water with us, making us a little edgy. It's sharky water, the heart of the Red Triangle, where there are more white shark–human encounters than anywhere else on the planet, an average of four or five bites a year, one death every few years. From the ocean I look up at the steep, green pine-covered hills rising above the beach. A rainbow's shadow appears on the clouds above us. I'm not only leaving Nancy and the Poose, I realize, but my other love, the sea. For half my life, I've lived within a mile of the Pacific, rode it, sailed on it, walked its shores.

Back at the Docks I can't swallow my tuna sandwich, nor can she, so at least we're reducing our mercury intake. She's sipping her latte. I feel numb and heartsick at the same time, a hollow feeling. I can't believe I'm doing this, destroying the life I know, leaving hers at risk. She looks young but she's already thirty-eight. Not much time really to decide, although I guess she already has. Tears are running down my cheeks. "I have to leave," I tell her. She nods.

If we were ever going to get married and have children, I

would have to be the one to push the issue because I knew she wouldn't. And I didn't want to suddenly find myself in my fifties and the decision made by default, and me resentful because we never had that final resolution. So now we have. And there are all these other reasons, although I can't identify them as clearly— still, they're there. In my first book's acknowledgments I'd called her my own life's love. I now have to wonder if that was just good writing. She says we'll see, we'll see if it was meant to be. What did I expect? I never expected it to hurt so much.

I move into an apartment on Connecticut Avenue in Washington, D.C., near Rock Creek Park. I soon find Ireland's 4 Provinces, the local Irish pub, where I start drinking too much, listening to Irish rebel songs from my youth. A friend asks why I moved to D.C. "Well, I was breaking up with my girlfriend of ten years and figured if I'm gonna traumatize myself, I might as well go all the way," I reply, not entirely in jest. Two weeks after I get there, having packed my dive gear and boogie board in the back of the closet, I get a call from Scott, my lawyer friend. He tells me he just won a multimillion-dollar jury verdict on the last wrongful death case we'd worked on together, when I was his private investigator, one involving a young man beaten to death outside a Central Valley bar named Shag Nasty's. He invites me to go diving with him in Cozumel, Mexico, his treat.

A few days later I'm looking down at the wild, unbroken rain forest of the Yucatán Peninsula. Before I have time to contemplate the lure of the jungle, the plane banks and the turquoise waters of the Caribbean now enthrall me.

Unlike the nearby resort city of Cancún, Cozumel is primarily a dive destination. Green jungle and mangrove swamps full of egrets, iguanas, wild pigs, and toothy caimans still cover much of the flat twenty-eight-by-eleven-mile island. Development is mainly low-rise along the west coast. On the east coast, there are long stretches of powdery white sea-turtle breeding beaches and a few palm-shaded cantinas. In the interior are some Mayan ruins dedicated to Ixchel, the goddess of childbirth, of medicine, and, more recently, of spring break.

The reef that fringes the rocky western shore was declared a national park in 1996, and despite its popularity among divers and its exposure to large cruise ships and hurricanes, it remains a vibrant refuge for marine wildlife.

I hook up with Scott and Brad, another friend from California, at the Scuba Club, a simple three-story whitewashed hotel with a red tile roof, lounging cats, and hibiscus trees. The rooms have tiled floors and outdoor racks for hanging wet suits. There are also dive lockers by the coral-encrusted quay just a few steps below the swimming pool.

We pick up weights and tanks and do a test dive off the quay. Everything seems to be functioning well in the white-rum-clear water. That evening, after testing the hammocks strung beneath the straw-roofed palapas, we have a chicken fajita dinner at the inn's Fat Grouper restaurant.

The next morning we head out on one of the resort's two catamarans. As we leave the dock, I look across the bright warm water and count three shades of blue: aquamarine in the sandy shallows changing to teal over the reef and finally cobalt in the deep sea.

Soon we're underwater, drifting above white sand channels that meander through towering columns of hard corals, sponges, and gorgonians. We spot the usual clutter of bright tropical fish: parrots and queen angels, triggers, hamlets, schooling goatfish, and small blue chromis, scattered like confetti through the water column. I notice a couple of electric rays cruising the bottom. Inside a sandy cave is a humongous green moray about eight feet long, with a toothy open mouth. Gentle-natured or not, he has razor-sharp teeth that could take your arm off at the elbow.

On the second dive, a large grouper approaches us, and I pat him on the side. When a smaller sixty-pound tiger grouper sidles up to me, I realize we're seeing a regulatory backlash. One of the new rules of the national park is no feeding the fish. Word apparently has not filtered down the food chain.

The next day, we visit Colombia Reef, near the southern tip of the island. We swim single file through ninety-foot-deep caverns whose walls are covered in soft star, flower and plate corals, barrel and vase sponges, and algae in red, white, orange, and green. The caves, where our bubbles hang on the ceiling like bits of quicksilver, are filled with squirrelfish, spiny lobsters, and rattle-shaped glassy sweepers.

The next cave ends abruptly as we swim out over a precipice, with nothing but pelagic blue before and below us. It's a little disconcerting when it catches you unaware. On another day, in another cave, I look out the entrance and see a column of sand swirling across the sea floor between underwater mesas and buttes, like a dust devil in Death Valley.

Our second night we walk into the main town of San Miguel, with its bustling waterfront traffic, exhaust-spewing buses, mopeds, dive shops, curio stores, and bars, including a Hooters, which is still a hell of a lot nicer than Shag Nasty's.

The next day, we're back underwater exploring Paraiso Reef.

I glimpse some spotted eels, sergeant majors, and a toadfish under a rock. There are also spotted drums; depending on their state of maturity, they resemble little red, white, and blue American flags or a tail without a fish. I search under a ledge and spook a large angelfish, which turns sideways and slips into a crevice like a manila envelope through a mail slot. A multihued parrot fish ignores our little drama, contentedly crunching away on the coral.

The following night, we dive on Chankanab Reef, halfway down the west coast. We attach green luminescence sticks to our tanks and check out our underwater lights. Beneath a three-quarter moon, we splash off the fantail. On reaching the bottom, we begin to search for nightlife. Within minutes, I spotlight a four-foot octopus. Caught in the open, he slides across the sandy floor, changing from green to bright blue to bumpy mottled sand brown, in almost perfect visual and tactile camouflage. Soon he finds a hole in the rocks and squishes into it, pulling his tentacles in behind him. I turn off my light and look up. Fifty feet above me the moonlight glitters on the surface, radiating silver beams through the water. A school of ocean triggerfish cruise by like moonlight shadows. I start humming "Moonshadow."

Drifting off on my own, I train my light on a barracuda swimming along the outside of the reef like a coyote tracking the edge of a mesa. It suddenly turns toward me and begins to approach. It looks to be over five feet of silver muscle and teeth, the Doberman of the sea. I lift a fin toward the lantern-jawed predator, but it keeps coming. At four feet distance, I chicken out and turn the light away. The barracuda stops, hesitates, then streaks past my head about six inches from my ear like a misfired rocket grenade and is gone. That takes some air out of my tank.

Our last day's dives are fast drifts over a runner reef full of barracuda, jacks, and groupers. We quietly check out a six-foot nurse shark sleeping in a narrow cave. Twenty minutes later, floating cross-legged, I look down and see a huge eagle ray with a ten-foot wingspan cruising by, a couple of remoras clinging to its handsome spotted back. I try to catch up, but a few graceful beats of those wings send it soaring off across the sea grass plains in search of some tasty conch.

Back on the boat, we're giddy with delight. Above us a split-tailed frigate bird is tracking something in the water. Suddenly, a dozen flying fish take to the air, skimming a foot or two above the sea. The black-and-white frigate swoops down, grabbing one of the winged fish in midflight. I have to laugh. Frigates look for wahoo, jack, or barracuda chasing prey, then wait. The flying fish take to the air to escape the predators below only to end up being grasped in beaks of death from above.

A week earlier, drinking alone in D.C., I'd felt a bit like one of those flying fish. But today, buoyed by the light and clarity of the sea, I feel more like that frigate, the wind whistling under my wings.

Two months after we split up Nancy comes to visit me in D.C., to see my new apartment and make sure I'm eating well and cleaning up after myself. I take her around the Washington Mall, the free museums, and the zoo as we play tourist for a few days. Later that spring I propose taking her on a trip to Alaska, something we'd talked about for a long time. She's now being pursued by a man she's known for years, who says he wants to marry her. She thinks he's too much of a ladies' man to take the offer seriously. Since I also haven't had much luck finding the theoretical mother of my children, off we go on our next grand adventure, if only for the sake of adventure.

We're three miles up the trail in Kachemak Bay State Park after being dropped off by water taxi from the Homer Spit. The spongy old-growth forest full of giant prickly devil's club, cranberries, mushrooms, moss- and lichen-covered Sitka spruce and hemlock is giving way to rocky higher ground of alder, fireweed, and snowcapped mountain ranges. Here the prints of bear and moose are clear on the open trail, as is their scat, the grizzly scat like mounds of half-digested berries, fresh but not steaming, not yet a warning sign of danger ahead.

"Hey, bear," I call out as I enter high brush, not wanting to surprise one at its feeding.

"Hey, man!" Nancy responds from behind me. A pheasant-like ptarmigan flushes in front of me, leaving my heart beating to the rhythm of its wings.

That morning's paper had a report about a man whose face was ripped by a grizzly in Chugach State Park, just above Anchorage.

"She was a pretty majestic animal," the victim, thirty-seven-year-old Blaine Smith, a mountain guide, claimed, his right eye still swollen shut, the bones beneath it broken from where the bear swatted him.

He and his wife, speaking loudly and calling, "Hey, bear," still managed to startle a cub on the trail and were then charged by its mother, who was only fifteen feet away in dense trailside woods. Smith says he didn't like the look of the bear's flattened ears or bared teeth, and who can blame him? After being pawed, he landed in a fetal position and played dead, as did his wife. The bear then ambled away. "Alaska is a great place where nature often has the upper hand," he explained. "That's what makes Alaska special, and bears are part of that scene. They're to be cherished for it."

We lunch alone by the milky melt pond of a high blue glacier, its light-absorbing density allowing only sky color to reflect back on us. The glacier's ice-sculpture floes sound like tin cans as they crack apart. Theirs is the only sound to be heard beyond the occasional caws of circling gulls and jays and the hammer clacking of a woodpecker. A peregrine falcon lands silently on a nearby tree branch.

A few hours later Nancy and I climb down over tangled roots through the thick green canopy to our rocky takeout point. We wait by a cold-water bay sheltered by snow-streaked green escarpments, backed by wild mountain ranges under rolling clouds, quilting up with the threat of rain. I glass the cliffs with my binoculars, searching for mountain goats. Half a mile across the water a rustic cabin with river rock chimney is set into the shore, as natural-seeming as a deadfall snag.

Mako, an ex-fisherman turned water taxi captain, arrives in his open yellow boat. He's already picked up two campers from another cove who'd gotten treed by a black bear going after their food. We clamber aboard across shoreside boulders and head out across the rough chop of Cook Inlet. Facing into the wind, we spot a couple of harbor porpoises, and Mako points up at a rare Arctic visitor, a black-and-white parasitic jaeger with diamond club tail. It's like a large magpie with attitude. It chases other seabirds until they drop their catch or throw up. Then it feeds.

Back ashore, we share a few drinks with Mako at the Salty Dawg, the log fishermen's bar on the spit, a natural spur of land that, like a compass needle, points Homer toward the sea. He tells us how they overfished the crab that was once abundant in Cook Inlet. A few years later it will be the inlet's white, blunt-headed beluga whales whose population begins to crash. In 2008 NOAA will protect these whales under the Endangered Species Act, despite opposition from then governor Sarah Palin. Illegal hunting and pollution of Cook Inlet are the main culprits suspected in the belugas' decline.

After five days on the Kenai Peninsula we fly south. Juneau, the state capital, is located in southeast Alaska, a kind of five-hundred-mile-long kite tail to the main body of the state. The area is made up of forested islands and federal lands containing some 30 percent of the world's remaining unlogged temperate rain forests, also the world's highest concentration of grizzly bears, bald eagles, and Sitka deer.

We decide to check out Alaska's biggest creatures, bigger even than the grizzlies, on a daylong trip aboard the Gustavus ferry through Icy Strait.

Heading north out of Auke Bay, we count the winged bounty of a healthy marine ecosystem: clownlike puffins, stately cormorants, pigeon guillemots, speedy little marbled murrelets (endangered in the Lower 48 because they require large tracts of old-growth forest for nesting), and common murres with their uncommon ability to drop from the sky to depths of several hundred feet underwater in pursuit of their piscine prey.

Off Lemesurier Island we check out lounging harbor seals and a dozen large sea otters grooming themselves in the kelp, including a mother otter trying to get her oversized kid to stop riding on her stomach and go catch a crab or something. Soon we cross paths with a pod of orcas. Among the group is a male with a six-foot dorsal fin cutting through the water like a scythe and, not far behind, a baby black-and-white orca leaping in pursuit of its family. Two of the killer whales head toward the starboard side of our boat, as if on a torpedo run, and then, twenty yards out, disappear from sight.

This drama is followed by the appearance of humpback whales feeding and breaching off Point Adolphus. A mother whale slaps her fifteen-foot-long pectoral fin on the water as her baby swims nearby. A forty-five-foot-long show-off breaches full out of the water, jumping eight or nine times in front of and next to our boat. Other whales swim so close that all you can hear is the humphing exhalation of their breaths and the snapping of camera shutters. Since the end of commercial whaling, humpbacks by the thousands now spend their summers feeding off Alaska and their winters making babies in the warm waters off Hawaii.

"That certainly convinces me these animals are highly intelligent," I tell Nancy.

"Write it down," she responds with a grin, changing film.

As we head back to the mainland, an arching rainbow appears in the straits ahead of us while the boat's loudspeakers play Paul Simon's "Graceland." We're in our own moment of grace, at peace with each other and the world.

Just before leaving Alaska, we stop at Eagle River Beach, a family picnic area outside a state campground. It proves true to its name—we spot a couple of bald eagles on a driftwood log by the beach's sandbar flats. Also out there are hundreds of cawing gulls and thousands of big spawning coho salmon finning through the shallows, playing out their role in an ocean-spanning cycle of life and death, with some end-of-life spawning activity thrown in 'cause even in cold river gravel water it's still to die for; plus, they sort of get reincarnated when their rotted flesh is consumed by bears and eagles and then deposited as scat nutrient at the base of wild forest trees. So there's a salmon soul in every Sitka spruce.

Across the water are the snow-brushed peaks of the Chilkat Range. As we walk onto the beach we pass under a tree full of ravens that take wing, shotgun-peppering the sky in front of us like a hundred jagged black holes in a painted seascape so pretty it makes your heart ache. We turn toward the grassy river mouth, where the salmon are now so numerous they're creating their own whitewater chop, and looking upriver with an unstated expectation, we see . . . nothing.

"There's an old Alaska saying I've just made up: if you don't see a bear on your first trip to Alaska you'll have to come back again," I tell the Gal.

"Of course we will," she assures me with more confidence than I'd expected.

I return to Washington, where I report on environmental politics for various magazines and begin doing stories and commentaries for Marketplace radio. I've joined the Society of Environmental Journalists and increasingly identify myself as one. This is a case of finding an ecological niche that needs to be filled. I'd noticed that most political and investigative reporters tend to view the environmental beat as either uninteresting or low-prestige, while many environmental reporters come from a science or nature-writing background. My own instincts have been to follow the issues by following the money, looking at how contending political and economic forces respond to changing environmental science and policy.

You can write all you want about how coastal wetlands and salt marshes function as habitat for wildlife, nurseries for juvenile

marine fish, filters of pollution, or rechargers of our groundwater supply, but if your local politician's major campaign contributor
is the Homebuilder's Association or local real-estate developers,
you can kiss that swamp good-bye. Federal coastal and ocean
policy, I've learned, is largely driven by what I call the five big
fish: the offshore oil and gas industry, the shipping industry, the
navy, commercial fishing interests, and coastal real-estate developers.

Among their other transgressions, almost all of them were, at
the turn of the century, ignoring the growing threat of anthropogenic (human-driven) climate change to the world's seas. I decided to follow the lead of thousands of scientist members of the
UN's Intergovernmental Panel on Climate Change (IPCC), who
say the most visible effects of global warming will come earliest
and be most pronounced at the planet's poles and in our polar
seas.

When the National Science Foundation (NSF) accepted me
for one of its journalist-in-residence slots in Antarctica, I e-mailed
Nancy, saying, "If I can't be with you I'll be with the penguins."

Clouds, snow, rock, and water hard as black marble is all we can
see as we approach the end of our four-day, nine-hundred-mile
journey from Punta Arenas, Chile, across the Southern Ocean.
Up on the bridge of the *Laurence M. Gould*, Robert, the first mate,
is playing Led Zeppelin and talking on the radio with Palmer.
"Never been this far south without seein' ice," he notes in a lilting Cajun accent.

We round Bonaparte Point, and there it is, set in a boulder
field below a blue-white glacier—Palmer Station, Antarctica.

Palmer, one of three U.S. Antarctic bases run by the National Science Foundation, is located on Anvers Island, thirty-eight miles of granite rock covered by ice up to two thousand feet thick. Anvers is part of the Antarctic Peninsula, a seven-hundred-mile-long tail to the coldest, driest, highest continent on Earth—a landmass bigger than the United States and Mexico combined, containing 70 percent of the world's fresh water and 90 percent of its ice. The peninsula, where polar and marine climates converge, is also a wildlife-rich habitat that researchers refer to as Antarctica's "banana belt." And that was before global warming.

While docking, we're greeted by a small welcoming committee of people, Adélie penguins, skua birds, and elephant seals. Palmer Station has the look of a low-rent ski resort next to an outdoor equipment dealership. It is made up of a group of blue and white prefab metal buildings, with two big fuel tanks, front loaders, snowmobiles, and MILVANs (shipping containers) scattered around. The two main buildings, Biolab and GWR (garage, warehouse, and recreation), are separated so that if one burns down, the other can act as a refuge for the twenty to forty scientists and support personnel who work here year-round.

The short, oblong pier on the inlet with its giant rubber fenders is where the *Gould*, our 240-foot supply and research vessel, docks every six to eight weeks during the austral summer. January and February's warm temperatures may drift between a balmy zero and forty degrees Fahrenheit, with twenty-three hours of daylight to enjoy the views across the island and iceberg-studded Bismarck Strait toward Cape Renard on the continental mainland, with its unnamed dragon's teeth mountain ranges of black rock and white snow.

The weather is variable, with sun, clouds, rain, snow, and gale-force winds, often all on the same day, kind of like San Francisco on steroids. Next to the pier is the boathouse and its string of black and gray Zodiacs, Mark 3s, and Mark 5s. Fifteen and twenty feet in length, they provide the main means of transport at Palmer, along with thick Sorel boots and ice crampons for glacier climbing. We'll get to operate these fast rubber rafts in the subfreezing waters of the Southern Ocean on those days when the winds drop below twenty knots.

Bill Fraser, a rangy, sun-weathered fifty-something ice veteran from Montana, is chief scientist at Palmer. "The Marr Glacier used to come within one hundred yards of the station," he tells me, pointing upslope. "Its meltwater was the source of our fresh water." By the time I arrive, the Marr has retreated a quarter mile from Palmer, across granite rocks and boulders. Skuas now splash in the old melt pond, while the station is forced to use a saltwater intake pipe and desalinization system to generate its fresh water. Periodically, the artillery rumble and boom of moving ice alerts us to continued glacial retreat while offering spectacular views of irregular ice faces calving off the glacier into Arthur Harbor, setting off a blue pall of ice crystals and a rolling turquoise wave under a newborn scree of chunky brash ice, some of which we'll use in our bar drinks.

A few years later I'll visit a long-wall coal mine deep underground in western Pennsylvania where the coal face being removed is a quarter mile wide, and I'll have an epiphany, realizing I've now seen both ends of the carbon cycle. In the mine a giant blade like an oversized salami slicer runs along the coal face, calving off big chunks of coal, which fall onto a conveyor belt that takes them one thousand feet up to the surface. There, trains take the coal to power plants, where it's burned for electricity, putting massive plumes of carbon dioxide into the atmosphere, which heats it up. As a result, the glaciers in Antarctica are now calving into the sea at an alarming rate.

"When I was a graduate student we were told that climate change occurs, but you'll never see it in your lifetime," Bill Fraser tells me. "But in the last twenty years I've seen tremendous effects. I've seen islands pop out from under glaciers, I've seen species changing places and landscape ecology altered."

While global temperatures have warmed an average one degree Fahrenheit over the last century—paralleling increased industrial output of carbon dioxide and other greenhouse gases—the Antarctic Peninsula has seen a jump of more than five degrees in just fifty years, including an incredible nine-degree average warming during its winter months.

One way we know there is more heat-trapping carbon dioxide in our atmosphere today than at any time in at least 420,000 years is through ice core samples taken from Siple Dome, Vostok Station, and other sites in the Antarctic interior. These cores contain trapped bubbles of ancient air that have been isolated, dated, and chemically analyzed. They also show that climate is far less stable than we've imagined, and that the past ten thousand years—the period that has seen the rise of human civilization— has also been a period of atypical climate stability, at least until recently.

"Climate is an angry beast, and we're poking it with a sharp stick" is how a scientist at the NSF's McMurdo Station explained it to Eugene Linden of *Time* magazine.

The Antarctic Peninsula has also made news over the years as huge pieces of the Larson B Ice Shelf, including one iceberg twice the size of the state of Delaware, began calving off its eastern shore. In 2009 the Wilkins Ice Shelf, about the size of Jamaica, also began breaking apart on the western side of the peninsula.

Scientists worry that the western Antarctic ice sheet, adjacent to the peninsula, could experience a sudden meltdown, raising global sea levels by sixteen to twenty-one feet (instead of the estimated three feet currently predicted by 2100). This would eliminate much of Florida and Bangladesh and put Washington, D.C., underwater. While most experts believe this melting will occur sometime after this century, by the time they know for sure, it will be too late to do anything about it. In the far north, Greenland, with its accelerating glacial melt, poses a similar but more immediate threat of rapid, uncontrollable sea-level rise.

So I can argue that I'm learning a survival skill when, immediately after helping unload the ship's "freshies" (fresh fruits and vegetables for the station), I learn how to operate one of the Zodiacs and take it for a test run. Steering the fifteen-foot rubber boat through floating fragments of brash ice, I spot a leopard seal lazing on an ice floe. As I maneuver around to take some photos of the snaky, blunt-headed marine predator, a panicked penguin jumps into the boat, tripping over the outboard's gas can. We exchange looks of mutual bewilderment before it leaps onto a pontoon and dives back into the icy blue water.

A few days later I'm out with Bill Fraser and his "Schnappers" (the boat-radio moniker for his seabird researchers, in honor of a Wisconsin polka band). We tie off our bowline on the rocky edge of Humble Island. Removing our orange float coats, we walk up to a wide, pebbly flat past a dozen burbling, one-thousand-pound elephant seals lying in their own green waste. One of them rises up just enough to show us a wide pink mouth and issue a belching challenge that means, Stay back or I might have to rouse myself from complete stupor in order to attack you. The elephant seal population, once restricted to more northerly climes, is now booming along the peninsula because of the warming conditions.

Their belching and grunting are soon complemented by the loud, hectic squawking, flipper-flapping, and cow-barn odor of three thousand Adélie penguins and their downy chicks, who occupy a series of rocky benches stained the color of Georgia red clay by their krill-rich droppings. Brown gull-like skuas glide overhead, looking for a weak chick to kill and feed on.

"These penguins are the ultimate canaries in the mine shaft. They're extremely sensitive indicators of climate change," Fraser tells me as we walk past a group of two-foot-tall adults waddling up from the sea, their bellies full of tiny shrimplike krill.

On another day I'll watch Fraser and his team "diet-sample" the Adélies, a process in which they run warm water down a bird's gullet, then turn the penguin upside down over a bucket to collect the krill it's eaten. I'll record the sound of the regurgitating birds for Marketplace radio, one of the perks of being a far-flung correspondent. It doesn't sound as bad as a drunken freshman getting sick at a frat party, more like a pitcher of ice water being poured out. Nor does the process, which involves a long-handled net, a garden pump, a bucket, some ziplock baggies, and two strong thighs, hurt the animal.

As they right the bird, it shakes its head vigorously, getting recycled krill on everyone's boat pants and fleece jackets, before it belly-slides and paddle-walks away, looking somewhat indignant, as penguins often do. By sorting through the partly digested krill, the scientists can see which species a bird's been going after and how long it has taken it to forage.

"Some of our birds are eating *Thysanoessa macrura*, a smaller species, which means they might be having a hard time finding their regular prey," Fraser explains to me back in the lab. His krill look blacker and lumpier than those of his researchers because they are a different species and more digested. I decide to skip the jambalaya listed as that evening's main course on Biolab's cafeteria blackboard. Krill, which look like tiny, hyperkinetic shrimp, are the most abundant animal on earth in terms of their total biomass. They make up the broad base of Antarctica's foreshortened food chain and are consumed in vast quantities by penguins, seals, and whales (a single blue whale can eat four tons of krill in a day). The first three weeks at Palmer I don't see any whales. Then on a Wednesday swarms of krill fill Arthur Harbor. The next day there are some twenty humpbacks, sei, minke, and right whales swimming around the station, filling their bellies.

Krill also act as a biological pump, taking carbon from the algae they feed on and, through spitballs and fecal strings, sinking it deep into the ocean abyss, where the excess carbon may not appear again for over one thousand years. But without access to sea ice, krill can shrink, lose weight, and become vulnerable to early death.

"The bottom of the ice is where 70 percent of krill larvae are found," explains Dr. Robin Ross of the University of California at Santa Barbara, a prim and cautious scientist who'll spend the research season onboard the *Gould*, trolling for krill and plankton. "The ice is like an upside-down coral reef with lots of bumps and crevasses and caves for them to hide in," she says. "But in the early nineties the cycles of high and low ice began to fall apart. This year's winter sea ice was the lowest on record."

This year's trawls are also bringing up more salps than krill.

Salps are open-water filter-feeding jelly creatures, which look like floating condoms, foul the bowlines of our Zodiacs, and are prey for only a limited number of birds and fish. Unlike krill, salps reproduce in open water—and may soon fill the ecological niche created as shrinking sea ice leads to a long-term decline in krill. A decline in krill, of course, could wreck much of Antarctica's marine ecosystem.

Rising temperatures are also increasing precipitation—which in Antarctica takes the form of snow. Excessive spring snow has disrupted the nesting and breeding of Adélie penguins, leading to the extinction of many of their island colonies.

Back on Humble, I'm waving off a dive-bombing skua while Bill Fraser is conferring with Rick Sanchez of the U.S. Geological Survey. Rick is carrying a portable GPS, along with a satellite antenna sticking out of his backpack and a magnesium-shelled laptop strapped to an elaborate fold-down rig hanging from his waist and shoulders. He's trying to walk off the perimeter of an extinct colony of Adélies in order to confirm Bill's observations linking increased snowfall to declining numbers of penguins, but a burbling pile of elephant seals is blocking his mapping venture. If he tries to move them, they might stampede and crush still-living penguin chicks from an adjacent colony. Such are the quandaries of high-tech research projects in Antarctica.

Before we leave the island Bill shows me a large, polished granite boulder at one of the failing colonies. The shiny reflective rock, which looks like the kind of polished stone sculpture you might find in a contemporary art gallery, is the result of more than seven hundred years of penguin feet marching across it. I think it would be nice if our grandchildren had a chance to experience this kind of shock of discovery for themselves.

While Adélie populations are crashing, more adaptable species such as chinstrap penguins, elephant seals, and fur seals are increasing their numbers. These newcomers to the area threaten to displace sea ice–dependent animals such as Weddell seals, crabeater seals (which are actually krill eaters), and the continent's top predator, the leopard seal. One day, while driving a Zodiac a mile off the station, I spot a penguin shooting twenty feet up into the air only to drop back down into the open jaws of a leopard seal that had just struck it a powerful deathblow.

In a warmer world, "weedlike" species that are highly adaptable to disrupted habitat (pigeons, chinstrap penguins, and salps) will displace more specialized creatures (polar bears, leopard seals, and Adélies), which depend on unique ecosystems such as tropical forests, tropical oceans, and polar ice shelves. Rising temperatures will also impact plant species.

Tad Day, a sandy-haired, boyish-looking professor from Arizona State who drives his Mark 3 Zodiac *Lucille* like a Formula One race car, studies Antarctica's only two flowering plants, hair grass and pearlwort. Hair grass looks like stunted crabgrass and is the dominant species. Pearlwort looks more like clumps of moss. The main study site Day and his Sundevils team use is Stepping Stone, a small, surprisingly green, rocky island several miles south of Palmer, around the rough chop of Bonaparte Point.

"Step" is surrounded by pale blue icebergs, a rumbling blue-white glacier, and other islands and outcroppings, including Biscoe Point to the south. But with the retreat of the Marr Glacier, Biscoe Point has now become Biscoe Island. Step also has a number of nesting giant petrels—sharp-billed albatrosslike scavengers the size of eagles that can spit a vile fishy stomach oil at intruders. That has not stopped researcher Donna Patterson from becoming fast friends with them. At one point she will shove my hand under one of these glaring beady-eyed big birds, and I'll come out with a downy fluff ball of a chick that she'll then weigh, measure, and return to its brooding parent.

Tad Day maintains two gardens on Stepping Stone. Fenced (to keep out fur seals), they contain more than ninety wire plant frames surrounding banks of hair grass and pearlwort growing not in true soil but a close approximation made up of glacial sand and guano.

He has found that warming improves the growth of pearlwort but appears to have a negative impact on hair grass. "Global warming," he explains, "has the capacity to shift the competitive balance of species in ways . . . that could have important consequences on our ability to produce [grow] food and fiber."

Increasingly reliable climate models now predict planetary warming of three to ten degrees Fahrenheit during this century. (By contrast, the last ice age was only five to nine degrees colder.) This will result in shifts in agricultural production; the spread of tropical insects, wood beetles, and diseases such as malaria; increases in extreme weather events, flooding, and droughts; more intense coastal storms and hurricanes; erosion of beaches; coral bleaching; rising sea levels; impacts on ocean productivity and upwellings and changes in ocean chemistry—all of which have already begun.

Still, it's hard to maintain a sense of gloom and doom on the last wild continent, at least for more than a few hours at a time. Along with nightly discussions over Pisco sours packed with sun-dappled glacier ice at the Penguin Pub, the open bar above the machine shop, I manage to distract myself with sojourns on the Southern Ocean. You need at least two people with radios to take out one of the Zodiacs, so on the days when I'm not working with the scientists and the winds aren't blowing above twenty-five knots I spend time looking for a boating partner.

Doc Labarre, the station's big, balding, fatalistic physician, who used to work in the emergency room in Kodiak, Alaska, is among those regularly up for an adventure.

One day we cruise past Torgersen Island, where I take the Zodiac up "on platform" (as you speed up, the bow drops down, giving increased visibility, stability, and control) and head toward Loudwater Cove, on the other side of Norsel Point. The following seas allow us to surf the fifteen-foot craft past the rocky spires of Litchfield Island and around the big breaking waves at Norsel. We then motor around a few apartment building–sized icebergs, crossing over to a landing opposite the glacier wall, where we tie off our bowline, watching a serpentine leopard seal sleeping on an adjacent ice floe. Dumping our float coats, we climb several hundred feet up and over some rocky scree and down a snowfield splotched with red algae, to the opening of an ice cave. The cave is like a dripping blue tunnel with slush over a clear ice floor that shows the rocky piedmont below. Hard blue glacier ice forms the bumpy roof, where icicles hang like stalactites and delicate rills form pressure joints along its edges under thousands of tons of slowly moving ice.

Outside, we hike the loose granite, feldspar, and glacial sand until we encounter a fur seal hauled up several hundred yards from the water on the sharp, broken rocks. He barks and whines a warning at us. Nearby ponds and one-hundred-year-old moss beds have attracted crowded colonies of brown skuas, who soon begin dive-bombing us. I get whacked from behind by one of the five-pound scavengers. It feels like getting slapped hard in the back of the head by a large man. We quickly move away from their nests, climbing back over the exposed glacier rock, past middens of limpet shells and down a rock chimney to where our boat is tied up.

The leopard seal is awake now, checking us out as we take off. I notice bloodstains on the ice where he's been resting.

We next drop by Christine, a big bouldery island. We walk past a large congregation of elephant seals hanging out opposite a colony of squawking Adélies. Crossing the heights, we find mossy green swales with ponds full of brine shrimp. We stretch ourselves out on a rocky beach at the end of a narrow blue channel, sharing the space with two elephant seals weighing about five hundred and one thousand pounds. The Southern Ocean is crystal clear; the sun has come out and turned the sky cobalt blue. It feels almost tropical as we lounge to the sound of the waves rolling and retreating across smooth fist-sized stones. Farther out are several flat islands with big breakers crashing over them, sending spray fifty feet into the air. The elephant seals are blowing snot and blinking their huge red eyes; their black pupils the size of teaspoons are used for gathering light in deep-diving forays after squid. A fur seal comes corkscrewing through the channel's water before paddle-walking ashore and scratching itself with a hind flipper, a blissful expression on its wolfy face. And there we are, just five lazy mammals enjoying a bit of sun and sea.

Driving the Zodiac back to station, we're accompanied by a flight of blue-eyed shags (also known as royal cormorants) and squads of porpoising penguins in the water. Doc steers while I keep an eye out for whales, like the minke that rammed the boat I was riding in a few days earlier (it was a real Melville moment, watching its huge brown back and blowhole rolling out from under us). The sky has again quilted over with clouds, turning the water the color of hammered tin; with the buck and slap of the boat and the icy cold saltwater spray in our faces, it feels like all's right with the wild.

Antarctica is vast and awesome in its indifference to the human condition. Yet it is also a world center for scientific research and has provided us fair warning about the human impact on climate change. The message from the ice is as plain as the penguin bones I found scattered around a dying Adélie colony: our world and theirs—Antarctica's Southern Ocean and our urban coastlines, tropical seas, and coral reefs—are much more closely linked than we imagine.

Nearly anywhere you go on our blue planet these messages are being broadcast with increased urgency. While Antarctica is a continent surrounded by ice, the Arctic is an ice sheet surrounded by land—but not for long. Since 1979, over 20 percent of the polar ice cap has melted away, opening up blue-water summer seas. By 2009 spring ice was the thinnest ever recorded.

In November 2004 a three-year collaboration of scientists from eight nations with Arctic lands, including the United States and Canada, concluded that the Arctic is warming at nearly twice the rate of the rest of the planet and could be as much as thirteen degrees warmer by 2100, melting the Greenland ice sheet, rapidly accelerating sea-level rise, and leading to the extinction of polar bears, narwhals, beluga whales, ringed seals, and other ice-dependent marine wildlife.

Predictions from the past decade that the Arctic Ocean would be largely ice-free by the middle of the twenty-first century failed to account for what scientists call positive-feedback loops. In this case, ice reflects solar radiation back into space while open water absorbs it, so as more water is exposed along the edge of the ice, the warming/melting effect is accelerated. It now appears that low-ice or ice-free summers have become a permanent feature of the Arctic Ocean. At the same time, a permafrost layer of decayed vegetation at the bottom of the Arctic Sea is beginning to unfreeze (as it is on the tundra). This could potentially release vast quantities of methane, a greenhouse warming gas twenty times as potent as carbon dioxide.

By 2007 the melting of the Arctic ice had also turned into an international "Cold Rush" for resources as Russia planted a titanium flag on the seabed beneath the North Pole and Canada war-gamed armed interdictions in the Northwest Passage.

The Arctic powers—Canada, Denmark, Finland, Iceland, Norway, Russia, Sweden, and the United States—rather than seeing the accelerated melting as a global alarm bell requiring a rapid transition from fossil fuels before positive feedback loops make human actions to stop the warming irrelevant, are instead moving to stake new claims in the Arctic and seize new riches, including oil and gas, minerals, fish, and commercial trade routes.

Among the changes an ice-free Arctic is expected to bring in the near term is a dramatic shift in shipping routes between Asia and Europe, with commercial fleets of container ships, bulk carriers, and ice-hardened oil tankers saving 20 to 40 percent on their fuel costs using either the Northern Sea Route above Russia or moving through the Northwest Passage, which Canada considers domestic waters but which the United States and other countries claim is an international strait. One of the legal requirements for declaring an international strait is its historic— and unchallenged—use by foreign vessels. Dogsleds don't count. These days the United States always "informs" Canada when it's transiting the passage with Coast Guard icebreakers but doesn't consider this a "request." Canada considers it a request but never denies permission.

A surprise during the ice-free summer of 2007 was the

movement of three cruise ships through the Northwest Passage and the unannounced arrival of a shipload of four hundred German-speaking tourists on the beach in the mainly Inuit town of Barrow, Alaska. A number of fishing boats were also seen moving from the Bering Sea into the Arctic Circle, following a shift of edible fish species north. In 2009, in an outbreak of sanity, the Secretary of Commerce (who oversees NOAA) banned commercial fishing on 250,000 square miles of U.S. Arctic waters north of the Bering Sea until the impacts of the rapidly changing ecosystem are better understood. His precautionary approach was supported and encouraged by both commercial fishermen and conservationists. At the same time, the U.S. and Canadian Coast Guards began expanding their safety and security patrols in the Arctic under a cooperative agreement.

Although I've yet to make it inside the Arctic Circle, I did recently spend some time flying around the Aleutians and Bering Sea with the U.S. Coast Guard and was impressed by the harsh and rapidly changing weather conditions people will have to deal with as new blue-water coasts emerge along the world's Arctic shoreline.

After my 1999 return from Antarctica, the nonprofit International Center for Journalists asked me to lead training workshops on environmental reporting for some of my overseas colleagues. I ended up working with reporters in Poland, Turkey, Slovakia, and Tunisia and with staffers at Radio Free Asia in Washington, D.C.

In Tunisia, Egyptian reporter Mohammad al-Mofty explained how, after he'd done a story on U.S. and Egyptian warships dropping depth charges on coral reefs during a naval exercise, he was called in to a military court and questioned for hours. Later, over dinner in the medina (the old quarter), I asked him if he still planned to write stories like that one. "For sure. They couldn't shake me. I had my facts right!" he insisted, reflecting the courage of many journalists across the planet who remain willing to face intimidation, death threats, beatings, even death in order to act out their role as the eyes and ears of the world.

Later we took a five-hour bus trip to El Feidja National Park, on the Algerian border, where the last herd of Barbary deer are kept behind a fence line and the World Wildlife Fund has worked with neighboring villagers to replace goats that were overgrazing the park with beehives that are producing organic honey and bringing in greater revenue for the locals. The new issue is a proposed pipeline that will drain the park's mountain aquifer to provide fresh water to Sousse and other Mediterranean beachfront resort areas popular with European tourists.

The park area is high desert, with live oak, chaparral, and cork trees. It reminds me of eastern San Diego's hiking parks. Climbing back on the bus for the long drive back to Tunis I sit down next to Mohammad. I'm a little peeved by the lack of organization that has gone into our field trip. We haven't eaten anything but honey and flat bread all day, and we've been too long on the road. "What did you think of the park?" I ask him.

"I don't want to leave. I want to live here forever," he says. I smile curiously. "I'm forty-two. I've never been in a forest before," he explains. "All these trees and the light. It's just amazing."

We forget how essential our connection with the natural world can be, the V formations of migrating geese, the burble of a mountain stream, the interplay of light and shadow in a forest. The allure of the everlasting sea is another example of this deep genetic bond, although sometimes it can be a cautionary one.

After my colleague Monica Allen and I spent our first week in Turkey with more than a dozen journalists from countries bordering the Black Sea, we'd pretty thoroughly reviewed the huge pollution loads that that historic body of water has absorbed from industrial and agricultural runoff, also problems related to invasive species like jellyfish, oil spills, sedimentation, sewage, and garbage, and how best to turn these environmental disasters into engaging stories in print, radio, television, and on the Internet.

To help out a nervous Turkish reporter working with us, I'd sat down with the government spy who'd been shadowing our meetings and explained to him all about low-oxygen hypoxia and no-oxygen anoxia and how oxygen-depleted waters generate dead zones through a process called eutrophication until he was convinced that environmental reporting had nothing to do with politics or religion or anything of interest to him. The next day he brought me a newspaper clipping about an American scientist working with shamans in the Amazon to find medicinal plants. The day after that I convinced him to procure an army bus to take us to the beach.

Of course, as soon as we got there we all stripped down and went running into the waves, completely ignoring everything we'd just learned from UN and other experts we'd brought in, not to mention all the oil-stained cans, lightbulbs, broken bottles, and used nappies I spotted in the sand after coming out of the water. When I got home eight days later I had a terrible pseudomonas infection in my left ear. "That's because you have soft, pampered American ears," Stefan Razvan, an ex-Romanian merchant sailor turned TV reporter, e-mailed me. "We Romanians have ears like pigs to take the Black Sea pollution."

Obviously, the size of a body of water will help determine its resiliency in the face of cascading environmental insults. The Aral Sea in Central Asia was drained for cotton growing by the old Soviet Union and is now mostly a dusty toxic wasteland. The larger Caspian Sea is awash in oil seepage and its sturgeon almost extinct as a result of the caviar trade that degenerated into armed shoot-outs among "Caviar Mafia" factions. The larger still Black Sea was close to dead in the 1980s but has seen some modest recovery, mostly as a result of the rapid decline of the industrial economies along its shores following the collapse of the Soviet Union and more recently because of the global recession. The Mediterranean is seriously overfished and impacted by both pollution and *Caulerpa*, an invasive seaweed (labeled "killer algae") that smothers native plants and has been spreading rapidly since it was accidentally introduced into the Med's waters in the 1980s. Italy also continues to tolerate illegal longline fishing vessels operating out of its ports while Spanish fishermen have gained a reputation for resource piracy both in the Med and around the world. The Atlantic Ocean is in worse shape than the vast Pacific, but the Pacific Ocean also, along with the Indian and Southern Oceans, is threatened by overfishing, pollution, marine debris, and climate change.

After my return from Turkey, and after years of living in D.C., I'd begun to think about moving back to California and the Pacific Ocean that I loved. I'd finally gotten an advance from a publisher and was about to begin work on the book I'd wanted to write for years. Titled *Blue Frontier*, it was the story of the ocean and America's two-hundred-mile Exclusive Economic Zone, a new wilderness range six times the size of the Louisiana Purchase. I was planning to start the work in Florida and then stay with Nancy during a summer research trip to California. It would be a problematic encounter for both of us, the unstated question being, If I did come back to California might we reconcile as a couple?

As with all human plans, fate, luck, or disaster would determine our course with far greater certainty than we could. We're just drifters in the sea of life.

9

Deeper Water

Oh! make her a grave, where the sun-beams rest,
When they promise a glorious morrow;
They'll shine o'er her sleep, like a smile from the West,
From her own lov'd Island of sorrow!

THOMAS MOORE,

"SHE IS FAR FROM THE LAND"

When our losses seem immeasurable all we can do is take the measure of ourselves, determine whether we want to continue, and if so to what end. I would write about my love of the sea and fear for its health even as my own love lost her health, fighting a personal battle for independence and control in the face of an invasive, aggressive cancer.

I'm diving in warm blue-green waters some five miles off Key Largo, headed down to Aquarius, the last underwater research laboratory. Its forty-eight-foot cylindrical body resting on four steel legs has a well-salted look about it, with orange rust spots and weedy growths being grazed by roving schools of fish. As I swim by one of its round view ports a resident scientist inside waves from his seat in front of a laptop before dipping into a can of salted peanuts. I turn and notice three big silvery tarpon, between 100 and 150 pounds, shadowing me. Steve Miller of the National Undersea Research Center leads me under the skirt of the habitat through a low-slung entryway. We pop up in the warm, humid "wet room" next to Greg Stone and another researcher from the New England Aquarium on their way out to the reef. A school of yellowtail snappers huddle discreetly toward the back of the room's moon pool, not going anywhere.

We strip off our scuba gear and climb up a short ladder. Inside, the habitat is cramped but comfortable, with blue industrial carpeting, a lab, kitchen, and two sets of triple bunks for the scientists and two support staff who will live and work down here during their eight-day mission. We can only stay about an hour before the nitrogen building up in our bodies threatens us with the bends. When the scientists and crew are done with their work they'll decompress for seventeen hours inside Aquarius before heading back to the surface.

While Aquarius provides a great opportunity for them to do extended underwater studies of the surrounding reef, the coral reef itself looks like it's been nuked. On a later dive, tagging along with a *National Geographic* film crew, I notice branching corals that once grew here are now only skeletal sticks in bleached rubble fields. Many of the rock corals are being eaten away by diseases that have spread through the Keys in an epidemic wave. Their names tell the story: black band, white band, white plague, and aspergillus, a fungus normally found in tomato fields that can shred purple fan corals like moths shred Irish lace. The corals are also being smothered under sediment and algal growth linked to polluted runoff and cruise ship discharges as well as impacted by periodic bleaching from warming water. Billy Causey, the manager of the Florida Keys National Marine Sanctuary, who will go on to become the National Sanctuaries' regional director, moved here back in 1973. He now sounds like an Old Testament Jeremiah as he recalls witnessing the year-by-year decline of the reef.

While among the most diverse of marine habitats, the world's massive coral colonies are also fragile structures in terms of what they require from water clarity, salinity, low-nutrient chemistry, and temperature range. They're high-maintenance beauties living within a narrow spectrum of options.

"Throughout the seventies we saw various problems but constantly clear waters with typical hundred-foot visibility," Billy Causey recalls. "In 1979, we had a warm water spell and big vase sponges started dying," he continues. "In June of 1980 we had a pattern of slick calm weather and thousands of fish were killed. This was the first signal to me that things were tilting the wrong way. Then in 1983, with an explosion of onshore development, there was an urchin die-off. In 1984 there was another doldrums, and the reefs bleached down to Key West. Maybe 5 percent of the coral died. In May of 1986, when we had hardly seen black band disease [characterized by dark bands of dead coral on otherwise healthy specimens], I went out to take a picture of it. I saw four-dozen massive outbreaks within an area about four hundred feet in length."

"In June of 1987 we got a slick calm," he continues. "On July 13 we went out and saw all the corals turning mustard yellow. Then they went stark white. Then we began getting reports of similar bleaching in the Caribbean and on the Indo/Pacific reefs, and we realized something global was going on. We began looking at this as the canary in the coal mine. Meanwhile, NOAA was reporting 1987 as the hottest year on record and the 1980s as the hottest decade." These records would fall in the 1990s and again in the first decade of the new century.

The bad news kept multiplying, Causey recalls. "In 1990, we had the first big losses linked to bleaching where the coral didn't come back. We lost most of our fire coral that year. There was another benchmark year in 1997, with coral bleaching all around the Caribbean. Lots of living coral just went away in 1998, a catastrophic bleaching event. But remote reefs in the Pacific were also being lost, so it gave me a sense that this wasn't an isolated event. There was back-to-back severe bleaching in 1997 and 1998, then Hurricane George hit."

He shakes his head, as if unwilling to believe his own unremittingly bleak narrative. "You look at old photos and film of the reef and you realize what was lost," he says. "If you were lucky enough to be here twenty to thirty years ago, you know."

By 2006 NOAA will list staghorn and elkhorn, once abundant branching corals in the Florida Keys, Puerto Rico, and the U.S. Virgin Islands, as threatened species under the Endangered Species Act.

I'm finally writing my ocean book, *Blue Frontier*, even if it sometimes feels like I'm reporting on the end of the frontier. Its title and theme are based on the fact that while the Census Bureau declared the western frontier closed in 1890, on March 10, 1983, President Ronald Reagan, in one of the most significant but least noted acts of his administration, established the U.S. Exclusive Economic Zone (EEZ), which extends two hundred miles out to sea from America's shores. At 3.4 million square nautical miles, the U.S. EEZ is 30 percent larger than the continental land base of the United States. It is a wilder, more challenging frontier than any known to past generations, one that is also part of a larger global ocean one-third of which is now enclosed in EEZs established by various coastal states. While President Reagan created the U.S. EEZ to promote deep-ocean mining opportunities for major corporations that then decided it wasn't economically feasible, I figure once you put markers in the ocean and claim it as your own you're also taking on a greater responsibility for its care and stewardship. In writing a comprehensive account of the history and condition of our ocean frontier, I've also given myself an excuse to venture on and below the sea.

I wander south Florida, doing interviews and visiting the Everglades, sometimes called the River of Grass, whose restoration is also vital to restoring the Keys' reef line by increasing water flow and reducing pollution. I ride along with Florida Marine Patrol cops during lobster "mini season," when forty thousand recreational boaters and divers poke around on the Keys' reef, chasing "bugs." Each person is allowed to take six. We pull up by a yacht pulling a second boat and a raft. There are nine people on board the main craft, including an infant. "You count for six [lobsters]," the baby's aunt coos, holding her up for our inspection.

Another day I help a former navy dolphin trainer named Rick Trout push a couple of five-foot nurse sharks around an open

pen before releasing the pet shop–reared predators back into the wild from a dive boat off Key Largo. This effort is supposed to help educate the public about respecting marine wildlife, but two days later a time-share tourist in a Boston Whaler spots fins in the water and thinks, Cool, I'm going to swim with the dolphins. The tourist jumps into a school of bull sharks and is bitten in the foot.

I return from the Keys to Miami, where I'm staying with my reporter friends Carl and Kathy Hersh. I give Nancy a call and leave a message on her machine. She calls back. I tell her we're about to have dinner. She says she's leaving in half an hour, going to a movie. She sounds strange. I say I'll call back before she goes. Twenty minutes later I do.

"I've got some weird news," she says. I say I'm sitting down.

"That's good," she says, not joking. "I went to the doctor. I have a lump in my breast." She starts to cry. I wait, stunned. She calms after a few moments. "I've had it about a month, but then my lymph glands swelled up the last few days so I went in. They stuck all these needles in my boob and took out cells. It really hurt. Then I had to have a mammogram. I had one in November [on her fortieth birthday] and everything was all right. This woman—this surgeon's now telling me about disfigurement and chemotherapy. . . ." She begins to cry again. "I don't want them to cut off my tit" is what I think I hear her say through the sobbing. I go outside so Carl and Kathy won't see me choking up.

I fly back to D.C. the next day. I'm seated next to a young woman with a baby who works for the Inter-American Development Bank on biodiversity issues, mainly attempts to save the world's rain forests. I ask if there are any examples of good programs that are working. She says no. I have to turn toward the window so she doesn't see my face contorting. I'm losing control again.

When I get home I call Nancy. She's just returned from Marin General Hospital.

"The surgeon says I have cancer," she tells me, and cries. "She says it's a weird-looking tumor, fast growing, aggressive.

"I'm just sitting here looking out at the water like a picture postcard, thinking how beautiful it is, and it feels so weird, it's just so weird," she says. "I'm a statistic, forty-year-old woman with no children living in Marin (which has one of the highest rates of breast cancer in North America). You know I've always eaten well, been healthy. I don't have it in my family, at least if I do no one's ever mentioned it. Everything suddenly feels irrelevant. I don't know what to do. It's just so strange. I guess this is a wake-up call for what's important in life."

I go to California and stay with her for several months while she goes through chemotherapy. Her mother visits and glares at me. They put her on AC: Adriamycin and Cytoxan. Her silky long hair falls out in clumps, covering the pillows on the bed until there's just a last long pinkie-thin top braid that she finally cuts off. She sobs silently. Then she makes a hair beret for the cat.

I give her backrubs and help her to the bathroom when she's going to be sick. The chemo is terrible but seems to work. By the second treatment her tumor is shrinking.

I head down to San Diego to fly out to the USS *John C. Stennis*, an aircraft carrier that will be in one of my book chapters. I watch combat jets landing and launching and pilots in training who are "bolting" the deck with their tailhooks, setting off showers of sparks before escaping on full afterburners like double dragon tails in the night. Before I'm catapulted back off the carrier a few days later I've been given the Cook's tour of the ship, from the rudder stems to the air control tower, but decline to check out the hospital ward for fear of picking up germs I might carry back to Nancy, whose white cell count has crashed from the chemo, leaving her immune system terribly compromised.

The Tuesday after I return we go in for her last infusion. We're there for five hours. Her doctor and nurse have a hard time even finding the lump in her breast. They take this as a very good sign.

In the infusion center we sit next to a lesbian couple from the city and begin to chat while the first IV bag is run into Nancy's veins.

Susan, the sick one, is fighting invasive cancer that has gone into her bones, hoping for a remission two and a half years after first diagnosis. She's tried AC, raw foods, and a range of other activities, including swimming with wild dolphins off Kona, Hawaii, a few days earlier. We tell them we'd gone swimming with wild spinner dolphins off a nude black-sand beach on the other side of the Big Island. I can't help but think this is a very California conversation.

After Nancy's done "sitting on the bag," she shares a big hug with her nurse and we boogie. She's in buoyant spirits. We take a short walk by a wild strand of cobble beach strewn with dried kelp, within sight of the Golden Gate Bridge. I dip my hands in the cold Pacific and say a kind of silent prayer, Let her be well. She sleeps well that night and seems happy the next day till around five, when she starts throwing up again. Later we watch a video, *G.I. Jane*. I tell her she looks better bald than Demi Moore does.

"Big deal. You don't like Demi Moore. What about Michelle Pfeiffer?"

"I haven't seen her bald."

We go to the seashore at Point Reyes and hike to Dream Beach, where we sit on a driftwood log in the sand.

"So are you going to move back in with me?" she asks.

I say it may not be the right time. I'm scared things won't go well. I'm angry that, other than her upcoming lumpectomy surgery, she's decided against any more treatment. Also, I'm a stupid male, always thinking someone better is going to come along, the theoretical wife and kid(s). If Nancy were to have a child after her treatment (assuming her medically induced menopause from the chemo faded), it would elevate her hormonal estrogen levels, bring back the cancer, and kill her.

She nods at my half answer, doesn't make the offer again.

We see a covey of quails on our way up from the beach, also a large bobcat bounding across the road, thrilling in its muscular grace.

We go to a sporting goods store, and she helps me select a pair of steel-toed boots that I'll need for an upcoming trip to Louisiana. Then I'll be heading back to D.C.

In Louisiana I fly out to a couple of BP deepwater oilrigs. They're marvels of modern engineering. Some of the roughnecks and roustabouts working the drill decks wear T-shirts reading "New Rigs, New People, New Records." Everyone wants to drill the deepest well in the Gulf of Mexico. I ask the "company man" (rig boss) what happens if they get an oil leak a mile or two down. "Guess we'll find out when it happens," he tells me.

Ten years later we find out when another BP rig, *Deepwater Horizon*, has a massive uncontrolled blowout that kills eleven workers and generates the worst oil spill disaster in U.S. history. Of course, even without world historical disasters, offshore drilling has become a climate threat.

Maybe to encourage a rapid transition off storm-intensifying fossil fuel energy we should have NOAA start naming alphabetically listed hurricanes after fossil fuel companies: Hurricane Aramco, Hurricane BP, Chevron, Dynegy, Exxon, and so on.

Flying into New Orleans, I look down over Lake Pontchartrain's levees. Ten feet below the lake level on the other side of the levees I see curving tree-lined suburban streets, homes, lawns, kids on bikes, and parked cars. Atlantis Gardens would be a good name for this development, I think, in the year 2000.

New Orleans itself averages eight feet below sea level. While its pumps keep working, it's been losing its protective wetlands, the bayou, that's afforded it some level of flood protection since the French settled the "Isle of Orleans" in 1718 (and immediately got hit by a hurricane). Its protective wetlands have been reduced from a 150-mile-wide buffer to less than thirty miles in some areas. The Army Corps of Engineers has worked to dredge and straighten out the Mississippi River for generations so that the slow-moving sediment that used to build up its delta now rushes deep into the gulf, carrying all sorts of synthetic fertilizers and pollutants from midwestern corn fields along with it, creating a massive oxygen-depleted dead zone in lieu of raising up new bayou swamplands. Land subsidence from oil company drilling and canal building, along with sea-level rise, have also contributed to the disappearance of over twenty-five square miles per year of what an oil company front group calls "America's Wetland" (meaning they shouldn't have to pay to rebuild it). A restoration effort has been proposed under the rubric Coast 2050; it calls for a fourteen-billion-dollar local, state, and federal effort over five decades. I meet Mark Davis, executive director of the Coalition to Restore Coastal Louisiana, in a French Quarter surfers' bar.

"The Army Corps has given us a levee system that's traded periodic river flooding for permanent coastal flooding, and that to me is a bad deal," he tells me over a couple of beers.

Does that mean he thinks he can mobilize enough popular will to turn around the forces of sprawl and development, also the Army Corps and the oil companies? I ask.

"If our advocacy is inadequate to the task, then a hurricane will make the case for us," he warns. That case would be made five years later with the arrival of Hurricane Katrina.

When I next visit California, Nancy's hair has grown back short and curly and nicely streaked with silver. She has a hairline scar in her left pit, and her left breast looks fine, its usual full, pear-shaped self. "I'm like somebody else," she says, looking at her salt-and-pepper poodle cut in the mirror, but really she's like herself again.

We're quietly working on our new relationship: loving friends without expectations. Remaining apart, we're trying to find a level of comfort that can take us through the coming years now that we think there will be coming years. We're both dating but don't really talk about it with each other. We're also trying to get past my anger over her decision not to do any follow-up, any additional chemo or radiation. At first she'd said she couldn't stand any more chemo but might do the radiation, then decided against that. My sister, Deborah, points out that, right or wrong, it's her decision to make, and once she's made a final decision, I should just shut up and support it. Sometimes I think there've been too many strong women in my life.

We walk to dinner on the Sausalito waterfront, bringing along Nancy's new Razor scooter so that I can try it out. "I just bought two of these for [my nephews] Adam and Ethan," I tell her. "Of course, they're nine and eleven."

"So get off it if you think it's only for kids, you old geez." she says with a grin. I kick away down the street.

I finish my ocean book *Blue Frontier* and am happy with it. A short time later, nine months after her lumpectomy, Nancy calls to tell me there's a new lump in her breast. "It's really creepy. The new tumor is twice as large as the first one. The doctors are freaked out by how rapidly it's come back." This time they're recommending chemo, radiation, and a mastectomy.

I fly out to California to be with her. This time she's shaved her head, refusing to watch her hair fall out in clumps again. I tell her she looks like Sinead O'Connor.

"Telly Savalas," she replies, "but what I really look like is someone with cancer. People used to say I looked younger than my age, but I think this has caught me up."

She's upset that some developer wants to tear up the blackberry bushes down the street in order to put up new housing units.

"Greed's destroying everything," she despairs. "We're poisoning the planet, tearing up the natural world . . ."

"Plus, those are some of the best blackberry bushes in the neighborhood," I agree.

A few days later she's feeling better. We drive to McClures Beach on Point Reyes. To get onto it we have to hike down a stream-cut canyon path with fierce winds funneling up it. We find no relief on the beach. The wind is whipping the sand into ghostly ankle-high sheets of flying silicate. The sun reflects a dazzling sparkle off the rippled stream's surface as it meanders out to sea. We unpack turkey sandwiches and Cokes and eat on a rock below the cliffs, our backs turned to the wind. A few dozen gulls are huddled along the ocean's edge, where the sand is wet and firm. Just beyond them cold cobalt blue breakers are showing hollow faces before thundering onto the beach, rock piles, and sea stacks, sending spray thirty feet into the air. Nancy takes pictures of the gulls and their web prints in the wet sand, also long translucent green/brown bulbs and strands of bull kelp. We notice three turkey vultures feeding down the beach. As we approach they reluctantly flap off their carrion feast. It's the remains of a sea lion, its upper body freshly pecked at. The lower half of the torso is missing, the jagged scoop of meat suggesting the work of a white ·shark. Nancy begins photographing the pungent half-eaten pinniped.

In the 1960s there were plans to build massive upscale housing developments here on Point Reyes, expand scenic Highway 1 into an eight-lane freeway, and construct a nuclear power plant on Bodega Bay, just to the north, where twenty-three gray whales recently returned to summer. It was only through the organized protest and participation of tens of thousands of dedicated conservationists, such as the Sierra Club's Dave Brower and progressive politicians like the late congressman Phil Burton, that these urban/industrial schemes were turned back and the Point Reyes National Seashore established in their place.

I tell this to Nancy in the hope of reviving her spirits, but the sun and wind and waves have already done that. She scrambles atop slick boulders for more pictures or just for the pure, unadulterated buzz of it.

You can argue about tourist revenues and fishing licenses and other ways that nature generates income, but this is the real value of protecting wildlands, beaches, and seas. Beyond their intrinsic worth and productivity, they also provide us the escape, sanctuary, and spiritual renewal we need in times of pain and trouble.

That evening I take Nancy to dinner at the Pine Cone Diner, and we talk about Dave Brower and his wife, Anne. Dave, whom we knew, has just passed away at the age of eighty-eight.

"What a good life he had," she says wistfully, tasting her acorn squash soup. "I wonder what he'd have had to say about what's going on in Florida?"

The 2000 presidential election is now forty-eight hours into its Florida vote recount without a decision. Eight days later, when I take Nancy to the breast care clinic for her next infusion, there still isn't a declared winner.

Two months after the chemo, she is to have her surgery. Her mother is there and Nancy tells me I don't have to come. I call the night before the operation.

"How'd I get this job?" she squeaks. "I wish you were here."

"I'm sorry. I offered."

"Call me in the hospital tomorrow, will you?"

"Sure."

"Bye," she says in a tiny, childlike voice that brings tears to my eyes.

"Hello?" she says, picking up the phone when I call through to the hospital the next evening. I'm surprised she's the one answering.

"How are you, gal? How'd it go?"

"I'm just glad I woke up," she says.

Later I return to California and begin taking her in for her radiation treatments. She's started reading *The Feisty Woman's Breast Cancer Book* and joined a support group. They do a quilt. Her square reads, "Cancer Sucks." She goes to see a plastic surgeon about reconstructive surgery and doesn't like what he has to say.

"He totally freaked me out," she reports.

I tell her this is one procedure she doesn't have to do.

Still, she wants me to read all about it, the attached and free-flap techniques, the tunneling of the muscles under the skin, the expander bags . . .

"Why?" I ask.

"You should just see for yourself how gross it is."

This is based on what I call the "refrigerator principle" by which whenever she eats or drinks something that tastes bad or is going sour, she wants me to try it too.

"Just tell me, does this milk taste curdled?"

We finish up her treatments and again, reluctantly this time, I leave.

Even with her Blue Cross coverage the bills keep adding up. Plus, she can't do much work anymore. The landlord wants to raise the rent. Her family helps out but also pressures her to move back to Wisconsin. She's increasingly stressed, worried she may have to declare bankruptcy.

As a freelance journalist, I've always traded my own economic security for a life of adventure and never regretted it. Now, although I send what money I can, I wish I were rich enough that I could just say, "Here, gal, here's a hundred grand, don't sweat the small stuff." Alternately, I'd settle for a universal health care system in the United States that doesn't penalize and bankrupt people for getting ill.

I read an article in the sports section of the *Washington Post*, a typical breast-cancer-survivor story about a woman with a double mastectomy competing in the winter Olympics. She's a Hungarian bobsledder. She also skydives, swims, and has a brown belt in judo.

I call Nancy and read it to her, saying, "This is the standard they're setting for you." She laughs. She tells me the Poose was up with the full moon, howling and running on the porch, then attacked her, then calmed down. We discuss the spectacular oceanic images that have run on the "Blue Planet" documentary series on the Discovery Channel. "I'll probably never dive again," she worries.

I'm writing dedications for my book. I decide to include Rell Sunn, a pioneer of Hawaiian women's surfing who died at forty-seven after a fifteen-year battle with breast cancer.

Our conversations have begun to flow like the ocean tides, running between Nancy's health and the health of the world, between the parts of life that bring us pleasure and those that worry us and limit our choices. The separations between subjects that are painful and joyous seem to be shrinking with time, shrinking with the time she has left.

My book comes out. I fly into the San Francisco airport on a Thursday and am picked up by Anne Rowley of Save Our Shores (SOS), an ocean protection group based in Santa Cruz. They started out fighting the threat of offshore oil drilling off central California back in the 1980s and now function as a citizen advisory group and watchdog for the Monterey Bay National Marine Sanctuary they helped establish. Among its other purposes, the sanctuary forbids drilling within its expansive waters.

Nancy and I had attended the sanctuary's dedication in Monterey back in 1992 and had been part of the shoreline crowd watching a flotilla of tall ships flying Old Glory, fishing boats, research vessels, Coast Guard cutters, and kayakers. As the Monterey Symphony struck up "Fanfare for the Common Man," the *Californian*, a 145-foot replica of a nineteenth-century revenue cutter, fired a loud, smoky volley. The cannon fire didn't seem to deter the dozens of curious sea lions that were leaping and nosing their way among the somewhat nervous kayakers. A woman next to us turned to her husband and asked, "How'd they get them to do that?"

I give a book talk at the Monterey Bay Aquarium that's taped for C-SPAN. From the aquarium's back deck you can see sea otters swimming through the coastal kelp forest. The aquarium has a project to rescue injured or abandoned pups and later return them to the wild, although it doesn't always work out.

"We had this one otter we released who had gotten too habituated to people and was always swimming up to boats or climbing onto kayaks," the aquarium's Sean Breheney tells me. "Then he climbed onto the front of this surfer's longboard. So the dude paddles in to shore and drapes the otter over his shoulder and walks him up the street to the aquarium. You have to remember this is a sixty-pound wild animal (a marine weasel) that could have bitten the guy's face off, but instead it's just lying there loving it. So he gets here and we grab the otter and toss it in this back room, but then realize the room has another door to a public area and race around to block it."

"So what became of the otter?" I ask.

"He's staying here with us."

Sea otters, of course, have become the icons of Monterey Bay, which is why few locals are willing to discuss how these terminally cute and cuddly animals are also voracious predators (eating about 25 percent of their body weight every day) and into rough sex. While effective for grooming their fine pelts and cracking clam and abalone shells against rocks they put on their bellies, the male otter's forelegs are too short to get a good grip on a potential mate. So the male gets firm purchase by biting down on the nose of the female before going for a little splendor in the kelp. Afterward you can often spot the females hauled up on rocks along the shore with matted fur and bloody noses. Breeding females are easily distinguished by the scars on and around their black nose leather. Knowing this, it's hard not to imagine that a female with a heavily scarred nose might get a reputation as an easy otter. While they are no role models for America's youth, we still owe these marine weasels big-time for the more than one million we killed just for their fine pelts. Today, while otters are protected from hunting, they face new threats from waterborne pathogens linked to cat feces and other land-based runoff. Sea otter research professor Pat Conrad of the University of California–Davis has shown her dedication to science by analyzing how much of 105 tons of cat feces deposited outdoors around Morro Bay, California, is from domestic cats that people let outdoors (70 percent) and how much from feral cats (30 percent), which can help educate the public, particularly cat owners.

The morning after I arrive, with no domestic cats in sight, I go for a swim on the beach at Davenport, just north of Santa Cruz. I'm wearing a full wet suit, but since I don't have gloves or booties, I'm out of the water in ten minutes, my hands and feet aching and blue from the cold. Nancy, who's feeling better, is supposed to meet me at Moss Landing, across from Elkhorn Slough. That's where I'm speaking, aboard a whale-watching boat for an SOS fund-raiser.

Nancy pulls in to the gravel parking lot moments before we're set to sail. She's traffic-harried but happy as we hug, lug her day bag, and of course wait for her to take a few pictures on the dock.

The *Princess of Whales* is a large motor catamaran, the best-equipped whale-watching boat on Monterey Bay. Along with

Captains Heidi and Steph, their dog Fluke, and some sixty guests, it's been outfitted for the day with catered organic food, wine, chocolates, and fresh flowers in abalone shells.

We're grinning widely as we pull out of the channel, with pelicans, cormorants, and sea otters working the waters around us. Within moments of clearing the harbor and passing the massive Monterey Bay Aquarium Research Institute on the outer spit, we encounter a huge congregation of sea lions in the water. There are literally hundreds of them packed so close together they form a barking, frothing raft twenty yards across, a furry brown mob scene, and in fact the proper term for their congregations is a "mob." Nancy and I agree we've never seen anything quite like it.

Within half an hour we've also spotted the rolling backs and tails of gray and humpback whales transiting the deep, nutrient-rich waters of Monterey's submarine canyon. Back at the dock I give a short talk on "seaweed rebels," marine grassroots activists like Save Our Shores that are making a difference. Nancy takes pictures.

We then spend the night with SOS's Anne Rowley and her husband, Matt, in the pine-forested hills behind Davenport. Anne and Matt had lived on a seventy-two-foot trimaran sailboat for a number of years until Matt had a diving accident off one of the islands of Indonesia. They now live in a beautiful river-stone and timber home with their new baby boy. Matt's done much of the design and construction work on the house. Nancy and I share a guest room that has the nicer aspects of a ship's cabin (built-in wooden bunk beds, porthole-type windows) without the rolling and pitching. That night they stoke a nearby salt kiln for a couple of artist friends down from the city. Nancy documents the placement of the ceramics in the brick

kiln, the works under fire, and the breaking out of the glaze-
finished pottery in the morning.

We then hook up with Chris, their surfer neighbor from the
top of the hill, who lends me gloves, booties, and a longboard.
We head out on a morning surf safari, hoping to find rideable
waves. We tool up the coast and check out several spots where
it's closed out, the waves chopped up and windblown. He then
takes us through a farm gate and across coastal asparagus acre-
age that would have long ago gone to condos had not the people
of California voted to keep much of their coast undeveloped
back in 1972 with the establishment of the California Coastal
Commission. We get out and wander along a weedy path to a
trailhead leading to the bluffs. We reach the edge and see below
us miles of Pacific beach.

"Sorry you didn't get to freeze your butt off getting beat up in
the waves," Nancy commiserates with a grin as we climb down
the trail. On the beach we find a couple of people with a small
pack of giant Irish wolfhounds. Nancy plays with and photographs the dogs before we take off our shoes and begin hiking
north. The beach here is wide and smooth, a light yellow-tan in
color, cool under our bare feet. It's backed on the land side by
forty-foot-high cliff faces whose sharp shadows are the only
sign of disturbance on the sand. The long empty strand runs for
miles along the gentle crescent of Monterey Bay. With the coastal
fog burning off and cobalt ocean and cerulean blue sky contrasting with the crushed eggshell white of the shore break, it seems
a place more remote than you might hope to find along any
American coastline. It feels more like the end of the world if the
end of the world is a state of grace, something you really won't
know until you're there. Nancy takes my picture. She's barefoot
and windblown, and smiling radiantly from behind her camera,

satisfied with this image and this place and with being here at just this moment.

"Nice weather," Wayne, the ship's walrus-mustached boatswain, says in a gravelly smoker's voice.

"For a fish," I agree.

We're standing outside the main science lab on the weather deck of the Woods Hole research vessel *Atlantis* watching white-capped eighteen- to twenty-foot seas rolling across eight-thousand-foot-deep blue waters. Secure in its stern hanger, *Alvin*, the deep-diving submersible, will not be diving today. We're steaming west at twelve knots, trying to avoid the brunt of Hurricane Erin, which the shortwave radio assures us is headed "safely out to sea" in our direction. I'm here for two weeks on the Deep East Expedition off the Atlantic seaboard. Supported by NOAA's new Office of Ocean Exploration, the trip will include three teams of scientists/explorers hoping to develop a better understanding of America's last great wilderness range, including newly identified deep-sea coral habitats off New England and chemosynthetic mussels and other strange organisms living on vast, icy beds of gas hydrates (frozen natural gas that burns when you take a match to it) in the deep seas off the Carolinas. I'm hoping to catch a ride a mile or two down on *Alvin* sometime during the trip, but it's not to be.

A few days later we're 150 miles off Nantucket when someone comes into the lab and says a plane just hit the World Trade Center. I climb up the salt-encrusted external ladder to the bridge and join Captain Gary Chiljean and his chief mate, Mitzi Crane, listening to the shortwave radio, a static-filled 1010 WINS report out of New York with live descriptions of the jetliner terror attacks and the collapse of the World Trade Center's towers. Rebecca Cerroni, one of the expedition members, lives three blocks from the site. We put her on the satellite radiophone and she gets through to her husband, Joe, who is okay. One of his coworkers is at the World Trade Center and missing, however.

She tells me how, as a high school student, she had participated with five thousand other kids on a March of the Living from Auschwitz to Birkenau concentration camps in Poland. "I wonder if someday my kids will march down Broadway to the Trade Center," she says, trying not to cry.

Our first week at sea had seen *Alvin* unable to deploy three out of five days due to high winds and rough seas. The plan had been to make a transfer of scientists at sea off Staten Island at the end of the week, but that plan has been blown away, along with thousands of lives, by the terrorist attacks. The navy (which owns *Alvin*) cancels permission for us to dive in the steepest parts of the Hudson Canyon, the largely unexplored seaward extension of the Hudson Riverbed, the assumption being they are moving nuclear submarines through there as backup for the aircraft carrier battle group now deployed off New York City.

The night after the attacks I'm watching some of the video taken by *Alvin*'s cameras 4,500 feet down in the dark, crushing depths of Oceanographer Canyon. There are beautiful branching deep-sea corals in yellow, brown, and white, also deep sponges, cutthroat eels, rattail fish, red crabs, luminescent purple shimmering squid, and other life abundant amid the marine snow, organic detritus falling from above. Someone tells me we now have TV reception. I go up to the lounge on the fo'c'sle to see, through a weak and snowy signal, our first images of the jetliners hitting the towers and the towers coming down.

For the rest of my days I'll be stuck with those contrasting images of what we're capable of as a species, from exploring and discovering new life in the most remote and challenging parts of our ocean planet, to using modern technology to carry out mass murder in the heart of a great city.

When we dock back at the Woods Hole Oceanographic Institution on Cape Cod I go to the phone booth at the end of the quay and try calling my friends in New York City. I'd planned on staying with them if, as originally planned, we'd ended our expedition there. Unfortunately, living in Tribeca in the shadow of the World Trade Center, they've been forced to evacuate and aren't reachable. I then call a friend in Washington, D.C., where the Pentagon was attacked. She tells me of Humvees on the streets and F-16 fighter jets patrolling overhead. As a D.C.-based journalist, I feel particularly out of it at this moment, although how could I have known? In the past when I've covered war zones I've had to leave the country to find them.

I next call my sister, Deborah, in Boston—she's worried about what to tell her young boys—and then I call Nancy in Sausalito.

"It's so weird," Nancy says. "I just sat in front of the TV for the first two days, not getting any work done, just crying and feeling numb. My first impression was how it looked like something out of a movie. Remember when we saw *Independence Day*, where the aliens blow up New York?"

"A lot of people had that impression."

"And now Bush is on TV telling everyone we should go out and shop. I mean, how bizarre is that? I wouldn't want to go to the mall right now, even if I had any money."

"You sound like you're on a cell phone."

"I am. I have my answering machine forwarding to it. I'm taking a walk down by the water."

She tells me she just did a follow-up visit to her radiologist (it's been four months since she finished getting zapped). She has a kind of pimple by her surgical scar, which is what they indicated might appear if the cancer came back.

"But I'm not thinking about that right now. I've got an appointment on Friday and I'll deal with it then."

I don't know what to say, so I follow her lead. Denial sounds like a sensible strategy for now.

I visit in early December. I've got a cough that's been going around, but Nancy says come over anyway, she's got the same cough, though of course it's not the same.

It's cold and windy in Sausalito. We sit in the kitchen as she shows me all her eastern medicines, bulbs and musky-flavored herbs and brown powders in paper bags that she boils up every few days and drinks for medication and also uses for poultices. The fridge is full of big glass jars of these brown liquids. She boils a new potful, the kitchen filling with an earthy, not unpleasant steam that also soothes our throats a bit. She drinks the slightly foul-flavored herbal recipe. The "mud" from the bottom of the rendering pot she soaks in a T-shirt and wears across her chest for an hour, trying not to drip.

We head over to the Marin Headlands, driving up to the Point Bonita overlook and down the twisting one-lane coastal road to Fort Cronkhite. It's getting on toward sunset as we reach the sands of Rodeo Beach, where a few hardy cold-water surfers are still catching humpy three-foot waves. We're both coughing and hacking as we climb up the Bonita Trail to the south, a steep, ice plant–covered incline that leads to a couple of concrete pillboxes and big artillery batteries, part of a chain of coastal defenses installed at the beginning of World War Two. This is the same bunker, I point out, where Nancy once had a bat fly into her hair.

"No it isn't. That was up by the radar installation where the red-tailed hawks hang out," she corrects me. I think that if she dies all these shared experiences will be nothing more than unverifiable memories locked in my head.

We get to Bird Rock Overview just as the fog and darkness set in. We take a couple of flash photos that look eerie and foreboding. They show the fog-shrouded waves and dark waters and both of us wrapped up against the cold and the night. We slip-slide back down the steep, sandy ridgeline to the beach. Half an hour later we're warming up over a Chinese dinner in Mill Valley. I give her a last long backrub at home, we kiss good-bye, and I leave.

"Can I get anything for you?" the nurse asks.

"A new body," Nancy replies. It's about three in the morning, and the woman has come to take blood from her. I'm spending the night on a green hospital chair that folds out to a narrow cot. The doctors have said Nancy could die within days, but she won't.

I arrived from D.C. via Baltimore, Salt Lake, and the mazelike parking structure of UC–San Francisco's Moffitt-Long hospital complex. I track down her room on the cardiac ward, where they've taken a liter of fluid from around her heart.

On Thursday, my friend Buck Bagot had called from the infusion center, what he calls the "euphemism center," where his wife, Pattie, is getting treated for cancer. Nancy had come in for a CT scan but was being rushed to the hospital instead.

"Can you cure my daughter?" her mom had asked a nurse.

"We'll make her as comfortable as we can," the woman replied.

"She looked green and was having a hard time breathing,"

Buck said. "I went to hug her in the wheelchair and she looked scared, and when Nancy Ledansky is scared, I get scared, so I called you," Buck tells me.

I enter her room on the tenth floor just as Alan Glassberg, a white-haired oncologist who looks like Dr. Welby, is telling her that the cancer is in her heart and lungs and she should consider what he'd said to her about putting her things in order.

"I'm sorry you weren't the bearer of good news," she says, shaking his hand as he stands to leave.

"So am I," he replies.

I reach down and hug her. Her arms close around me.

"I'm fucked," she cries quietly in my ear, so her mom doesn't hear.

Nancy has been battling cancer for almost three years now. She's forty-three years old and dying. She's angry, she's frustrated, she doesn't want to be treated any differently. When Pattie calls to see if she's still alive, Nancy apologizes.

"I'm sorry I didn't get a chance to come over and say hi to you in the infusion center."

"That's okay," Pattie answers, nonplussed. "I could see you were busy."

At some level we all know that death is part of the big package, along with childbirth and the lives we lead, but in our culture we try to keep it on the margins. If forced, we'll attempt to seek meaning in death's awesome and capricious power. Meaning, of course, is what we higher mammals bring to the table in the form of self-consciousness, that disturbing awareness of our own mortality. Religions and their rituals of grief and renewal are attempts to create context and meaning for the cycles of life and death that define the natural world.

I realize that, over fifteen years, Nancy and I have had almost no discussion of theology or the afterlife. I think of her as some-thing of a Russian Orthodox pagan. She's got a kind of mix-and-match spiritualism, incorporating things she likes from Buddhism, Judaism, Christianity, and Animism (including a bit of Egyptian cat worship). She talks about wanting to be buried in a simple pine box on a hill overlooking the Pacific Ocean, where "my body could rot into the ground and my molecules become part of every-thing else." Still, she's agreed that her family can take her home to Wisconsin, but only after she's dead.

I remember our driving through Oregon on a cloudy Easter Sunday. She said she was feeling guilty because her mom would want her to be in church. We stopped at a state park where the spring snow was still thigh deep and the trails partially blocked by the downfall from what had been a major spring avalanche. We decided to hike to the source, and within half an hour were climbing over an apocalyptic tangle of snow-covered trunks, branches, and root balls. Thousands of trees over hundreds of acres had been knocked down by the terrific force of the great river of snow. After ninety minutes of rough hiking and some cursing (on my part), we emerged in a snowfield below a giant granite bowl, the exposed peaks stripped to their elemental rock. Just then the clouds parted and beacons of sunlight lit the rock walls before us.

"Here's your cathedral!" I said. "Happy Easter."

"God's here." She smiled.

My doctor friend Cathy puts us in touch with Steve McPhee, a palliative doc who becomes Nancy's doctor and friend in her final days, which stretch into months. A week after her hospital admittance there's an "opening" in his hospice suite and she's able to move into Room 1239. It's a double room with a panoramic view. In the foreground is a forest canopy of eucalyptus trees sprouting from a neighboring park; beyond there's the white city and slate-colored bay on which sailboats are scattered like carnations. Farther out is a vista of the Golden Gate Bridge, the Marin Headlands, and the vast ocean beyond.

She looks out at the breathtaking view and says, "Oh my God. This is *Soylent Green!*"

That 1973 sci-fi classic starring Charlton Heston depicts an overcrowded future in which those who volunteer for the suicide machine are taken to a large room where, as they're put to sleep, beautiful images of wild nature as it once existed on Earth are projected onto the walls. While Dr. McPhee will find her reaction disturbingly "negative," I can't deny the acuity of her gallows humor.

The dark thought passes quickly, and she's soon on the phone telling a family priest in Wisconsin how "I've got a lot of love pouring in." Her mom, sister, brother, and his family are all here now, as are many of her other friends and loved ones.

Later, when everyone leaves, I go into the bathroom with her and help her wipe down with disposable washcloths. She begins crying. "I'm in the Soylent Green room," she repeats, but seriously bothered this time. The crying becomes convulsive, and she starts shaking badly. She's so cold, she says, asks me to hold her. I hold her carefully so as not to cause more pain where they've cut and burned her.

"Shhh . . . Shhh . . ." She tries to calm herself, but the shakes just keep getting worse. "Hysterical anxiety" is the term a doctor will later use, but I think of it as battle shock. I'm hitting the bathroom buzzer for a nurse and trying to calm her. She's shaking like a bloody wounded combatant I remember from a graveyard battlefield in Nicaragua. "Shhh . . . Shhh . . . ," she's saying to herself as I hold her thin, ravaged body. Finally an aide taps on the door and gives her a new gown and changes the bedding, and she calms down and as soon as she gets back under the covers decides we need to have our big relationship talk, which we do. We cry some more and I'm thinking, This woman doesn't give it a break.

Dr. McPhee visits with Nancy and reads her a poem about feasting fully on one's life. Afterward I join him in the downstairs cafeteria. He asks me how I'm sleeping.

"I didn't sleep last night, but I figure that's just a sign of depression."

"There's a difference between depression and grieving," he points out. "The grieving process is normal, and you will get through it to the other side. I was once taking an Amtrak train through the Rockies. It was all rock and snow when we entered this tunnel on the continental divide, and it was a really long tunnel. We seemed to be in it for a long time, and when we emerged it was a whole other landscape. That's how I think of the grieving process."

The Gal and I once took that train, I think to myself.

After three weeks in the hospital Nancy has stabilized to the point where, rather than die here or at some hospice center, she's able to go home and do home hospice. Steve McPhee drops by, reads her a Mary Oliver poem, and promises to continue visiting with her in Sausalito.

We load up her oxygen and wheelchair and drive over the Golden Gate Bridge and down Alexander Avenue through Sausalito. There are sailboats and herring fishing boats anchored just offshore, and we can see the city, white on blue, like a postcard that we've left behind.

She's the first into the house. She walks around the big living room couch and kneels by the antique green chair where the cat's sitting, meowing in complaint at her long absence. She begins to rub and scratch the Poose.

"She looks a little sick? Is she okay?" Nancy wonders, and a lump forms in my throat.

Hospice of Marin is great and soon she's got her own hospital bed, oxygen generator, and other equipment she needs, along with visiting nurses who cajole her over her refusal to take the many meds she needs. Nancy fights the morphine and other drugs because she wants to be in control of her faculties and in control of her life.

I sleep on an air mattress in the living room except when her mother gets upset by my presence and then I stay overnight with friends, sometimes on a friend's houseboat nearby. It's okay when I'm with Nancy but devastating whenever I have to leave her.

I try to understand. My grandmother Emi came to visit when her daughter (my mother) was dying. Theirs was also a tense mother-daughter relationship. After they hugged awkwardly and talked for a while, Emi went outside and did something I'd never seen her do before. After kicking at the grass, she burst into tears. "It's not right!" she cried. "It's not right that a child should die before the parent."

"It's not the right order," Nancy's mother complains twenty-eight years later, and I still can't disagree.

After a few weeks the Gal pretty much stops eating. Her sister Deb has to return to her teaching job on St. John, so one evening I stay with friends so they can be alone. Before leaving, I give Nancy a foot rub. She hugs me around the neck. It's the hug of a child. She's losing strength. "I didn't get to go outside today. It looked like a nice day," she says wistfully.

Still, even at her sickest, the Gal will take a call or accept a visit if it will reassure or comfort a friend. Altruism, I think, is an underestimated part of our genetic makeup. She gives a couple of her nature photographs to Dr. McPhee as a gift. The UCSF Cancer Center has bought a dozen, including a shot from the Mendocino coast, for display in its hallways.

I take the wheelchair out to the front porch and bring out the portable oxygen and a second chair. She arranges herself, sits on her cushion, and basks in the sun. We can hear traffic on 101, the warbling of a nearby bird. Her mom brings her a small chicken sandwich and potato chips. Nancy eats it all and some melon as well. She nods contentedly, her head on her hand; her eyes flutter like curtains, then flick back open. We're in the moment.

"Ma and Pa Kettle on the porch," I say.

"You know those swings with the footrests?" she asks.

And I do, from the Mill Valley Arts Festival maybe six years ago, cloth swings that rock. It's like ESP, a kind of verbal shorthand you develop after years of shared experiences with someone you love. I nod. The bird warbles again. Time passes.

The Gal becomes emaciated, can only whisper now. I go to an Investigative Reporters & Editors conference in San Francisco, give a talk on covering the oceans, attend another one on covering traumas like September 11. They talk about trauma victims' distressed and reactionary behavior: avoidance and numbing, hyperarousal, insomnia. They pass out a thirty-page guide titled "Tragedies & Journalists."

On page fifteen it reads, "Understand that your problems may become overwhelming. Before he died in April 1945, war correspondent Ernie Pyle wrote, 'I've been immersed in it too long. My spirit is wobbly and my mind is confused. The hurt has become too great.'" I walk out, duck into the men's room, and try not to cry.

Nancy sleeps sitting up, leaning into her pillows with the cat curled up between her legs. She has a few visitors and writes out what she wants in a small notebook. After they leave I mention that the Poose's nails are getting long. Nancy tells me to get the clippers. I'm skeptical but find them on her side table. I get down on my knees to lure the cat out from under the drafting table and Nancy begins to scratch my butt and back like she would the Poose. I arch my back, look up at her with a smile, and she's smiling back, my reward. I get the Poose and place her in the Gal's arms and the cat snuggles and looks quite pleased but then gets all squirmy when Nancy tries to splay her footpads and expose her claws.

"Get out," she whispers to me, and I leave so she can calm the cat. Over the next twenty minutes I hear periodic clipping sounds and plaintive meows.

When I go back in, the Poose is out the sliding glass door onto the back porch and Nancy's lap is covered in fur and cat nails. I get some sponge wipes, then suggest using tape. She whispers that there's packing tape in the kitchen. I bring it back and make loops and pat all the hair and clippings off her lap. She directs my hand with hers, turning my pats into a caress. When her black stretch pants are clean again she indicates she needs help to the commode. Then her sister, who's returned from St. John, comes in and Nancy says, "Get Ma," and I go to the kitchen so her mom can help her out.

I wake up on my air mattress at six in the morning and check her out and she's sleeping folded forward, head down in her lap pillows. The low hum and thump of the oxygen generator has become the background noise of the household. I sit out on the porch for several hours, watching the trees and water below. The tide is turning. Nancy is sleeping. I read a book. Her mom and sister sit at the kitchen table in their housedresses.

At 11 A.M. I take a walk, feeling anxious. I get back at two in the afternoon and she's still asleep, folded up peacefully.

Dr. McPhee arrives and takes Nancy's pulse and blood pressure, which is around 50.

"She'll probably just sleep like this if her blood pressure doesn't change," he tells us. A short time later he goes back into Nancy's room with her mother and sister to help bathe her.

"David! Come in here! She's dying right now!" he calls out.

I enter the room and her mouth has fallen open and her mother is hugging her head and her sister is holding one arm and I take her other hand and kneel down by the metal edge of the bed and it's too sudden. I'm crying but thinking she's still here and then, at a certain moment, she's not. It's like her life force has moved. It's still here, too powerful to ignore, but no longer with her body. The corpse, with its eyes closed, suddenly looks like that of an old woman from the camps, where just a moment ago it was Nancy sleeping.

Steve McPhee pronounces her dead at 3:58 P.M. It's Saturday, June 8, 2002. Later, when he's comforting her mother and sister in the other room, I'll touch my lips to her temple, kiss her fine dark hair one last time.

He brings them back to the body and tells them to wash her and dress her and just take care of her till the undertaker arrives, and reads a short poem by Dag Hammarskjöld about finding your way over a new landscape.

I leave with the doctor around 4:30.

And Nancy pulled it off, I think. She wanted her mother, sister, and me there at the end. She then waited till her doctor arrived to mediate the final scene, but she had no intention of lingering once she no longer had control.

I drive back through town and over the Golden Gate Bridge

and it's a beautiful Bay Area day, sunny and in the seventies, and people are out on the water and jogging and riding their bikes, and it's the kind of day Nancy would have wanted to go for a hike along the coast.

Her family takes her body back to Wisconsin for her funeral while some sixty of us hold a memorial service at Rodeo Beach, one of her favorite places on the Marin Headlands. It's a gusty day, feisty like the Gal herself, with the winds whipping the sand and frothing the cold, translucent waves.

Nancy used to say I never looked happier than when I was coming out of the water after getting beat up by the waves. But the ocean can also provide solace, give you a sense of being part of something larger, even when large parts of your own soul have been torn away.

Shelley Hwang, Nancy's surgeon, comes up to me and tells me not to have any regrets about Nancy's decisions.

"Nothing she did or didn't do would have changed the outcome, that's my strong medical opinion," she says.

This gives me some comfort.

Marketplace radio plays one of my environmental commentaries, and I start to cry because she didn't get to hear it.

I put the Poose in Buck and Pattie's front room, where I'm staying, along with her litter box, food, and water. I close the door to avoid any confrontations with their dogs and cat. For two days she stays under the bed and doesn't eat anything. Then I buy a turkey sandwich and it's kind of like, I'm too upset to eat cat food but maybe a little turkey wouldn't hurt. . . . Pattie makes a full recovery from her cancer.

I fly the Poose home in a carrying case under my airline seat, doped up on a kitty downer. She quickly makes the adjustment to D.C. apartment living, once again becoming a model roommate. I comb her every day. It's a symbiotic thing. She purrs and stretches and claws the rug and I can feel my blood pressure drop.

I have a dream I'm with Nancy in San Francisco. I'm flying above her on a road leading up to Twin Peaks. I have wings like a hawk and she looks like a wild horse, racing up the hill. Then I'm next to her and she's standing in a tan trench coat that I mistook for her horsehide. We begin jogging up the hill together. We stop and look at each other. Her eyes are shining with delight.

"We both have the same eyes," she says. I feel a rush of pure joy. I begin to cry and then she cries with sudden realization. I hug her, only I'm hugging two of her. As I wake I think one is Nancy who was flesh and blood, the other is Nancy of dreams and memories.

As the days, weeks, and months pass I think and rethink the past and wonder about having done things differently. But it isn't really about regrets anymore. Most things were resolved or at least accepted between us. The reality is just that I still miss her. I still miss her very much.

10

The Seaweed Rebellion

Nothing of him that doth fade,
But doth suffer a Sea-change
Into something rich & strange.

WILLIAM SHAKESPEARE

I'd lost many loved ones and was about to lose another, but after
a time of pain and uncertainty I determined to fight for the one
love that still might (or might not) be saved, the one I will always

return to, whether for wave-gliding fun or as light gray ash. In seeking to protect our mother ocean I will also assure myself continued risk and adventure, a larger social purpose for living, and perhaps even the occasional moment of transcendence, something any one of us might aspire to by taking the plunge.

When I returned to D.C. I hadn't worked in months and was deeply in debt. I wasn't sure what to do next, not sure I wanted there to be a next. I drank. I raged. After a time of grief and reflection I found I had three options. I could return to California to do more private investigating for Scott Fielder, but I'd already done that. I could return to war reporting, as President Bush was then ginning up for a unilateral war on Iraq, and that had some appeal, war having proved an effective antidote to depression after my parents' deaths. I also started meeting with consumer advocate, public citizen, and Independent presidential candidate Ralph Nader, who had read my book and encouraged me to organize the Seaweed Rebellion of marine grassroots advocates that I describe in the book's final chapter. He offered me some support, including free office space amid a rabbit warren of public-interest start-ups in a building near Dupont Circle.

After some consideration I decided that while we'll probably always have wars, we may not always have wild fish, living reefs, or intact coastal wetlands. What was most frustrating about the cascading threats to our public seas was that we knew what the solutions were but just hadn't created the political will to do the things that are needed. I believe what South Seas anthropologist Margaret Mead once said: "Never doubt that a small group of dedicated people can change the world. Indeed, nothing else ever has." This could be my chance to help make a difference.

Plus, if I went to war I didn't know what I'd do with the cat. So the Poose, who hated getting even her paws wet, brought me back to the sea.

I established the nonprofit Blue Frontier Campaign in early 2003 with a mission statement to promote unity, provide tools to, and enhance public awareness of the solution-oriented ocean conservation movement. A Disney designer I met while speaking at the Aquarium of the Pacific drew up our Seaweed Rebel logo—a fist gripping a tangle of seaweed.

The years 2003 and 2004 also saw two reports published by two U.S. blue-ribbon panels on the ocean, the first ones since 1969. The independent Pew Oceans Commission was made up of scientists, fishermen, environmentalists, and elected officials, including the governor of New York. Its chair, Leon Panetta, a former congressman and Clinton White House chief of staff, would head the CIA and Department of Defense under President Obama.

In response to the establishment of the Pew Commission, the Bush administration appointed the U.S. Commission on Ocean Policy. It included representatives from the offshore oil industry, ports, navy admirals, academics, and *Titanic* explorer Bob Ballard. Its chair, Admiral Jim Watkins, was the Pentagon's former chief of naval operations and secretary of energy under the first President Bush.

Despite their very dissimilar makeups, their findings were remarkably similar. Both commissions concluded that the ecological degradation of the ocean represents a major threat to the nation's economy, security, and environment. They proposed a number of solutions for the restoration of ocean health, including an ecosystem-based management approach (also known as Marine Spatial Planning), a kind of ocean and coastal zoning that would incorporate a system of cleaned-up watersheds and estuaries; offshore shipping lanes and greener ports; wildlife migration corridors; clearly delineated clean-energy, national defense training, and fishing areas; recreational and marine wilderness parks; and other public benefits. They recognized that humans are a part of the marine ecosystem but also that the basic laws of nature—including biology, chemistry, and physics—are not amenable to negotiation or compromise. They also proposed a four-billion-dollar-a-year ocean trust fund to carry out their proposed initiatives.

In 2004, in response to these reports, our Blue Frontier Campaign organized its first three-day Blue Vision gathering in Washington, D.C., for some 250 leaders of marine conservation, recreation, and industry.

Our keynote speaker, the late marine conservationist and *Jaws* author Peter Benchley, contrasted his youth on Nantucket Island, when you couldn't haul in a swordfish without a shark taking a chunk out of it, with today's rapid decline of large predators. He recalled a dive off Costa Rica where he found the bottom littered with dead sharks whose fins had been cut off to sell for shark fin soup.

At one session we presented the first annual Blue Frontier Awards (now the Benchley Awards). The science winner was marine wildlife biologist Dr. Ransom Myers, of Dalhousie University in Nova Scotia, whose work included that disturbing 2003 study published in *Nature* explaining how 90 percent of large fish in the ocean have been scoured from the sea by overfishing just since the time I was born. "There is no blue frontier left," he worried. "The ocean is changing in ways that we simply cannot fathom and we're losing more and more biodiversity every day. There is no equivalent of a blue frontier organization in Europe or in Southeast Asia and I think we really need to take the vision and expand it worldwide." Myers passed away in 2007.

We honor people like Benchley and Myers by continuing their efforts to alert the public about policies and behaviors that threaten the crucible of life on our blue planet and by proposing practical alternatives and solutions that can work.

Another approach we took was to promote blue media by producing articles, opinion pieçes, a website, and a Blue Notes ocean policy newsletter, which I still write. I figured the one ocean resource not being fully exploited was good ocean stories. In 2005 we also published *The Ocean and Coastal Conservation Guide*, with Island Press, describing some two thousand groups, agencies, parks, schools, and marine labs linked to the sea, and we continue to update it on our bluefront.org website.

By this time I was giving a lot of public talks on the state of the seas only to be approached afterward by people saying they wished they could do something but they had full-time jobs and families to raise or classes to attend, and things like global warming and the collapse of marine wildlife just seemed too overwhelming for them to have any impact anyway. The answer, of course, is that they were already having an impact. Everything we do each day affects the seas around us, from the cars we drive to the things we do when we snorkel or dive. The only real question is, Will we be conscious of our impact and then make the right choices to help heal the ocean?

So I wrote a new book, *50 Ways to Save the Ocean*, to offer people options. It has a foreword by third-generation ocean explorer Philippe Cousteau and an illustrated fish and crab duo (Finley and Clawdia) drawn by *Sherman's Lagoon* cartoonist Jim Toomey. It explains in simple, fact-based chapters how, by making right choices for the sea, you also tend to do the right thing for your health ("Eat Organic and Vegetarian Foods"), your pocketbook ("Drive a Fuel-Efficient Car, Join a Car Pool, or Use Public Transit"), even your sense of well-being ("Talk About the Ocean in Your Place of Worship."). The book is broken down into five sections: Enjoy, Conserve, Clean, Protect, and finally Learn and Share. The number one thing to do is go to the beach, because you're more likely to protect the places that you love.

The book also highlights how things that you may not think of as being tied to the sea can actually have a huge impact on it. Take energy conservation. About a third of the electric power generated in the United States comes from coal-fired power plants. California, by contrast, is a state where over 90 percent of the power plants use natural gas and most of the rest renewable energies. Coal plants release both sulfur dioxide and nitrogen oxide, which create smog and acid rain. Rainfall washes these pollutants into rivers, bays, and the sea, where they contribute to oxygen-depleted dead zones. Coal-generated power plants also release mercury, a neurotoxin that accumulates through the food web and concentrates as methyl mercury in the flesh of top ocean predator fish like halibut, tuna, and swordfish, becoming a health risk for both marine life and seafood consumers, particularly pregnant women, as even tiny amounts of mercury can impact the neurological development of the human fetus in utero. In addition, burning coal adds a huge amount of climate-warming carbon dioxide to the atmosphere. Global warming, in turn, is causing sea-level rise and changing the ocean's temperature and chemistry, making it more acidic and reducing its overall productivity. While not as harmful as coal, other fossil fuels used to generate electricity—including diesel oil and natural gas—also contribute to global warming, and air and water pollution. Along with encouraging the reader to campaign for safe clean-energy alternatives, the book explains how we can reduce our energy footprint in ways that save both money and the sea. For example:

- Ask your utility provider for a free home energy audit.

- Properly insulate your home and weather-seal leaky windows.

- If you can't afford to double-pane windows, use window plastic to create a double layer.

- Turn off the lights and disconnect TVs, computers, and cell phone chargers when they're not in use.

- Replace incandescent lightbulbs with compact fluorescents.

- Purchase EPA-rated Energy Star appliances.

- Look for an Energy Star rating when you purchase a new home.

- Install a programmable thermostat to automatically adjust your home temperature while you're away or asleep. Also use comforters in cold weather.

- Use an energy-efficient humidifier in the winter. Moisture increases the "heat index," making sixty-eight degrees feel like seventy-six.

- Install solar paneling and water heating systems to save electricity.

- In the winter, open your curtains and blinds during the day to let in solar radiation and close them at night to keep heat in. In the summer reverse the process.

- Plant shade trees around your house and encourage your city to plant an urban forest to reduce the need for air-conditioning.

Along with written advice for the ocean lovelorn, Blue Frontier began holding regular Seaweed Happy Hours for the D.C. ocean community at a bar called the Reef (though encouraging the hardworking activists not to overindulge and drink like fish). We also sponsored Celebrations of the Sea and regional organizing and planning meetings around the country, our attempt at herding catfish. A Gulf regional meeting planned for New Orleans in early fall 2005 had to be called off on account of weather, however. Instead, I ended up working as a journalist once again, reporting on the impact of Hurricane Katrina.

I fly into the Gulf region by way of Ronald Reagan (Washington, D.C.) and George Bush (Houston) airports to see how the conservative philosophy of "less government" functions in the face of a coastal catastrophe. As with the deregulation of Wall Street, not so well, it turns out. The U.S. Coast Guard (which will rescue over thirty-three thousand people) and Louisiana Department of Wildlife seem to be the only functioning parts of government in the first critical days after the storm.

I arrive in Baton Rouge with a planeload of relief workers, FEMA functionaries, and crew-cut contractors, all working their cell phones and BlackBerrys. I call Mark Davis of the Coalition to Restore Coastal Louisiana, who five years earlier told me if they couldn't make the case for wetlands restoration a hurricane would. "Being right sure sucks," he now says. After renting a car

I head south on Interstate 10, tuning in to United Radio Broad-
casters of New Orleans, a consortium of local stations playing
24-7 information and call-in reports. One caller is complaining
it takes hours to get through on the Red Cross relief line but only
seconds if you switch to the contributions phone line.

Around the New Orleans airport in Jefferson Parish, I begin
to see box stores, warehouses, and motels with their roofs ripped
off or caved in; downed trees and broken street signs; house
roofs covered in blue tarps; and high-rises with glass windows
popped out like broken eyes. I hit a traffic jam and follow an
SUV across the median strip to an exit, where I stop to take a
picture of a small office complex with its second-story front and
roof gone. I get a call from a contact at the New Orleans aquarium. They lost most of their fish when the pumps failed but
managed to evacuate the penguins and sea otters to Monterey.

I get on a wide boulevard that leads to a roadblock where a
police officer checks my press identification. "This is only for
emergency vehicles, but go ahead," she says.

I drive into Lakeview, one of the large sections of the city that
sat underwater for two weeks and will likely have to be bull-
dozed. It reminds me of war zones I've been in after heavy street
fighting. There are trees and power poles down, electric lines
hanging, metal sheets and street signs on mud-caked pavement,
smashed cars, boats on sidewalks and torn-open houses, all colored in sepia tones of gray and brown.

Unable to drive far in the debris-chocked streets, I get out of
my car, half expecting the sweet, rotting-meat smell of death.
Instead, I'm confronted with an equally noxious odor. It's what
I'll come to think of as the smell of a dead city, like dried cow
pies and mold with a stinging chemical aftertaste. Fine yellow

dust starts rising up from under my boots and infiltrating the car. I retreat. The I-10 exit is barricaded, forcing me north again. I do a U-turn at a major roadblock and get chased down by some angry cops. I explain that I'm just following another cop's helpful directions and soon find myself speeding along a near-empty freeway bridge approaching downtown. I'm doing eighty and get passed by a cop car doing over one hundred.

The rusted, ruined roof of the Superdome inspires me to choose an exit and, after getting turned around at a friendly National Guard checkpoint, I'm soon in the deserted streets of the central business district amid abandoned hotels, rubble piles, and high-rises. A big wind-damaged Doubletree hotel sign reads D U L EE. The French Quarter is still intact, with even a few generator-powered bars open for soldiers, FBI agents, and firefighters. On Canal Street, it looks like a Woodstock for first responders, with Red Cross and media satellite trucks, tents, and RVs pulled up on the central streetcar median by the Sheraton. Red-bereted troops from the Eighty-second Airborne cruise by in open-sided trucks, M4s at the ready in case the undead should appear at sunset. Uptown, some boats lie in the middle of the street, along with cars crushed by a falling wall, and there's a pharmacy trashed by looters. Farther on are the smashed homes and muddied boulevards, the still-flooded underpasses and cemeteries, the abandoned cars and broken levees of an eerily hollow city.

In the coming days, I'll travel across this new urban landscape, tracing the brown floodwater line that marks tens of thousands of homes, schools, offices, banks, churches, grocery stores, and other ruined structures, including the main sewage plant. I'll cross paths with animal rescue crews, military patrols, utility crews from New York and Pennsylvania, and body-recovery search teams with K-9 dogs, and orange spray paint, which they use to mark the doors of still unexamined buildings, writing the date and adding a zero for no bodies or numbers where bodies have been found.

"I don't think anyone anticipated the breach of the levees," President Bush told Diane Sawyer shortly after this below-sea-level city went aquatic, perhaps his most memorable line since declaring "Mission Accomplished" onboard an aircraft carrier after the invasion of Iraq. Of course, the U.S. Commission on Ocean Policy, which he appointed, had highlighted the risk of the levees failing in its final report in the fall of 2004. My friend Mark Schleifstein of the New Orleans *Times-Picayune* newspaper had also been writing about the risk of a hurricane devastating the city for so many years that his editor started calling his stories "disaster porn." After Katrina struck, he and his workmates got out of their office in the back of big-wheeled newspaper delivery trucks with the flood waters up to their grilles. They then published the newspaper online out of an industrial park in Baton Rouge.

I stay with Cain Burdeau, an AP colleague, in the less damaged Algiers Point section of the city, just across the Mississippi from where the helicopter assault ship *Iwo Jima* and Carnival cruise ship *Ecstasy* are being used to house city employees and relief workers. Black Hawk helicopters fly overhead at sunset while a Red Cross truck down the street offers hot food to the handful of residents still here. We trade them warm beer for turkey chili.

Back in Lakeview, I encounter Bob Chick. Bob sneaked past the checkpoints to see if he could salvage anything from his green Cajun cottage, located near the breach in the Seventeenth Street floodwall. He hasn't had much luck. "Just some tools that might be okay," he says. "I left all my photos on top of a chest of drawers, thinking the water wouldn't get that high. They say if you have more than five inches of water in your house for five days it's a loss. We had eight feet for two weeks." He's found one of his cats dead but thinks the other two might have escaped, judging by a nest of fur on a ruined sofa. He invites me to look inside. From the door it's a jumble of furniture, including a sofa, table, twisted carpet, lamps, and wooden pieces all covered in black and gray gunk, reeking of mold and rotted cat food. I try not to breathe too deeply. "I had a collection of Jazz Fest T-shirts going back to 'seventy-nine but they're gone." He's wearing a mask, rubber boots, and gloves but still manages to give an expressive shrug of resignation when I take his picture. "I lived in this house sixteen years. We'd have been fine if the levee hadn't broke. We'd be moving back right now."

U.S. demographics have changed since Katrina. Baton Rouge is now the largest city in Louisiana, its arenas and hotels jammed with evacuees. Like the Dust Bowl of the 1930s, this new Storm Bowl could result in a new wave of homelessness. By mid-October, FEMA is spending eleven million dollars a day on hotel rooms to house the displaced.

I meet a group of a dozen Cajuns spending their days and nights in a carport under a damaged three-story office building in Belle Chasse, Louisiana. They've got two big coolers full of food and beer, which they insist on sharing with me. They sleep on patches of dry carpet in one of the abandoned law offices at night. There are black and white folks camped out in tents, campers, and an RV under the storm-torn Ocean Springs–Biloxi bridge in Mississippi; there are refugees in marine-lab dorms and KOAs and a Mormon tent colony by a lake; there are people staying in friends' and families' homes, barns, and yards, or—as a last resort—in government evacuation centers. I go to a Society of Environmental Journalists' conference in Austin, Texas, more than a month after Katrina and find my motel is full of New Orleans evacuees smoking cigarettes, playing dominoes, and waiting, just waiting.

I catch a ride along the west bank of the Mississippi in Plaquemines Parish, south of New Orleans, with Deputy Sheriff Ken Harvey. This is where towns of several thousand, like Empire and Buras, got washed away and some oil tank farms also ruptured. Where the road is cut by water, we drive up on the eroded levee and keep going. It's a world turned upside down, with boats on the land and houses in the water. At one point where the levee broke and the water poured through, there's nothing but a field where Diamond, an unincorporated town of some three hundred souls, including many trailer-park residents, stood. Those folks never seem to catch a break.

I take a picture of an antebellum white mansion in the water along with a floating pickup, a larger truck hanging off a tree, a semi-trailer cab under the bottom of an uplifted house, a speedboat through a picture window. Shrimp boats are everywhere, on the levee, on the road, and in the bushes, with military patrols passing by. We stare in awe at a two-hundred-foot barge tossed atop the levee like a bath toy on a tub rim. Approaching the Empire Bridge, I note the white church facing north toward us is still intact and suggest that's a hopeful sign. "It used to face the road," Harvey points out.

We listen to his boss, the sheriff, on Unity Radio threatening to lay off his people and make the state troopers take over the parish if he can't meet payroll by midnight. Late that evening, the governor agrees to hand him ten million dollars. In what's left of Port Sulphur, the sheriff's deputies are living in converted shipping containers (the same kind used on offshore oil rigs). Most of their homes have also washed away.

I spot a U.S. mail truck in a canal just before we stop to check out a long row of railroad boxcars knocked off their track; they acted as an accidental debris dam, saving a community of fifty homes.

We also examine oil that has spread across the road and into the wetlands, where a Shell pipeline burst. I take a picture of some collapsed oil storage tanks. Ken gets nervous when I take a picture of the Shell refinery.

The oil companies lost at least 52 rigs in the Gulf, with more than 110 others damaged. The Coast Guard's latest estimate is over eight million gallons of oil spilled (more than two-thirds of the quantity spilled by the *Exxon Valdez*) offshore and on, but since it's the Louisiana-Texas coastline, no one raises much of a fuss.

Professor Nancy Rabalais at the Louisiana Universities Marine Consortium in Cocodrie (which lost its roof to Katrina and its vehicles to Rita) still managed to get out on a research cruise between the storms. She spotted a seven-foot swamp alligator swimming fifteen miles out at sea, she tells me. Sixty feet down, diving in the murky water to see how the storm affected the Gulf of Mexico's massive nutrient-fed dead zone, she felt something touch her foot. She jumped, but then figured it was too deep to be the alligator. Three years later her lab would be trashed again, this time by Hurricane Ike.

Most of the region's shrimp and commercial fishing fleet was sunk or thrown up onto the land by Katrina. The thirty-mile-long crescent of the Chandeleur Islands, east of Louisiana, once a stronghold of French pirates, is now gone. One hundred sixty square miles of swampland has also been reclaimed by the sea.

The good news is that many of the live oak, hackberry, and cypress trees that look dead are starting to rebud. Some twenty-five-foot-tall trees survived because the storm waves were so high above them that they weren't scoured away.

Unfortunately, as I drive east through Mississippi and Alabama I find most of the trees and wetlands festooned with plastic, like Tibetan prayer flags if Buddhist monks prayed for the deaths of turtles and seabirds (they often choke on plastic, which they mistake for food). When thousands of homes are blown apart like piñatas, a lot of plastic comes streaming out. In Biloxi, along with the smashed casinos, Civil War–era homes, and flattened neighborhoods, I find miles of beachfront covered in plastic and fiberglass insulation; PVC pipe, kitchen appliances, plastic containers, chunks of cement and drywall, wire sheathing, and Styrofoam pellets, which the seabirds are eyeing as potential snack food.

I feel like an eco geek being more concerned about the gulls and wetlands than the lost revenue from the casinos, which is what everyone else seems to be obsessing about. The waterside wing of the new Hard Rock Casino is a smashed-up tangle of twisted girders and concrete rubble. I pull over by an eight-thousand-ton, six-hundred-foot-long casino barge that was pushed half a mile by the storm, landing on Beach Drive. Somewhere underneath its barnacle-encrusted black hull is a historic mansion. Nearby, the Grand Casino barge has taken out much of the stately façade of the six-story yellow brick Biloxi Yacht Club before grounding next to it. Another barge landed on the Holiday Inn, where more than twenty-five people may have been trying to ride out the hurricane. No one's been able to do a body recovery there yet. I talk with Phil Sturgeon, a Harrah's security agent hanging out with some cops from Winter Park, Florida. He's in jeans and a gray shirt with a toothbrush and pen sticking out of his pocket. He tells me the storm surge crested at about thirty-five feet, at least five feet higher than Hurricane Camille in 1969.

In Waveland, I drive over twisted railroad tracks where the eye of Katrina passed, into neighborhoods of jagged wooden debris. A middle-aged couple is trying to clear the drive to the lot where their home once stood. A surfboard leans up against one of the live oaks, which seem to have fared better than the houses in between them.

"Are you an adjuster?" the woman asks.

"No, a reporter."

"Good, because we don't like adjusters. Nationwide was not on our side."

Apparently they've been offered $1,700 on their $422,000 home.

"At least you've got your surfboard," I tell John, her husband. "Oh, that's not my surfboard." He grins, pointing around. "And that's not my boat, and that's not my Corvette (buried to its hood in the rubble), and that's not our roof. We think it might belong to the house at the end of the street."

Some fifty million tons of rubble and waste along the Gulf is another environmental challenge. The plan is to go after the "woody debris" (downed trees) first, then white debris (refrigerators, stoves, etc.), cars, boats, construction materials, building materials, hazardous waste, plastics, and so on. Authorities can't burn it without risking a huge spike in asthma and other lung diseases, as happened in Dade County, Florida, after Hurricane Andrew in 1992. But they also can't move much wood out of New Orleans without risking the spread of invasive Formosan termites that have riddled the city.

I'm back in New Orleans on Canal Street, where the Salvation

Army offers me cold water, a baloney sandwich (I decline), and a fruit cocktail. It's been a long day with the Army Corps of Engineers, who've leased helicopters that are dropping three-thousand- and seven-thousand-pound sandbags on the latest breach in the Industrial Canal, which has reflooded the Lower Ninth Ward. I enter the Sheraton after getting cleared by muscular Blackwater Security guys in tan and khaki T-shirts and shorts with Glock pistols on their hips. Another one sits by the elevators, checking room IDs. I wonder if being a professional mercenary in Iraq is good training for concierge duty. I sit by the Pelican Bar in the lobby, looking out the three-story-high glass window at the media RVs and SUVs on the street—feeling as if I've been in this hotel before. It reminds me of third-world trouble spots like Managua, Tegucigalpa, and Suva.

The Gulf region is now very much a war zone, only with fewer deaths (about 1,600 bodies recovered at the time of my visit), far more extensive damage, and a million environmental refugees. It also offers many of the same ironies and bizarre moments one finds in war. Unity Radio announces that if you're going to tonight's Louisiana State University football game in Baton Rouge you can return after curfew provided you show your game stubs to the armed deputies at the roadblocks.

Stranger still are the ways in which the federal government keeps putting people in harm's way, refusing to learn obvious lessons, even after a monumental disaster like Katrina. Subsidies are offered for bridges and road construction into high-impact areas, for beach replenishment and sand berms using dredged sand, and of course for federal flood insurance. FEMA's Flood Insurance Program has been a driver of high-risk coastal development in flood plains and on barrier islands for generations. Before the program got going in 1968, no private insurance company would cover these at-risk areas, and so people tended to build only what they could afford to lose to a storm or not build at all. Once the feds provided the flood insurance, however, banks started providing loans and mortgages to developers, and the coastal real-estate boom hasn't slowed since.

Unfortunately, barrier islands are like geology on amphetamines. They're made to move even when people build on top of them. Dauphin Island, Alabama, is fourteen miles by one and a half miles at its thickest. It's been hit and reshaped by hurricanes since it first emerged from the sea thousands of years ago, most recently by Frederic in 1979, Danny in 1997, Georges in 1998, Lili in 2002, Ivan in 2004, and Dennis, Katrina, and Wilma in 2005.

I'm walking with Dr. George Crozier, the lanky white-blond-haired director of Alabama's Dauphin Island Sea Lab and one of the nation's leading experts on coastal processes. We pass a police roadblock and hike down the narrow West End Beach through an apocalyptic scene of two hundred broken and vanished stilt houses, downed power lines, flooded roads, buried cars, knee-deep quicksand, and a massive oil rig, *Ocean Warwick*, that drifted sixty miles before grounding in the surf. A million-dollar protective sand berm built by FEMA after last year's Hurricane Ivan, which destroyed fifty homes, has now vanished into the sea.

Meanwhile, we're getting sandblasted and drenched by twenty-five-knot winds and rainsqualls that mark the outer bands of Hurricane Rita, which, at the moment, is threatening to do to Houston what Katrina did to New Orleans.

"Maybe instead of 'barrier islands,' we should rename them death-by-drowning islands," I suggest.

Crozier likes the idea but doesn't think it will stop the developers. "The rush to rebuild is understandable. It's basic human sympathy, but we have to build in a different way," he explains.

"What happened in Florida in 2004 and Louisiana in 2005 is no longer the exception—it's the new rule."

He means because of fossil fuel–fired climate change, sea-level rise, bigger storm surges, a possible increase in intensity and number of Category 4 and 5 hurricanes. But since the next really big hurricane season won't take place for another three years, people willfully forget and build even more stilt houses on cement pads on the sand. I'll see hundreds of them battered and broken flying over Galveston Island, Texas, in a Coast Guard helicopter the day after 2008's Hurricane Ike. Even greater devastation will be visited upon New York and much of the New Jersey shoreline by Superstorm Sandy in 2012. The real problem has little to do with natural disasters, however. The issue is why—through bad policies on coastal development, wetlands protection (or lack thereof), and the energy choices we make—we keep turning natural disasters into human catastrophes.

Hoping to promote practical alternatives, Blue Frontier organized a thirty-five-city book tour for *50 Ways to Save the Ocean*, including talks at major aquariums, marine science centers, activist meetings, and schools in a dozen states. My sister comes to hear me speak at the New England Aquarium and when we are driving back to her house tells me it was a good presentation. "You were loose and funny. Maybe you should have been a stand-up [comedian]," she suggests, always willing to reinvent my life, as older siblings tend to do.

After speaking to the annual meeting of the Florida Marine Science Educators Association I get to go snorkeling with manatees in Clearwater. At 6 A.M. my friend Drew and I slowly approach the first two we've spotted—they seem surprisingly active after what I've heard and read about these big marine herbivores. They're splashing around in a lively manner when the closer of the two slaps me with his big tail fluke and I realize we are interrupting an enthusiastic attempt to change their endangered species status. Embarrassed by our transgression, we return to the boat.

A little later I get to roll off the side of the float boat and am soon rubbing the algal backs of four big gray "sea cows" as they graze the shallow river bottom. They like having their backs and bellies scratched, also under their flippers. If they get bored of this they can retreat behind the MANATEE RESERVE sign sticking out of the water, where people aren't allowed to follow. The danger for manatees is not from swimmers but from powerboats that run them over as they glide through nearshore coastal waters or hang around the warm water outflows of power plants; also, they're at risk from toxic algal blooms that have killed hundreds of them and are on the increase worldwide.

Jim Toomey joins me for the Bay Area segment of the book tour, where we face our toughest crowd to date but are still able to keep the undivided attention of two hundred K–fifth graders for an hour, thanks to our descriptions of the wonders and terrors of the sea and Jim's lively illustrations of what we're saying. As I explain that penguin colonies are smelly as cow barns and loud as rock concerts he draws a tubby penguin playing an electric guitar. Afterward he draws and signs a few of his Sherman the shark pictures for the kids.

At the Aquarium of the Pacific in Long Beach I get to make friends with some giant halibut, groupers, rays, and reef sharks when they let me scuba dive their main 350,000-gallon tank after my talk there. I have to wear dark gloves because the sharks sometimes mistake loose pale fingers for the squid and fish they're fed.

The book's original publisher, Inner Ocean, is based in Maui and so I get to speak there and in Honolulu on the summer night in 2006 when George W. Bush gives the United States its first great wilderness park in the sea.

I am speaking at the invitation of KAHEA, an alliance of native Hawaiian and environmental groups, when word comes that the president had designated the Northwest Hawaiian Islands Ecosystem Reserve as a 140,000-square-mile national monument, today known as the Papahānaumokuākea Marine National Monument (that's Hawaiian for Yellowstone, I think). Stretching over 1,200 miles northwest from the main islands to Midway, it contains a string of postage-stamp-sized islets, vast atolls, and over 70 percent of the nation's coral reefs.

Certainly a strong case can be made that the Bush administration had the worst environmental record of any presidency. But just as Barry Bond's home-run record will always come with an asterisk relating to his steroid use, any recounting of the Bush administration will have to come with a blue asterisk noting the establishment of America's first fully protected ocean wilderness parks. The Northwest Hawaii monument is huge, almost eight times the size of the nation's thirteen National Marine Sanctuaries combined. The sanctuaries, the largest three established to prevent oil drilling off California, Massachusetts, and the Florida Keys, are also designated for multiple use, including recreational and commercial fishing, whereas Northwest Hawaii allows for no extractive uses (think national parks versus national forests).

Some larger national conservation groups were quick to claim the credit for the monument's designation, but that night in Honolulu I tell a local TV reporter that we couldn't have gotten to this historic moment without the work of local Hawaiian citizens groups. They turned out hundreds of people at public hearings over the previous five years, helping pressure and inspire Hawaii's

Republican governor and state congressional delegation to join in their call for full protection of the nation's greatest coral reef system. That, in turn, made it possible for the Republican president to take positive action.

The Northwest Hawaiian reef system was first given transitional protection as an "ecosystem reserve" under Bill Clinton back in 2000 after he was informed that if he did so he would have protected more wilderness area than Teddy Roosevelt.

Still, there had been fierce opposition to its final protection from the Western Pacific Fishery Management Council, one of eight regional advisory groups that, because they're the only federal regulatory bodies exempted from conflict-of-interest laws, are also dominated by the commercial and recreational fishing industries they're supposed to manage.

Yet because there'd been so little historic fishing pressure in the remote islands area (only eight commercial fishing boats had permits to make the long, fuel-costly journey) it still retains many of the pristine characteristics of the ocean before human impact. One of these is that it's a predator-dominated ecosystem, a kind of inverse food pyramid that has upended the way scientists have traditionally envisioned the sea. It turns out the greater part of this intact reef's biomass is made up of big carnivorous critters like tiger and Galapagos sharks, jacks, groupers, dolphins, and endangered Hawaiian monk seals. In the populated parts of the Hawaiian island chain, where people have been fishing for some 1,500 years, less than 5 percent of the marine biomass is made up of predators while the great majority of the wildlife consists of smaller herbivorous fish and turtles.

President Bush's interest in this had been piqued that spring when he attended a White House screening of a PBS documentary on Northwest Hawaii produced by Jean-Michel Cousteau.

The screening was arranged in collaboration with the National Marine Sanctuary Foundation and was attended by a number of ocean conservationists, including Sylvia Earle, who spent much of the evening briefing the president and his wife, Laura, who seemed particularly interested, on the state of the reef and the impact of the tons of plastic debris floating into the monument every year on the Pacific Gyre.

Midway Island, which anchors the reef chain, is the nesting site for thousands of albatross, also known as gooney birds. Of course, if you spent over 90 percent of your lifetime airborne, your landing and take-off skills might also appear somewhat ungainly. Adult albatross will forage far out over the Pacific, returning to the site of the famous World War Two sea battle with both natural food like squid and small pieces of plastic they mistake for food and then feed to their chicks. As a result, many chicks starve, dying with their bellies full of plastic. The president was clearly inspired to action by the documentary and subsequent dinner conversation with Sylvia Earle. Perhaps he wanted to protect the monk seals from religious persecution. For whatever reasons he gave Northwest Hawaii its monument status in June 2006. Afterward Laura Bush began speaking out publicly on the problem of marine debris.

Bush's final blue asterisks were announced two and a half years later, on January 6, 2009, during his final days in office, and were also huge victories for the sea. He gave monument status to the largely unspoiled and rarely visited islands of Kingman, Palmyra, Howland, Baker, Jarvis, Johnson, and Wake (the Line Islands), Rose Atoll in Samoa, and the Mariana Trench, the deepest canyon on earth. These are among the last great and unexplored wildernesses on our blue planet, and because they're located within the U.S. Exclusive Economic Zone, they now have been protected for all time. Spanning some 195,000 square miles, they are 50 percent larger than all U.S. national parks combined. About the size of Spain, they are just slightly bigger than the Phoenix Islands reserve established by the tiny Pacific island nation of Kiribati in 2008.

Reporting on the White House's internal decision-making process by *Washington Post* reporter Juliet Eilperin and others indicated the president's final decision on these monuments would be influenced either by his wife, Laura, who strongly supported the designations, or by Vice President Dick Cheney, who never saw much value in wildlife and habitat you couldn't hook, shoot, or drill. Luckily, Laura won the argument, probably because Cheney wouldn't be moving to Dallas with them.

In the calculus of history, the monument designations certainly won't balance President Bush's other blunders, high crimes, and misdemeanors (no one talks about Mussolini's commitment to mass transit); still, it proved to be a huge step forward for marine conservation and set a high bar for President Obama and other world leaders to meet (in 2014 Obama would expand the Pacific monuments' protected areas to almost half a million square miles). Scientists have long suggested that 20 percent of the ocean be set aside as fully protected marine reserves where no fishing, drilling, dumping, or mining take place, wilderness parks in the sea that can help assure the genetic and biological diversity of our blue planet. With the addition of the U.S. Pacific monuments, we're now at around 3 percent.

I was staying at someone's small *ohana*, or guest cottage, in up-country Maui in Hawaii, sharing the sink with a gecko lizard that liked to curl up in the drain trap, making it difficult for me to brush my teeth, when the phone rang one night. It was Cousin Jane in D.C.

"Do you know it's 3 A.M. here?" I asked, thinking she didn't know I was in Hawaii.

"You know no one calls you at 3 A.M. unless it's serious," she replied. "Your sister has lung cancer."

"Why didn't she call herself?"

"I think she was worried for you. You know, because of what you went through before."

Later that morning I called Deborah, who told me she'd already told the boys. A few months earlier their father, Patrick, had been diagnosed with a serious lung disease. Although my sister had smoked some in the past (I never knew how much because she hid it from me after our mother died), it seemed likely that she and Patrick had also been exposed to asbestos while rehabbing her first house on Boston's Mission Hill two decades earlier. I remembered how they'd stripped much of it, including the attic, down to the frame and how dusty everything had been.

Around noon I drove down to the waterfront by the old whaling town of Lahaina, feeling a familiar hollowness. There was a palm-lined rocky shoreline and longboarders catching small waves about two hundred yards out on a postcard-blue sea with the outlying islands beyond. I stripped down to my swimsuit, grabbed my short fins, and began walking out across the rocky bottom. On the third or fourth step I felt a sharp, searing pain as a black sea urchin spine went into the bottom of my foot. I hopped ashore and pulled out what I could of the spine. The sharp tip would stay in my footpad over the next four to five months. "It's calcium carbonate. It'll dissolve, but slowly, like a rusty nail," Sam Farr, the democratic congressman from Monterey and a good friend of the ocean, told me the next time we spoke. He'd also stepped on a sea urchin in Hawaii.

From Hawaii I flew to Alaska for my aunt Renate's eightieth birthday. It was a family reunion at Camp Denali, ninety miles into the national park, and even though Deborah couldn't be there because she was in the hospital, she wanted me to be there with the boys. Adam and Ethan and I hiked and canoed and saw loons and beaver, blond-colored grizzly bears, caribou, and a wolf tracking a caribou and its calf down a riverbed under heavy cloud cover. The tundra was soft enough that I could hobble across it with the urchin spine in my foot. After a long hike Ethan and I jumped into the camp's freezing cold pond. On our third day the clouds parted and we looked out on what appeared to be the Himalayas but was actually the Alaska Range. Cousin Eric leased a couple of bush planes so we could all fly over Mount Denali, at 20,320 feet the highest mountain peak in North America. We looked down to see rescue helicopters removing injured climbers. It was awesome. Terrestrial wilderness, I have to admit, can be as impressive as the sea. It's just that the wildlife is so much more scattered. One of the second-generation camp owners, although only in her early thirties, told us of the dramatic changes she's witnessed in glacial runoff and seasonal climate shifts around Mount Denali just since she was a girl.

We got back east after Deborah was released from the hospital. She'd now be able to stay home for her last six months.

"You know one nice effect of this is we're actually talking and seeing each other more than we have in years," she noted at one point after I'd made a few trips to visit her, Adam, and Ethan. On one trip I'd stayed in Ethan's room at his dad's place. Deborah had never seen it. "He has three big posters on the wall above his bed," I tell her. "Muhammad Ali, Jimi Hendrix, and Che Guevara,"

"Really?" She smiles. "That's me. That's my influence."

We're sitting on her porch in Brookline about a week before she passes, the early-winter sun warming our faces, both of us now in our fifties, set in our own ways, comfortable with our common history.

"I wonder how I would have turned out differently if not for the sixties," she muses.

"Maybe you wouldn't have ended up doing all your medical work or being the great mom you are," I suggest.

She looks unconvinced.

"Maybe we should just be in the moment," I say.

She gives me an odd look, then grins. "Right, that California stuff." But she is quiet and relaxed in the sun, pain-free for a time before getting back to worrying about Ethan and Adam, now sixteen and eighteen.

Adam was scheduled to go off to college that fall but decided he'd stay home, got a job with City Year helping low-income school kids, stopped fighting with his mom, and became a real mensch. Ethan was making beautiful pots in his high school ceramics class. One was a tall vase, unglazed on the outside, on which he etched a tree of life and a quote from the Jewish theologian Heschel: "Our life is beset with difficulties but is never devoid of meaning." It now sits on a shelf in my living room.

My sister had a wonderful last Thanksgiving with her family and friends, the matriarch of a table full of food, love, and life. She was fifty-seven. From there I headed down to the Coast Guard Academy in New London, Connecticut, to work on my next book. Two days later I had to turn around and get the train back to Boston to be there when she passed. It was a hard passage but not devoid of meaning.

Hundreds of people came to her service at Boston's Temple Israel, and we sat shivah at the house in Brookline for a week.

When the boys were ten and twelve she'd taken them on an educational tour organized through the synagogue to visit the (few hundred) Jews of Cuba. They told me they'd like to go back and scatter her ashes off a high bridge they remembered between Havana and the oceanside beach resort at Varadero, so that's what we did.

Along with running the Blue Frontier Campaign I was also writing my book *Rescue Warriors*, about the U.S. Coast Guard. This gave me a measure of comfort while I grieved over my sister's death. I enjoyed being with the "Coasties," not just because I was getting out on the water with them but also because of who they are.

Aboard the high-endurance cutter *Munro* in Kodiak, Alaska, Captain Craig "Bark" Lloyd told me that he asked all his new crew members what their moms and dads did, "and a really common answer I get from about 10 percent of them is their mom's a nurse. So you have this rescue personality—people whose mothers were nurturing for a living and they want a life like that, but with more adventure."

In the Coast Guard they get it. In Alaska their cutters and 'copters are like orcas and eagles, following the fishing fleet and acting as 911 for *The Deadliest Catch*. Two months after I visited the *Munro*, it was involved in a Bering Sea Easter storm rescue that saved forty-two of forty-seven fishermen's lives after the factory trawler *Alaska Ranger* sank at night in twenty-foot seas. How could I not like a military sea service whose main purpose is to save lives rather than take them? While not ignoring their shortcomings in *Rescue Warriors*, I still came to identify with the men and women of the Coast Guard and the way they combine the best of patriotism, altruism, and adrenaline.

In the spring of 2007, after nine years of self-imposed exile, I moved home to the San Francisco Bay Area. I sold my apartment in D.C. and bought a townhouse on the water in the East Bay community of Richmond, where I used to get a lot of my criminal defense cases, including homicides, as a private investigator. Of course, part of the struggle to protect our blue frontier is protecting culturally diverse and affordable waterfront communities like Richmond, a low-income city of just over 100,000, about 40 percent Hispanic, 30 percent African American, 20 percent white, and 10 percent Asian and other folks. It's the site of a century-old Chevron oil refinery that shares most of its risks (such as a 2012 fire that sent 15,000 people to area hospitals) and few of its rewards with its neighbors.

Still, I've now got ducks instead of trucks on my street and am adjacent to a sailboat marina that used to be part of the Kaiser shipbuilding basin during World War Two. Here 737 Liberty ships and 10 later-model Victory ships were built in just four years back when America was the arsenal of democracy. Along the San Francisco Bay Trail a few steps from my door is the Rosie the Riveter National Historical Park honoring the more than 90,000 wartime workers who transformed a small industrial swamp town into a bustling multiracial boomtown. With many white males drafted out of the workforce, women workers along with African American and Hispanic men and women were finally allowed to seek jobs in shipyards and defense factories. Their hard-hat labor helped save democracy while also advancing the nation's slow march toward equal rights. An original Victory ship, the *Red Oak Victory*, is still docked across the channel by the Port of Richmond, where car ships from Japan now offload.

World War Two cargo vessels like the *Red Oak Victory* are dwarfed by today's massive container ships. "Ships are so large now that you don't need an oil tanker for a major spill. Fuel can be a major spill," Admiral Craig Bone, former commander of the Coast Guard's Eleventh District (which includes California), told me. That morning, a Chinese-owned 902-foot container ship, the *Cosco Busan*, hit the base of the Bay Bridge in heavy fog, spilling more than fifty-three thousand gallons of toxic bunker fuel. This was on November 7, 2007, five months after I moved to Richmond.

In the wake of this disaster, I'm sitting on the dock of the bay—that's what Otis Redding called the Berkeley Municipal Pier in his famous song. On the rock pile below me, a surf sco-ter—a diving duck—is using the bottom of its red bill to preen its oil-blackened feathers. It shakes its head and carefully repeats the process for the half hour I'm there waiting for an animal rescue unit that never arrives. When I make too sudden a move, it flaps its wings like it's going to flee into the water, where it would likely die of hypothermia, its natural insulation ruined by the oil. I'll see dozens more oiled birds this day: scoters, grebes, gulls, a ruddy duck, and cormorants.

The marina is now covered by an oily sheen. "Rainbows of oil" is a misnomer. Gasoline leaves rainbow sheens. Bunker fuel, the dregs of the petroleum process, leaves green-and-brown streaks and smudges like marbled meat gone bad. It leaves float-ing tar balls and disks and globular curlicue pieces, and concen-trations of hard, asphalt-like toxic chips.

Even though a third of San Francisco Bay has been filled in

over time, it remains one of the nation's great urban estuaries, a vast shallow body of water with a broad delta to the north, where the fresh water of the Sacramento River meets the salty tidal surge from the Golden Gate's narrow opening halfway down the bay. This makes it a natural nursery for crab and fish, including spawning herring that in turn draw vast numbers of seabirds and fishing boats to its muddy fringes, along with seals and sea lions. In addition to its natural abundance, the bay is also a maritime ballet of commercial shipping, ferries, tankers, sailboats, kayakers, and kiteboarders.

The bunker fuel spreads out through the Golden Gate to San Francisco's Ocean Beach and north to Point Reyes National Seashore. In the bay, Angel Island and Alcatraz are hit. At the Marin Headlands, orange plastic fencing and oil-spill warning signs block access to the wide, cliff-framed strand at Rodeo Beach, where we held Nancy's memorial service and where workers in yellow hazmat suits are now removing oil-stained boulders and scraping away contaminated sand. This was her favorite local beach, and I feel deeply offended at its desecration.

A western grebe lies exhausted on a rock in my marina. Stained black, it has red eyes that seem to burn at me with anger and reproach. I know that's anthropomorphic thinking. As humans, we understand that we're killing them, whereas they have no idea what's killing them. I walk over to Shimada Friendship Park. There's a couple, early twenties, Amber Kirst and Scott Egan. She's walking the shoreline at dusk, her white pants oil-stained at the ankles, wearing a protective rubber glove and holding a bag full of oiled litter and dead crabs.

"We've got a live crab too. He was in a Cheetos bag," she tells me, climbing up the rocks to the pathway. "We drove down from Lodi to volunteer, but they said they'd get back to us. It's an hour-and-a-half drive. We needed to do something."

The Cheetos crab is still alive. She shows me the small critter, with its dark shell. "Should I put it back? Is it too oiled for them to feed on?" She looks at the hundreds of shorebirds hunting in the exposed mudflats and floating just beyond. "It's all so depressing," she concludes before climbing back down to pick up more oiled litter.

Amber and Scott came from Lodi. They needed to do something. We all do.

I visit the incident command center, where the spill is being tracked, and go out with the Coast Guard to do beach surveys around Sausalito and Richardson Bay, where I used to live. Luckily, the damage here isn't too bad, though we do run into some more oiled birds including a dead cormorant. Over twenty thousand will die in the coming days.

Nine days after the spill, with 1,500 people now involved in the ongoing cleanup, I fly to Bahrain to report on the U.S. Coast Guard in Iraq. I catch a Navy Seahawk helicopter headed north and join up with 110-foot Coast Guard cutters protecting Iraq's two big offshore oil terminals in the northern Persian Gulf. Along with chasing off ships that threaten to enter the security zone around the terminals, doing armed boardings of Iraqi fishing dhows, and patrolling a disputed maritime line between Iraq and Iran, we also do security boardings of supertankers before they fill up at the terminals.

One of the tankers, the red and green *BW Noto*, weighs 286,000 tons, is 1,100 feet long, and, when fully loaded, can carry two million barrels of oil. That's two hundred million dollars' worth of product at the time of our boarding. Later that night Gordon Hood, the twenty-four-year-old executive officer of the cutter *Wrangell*, stands next to me on the darkened bridge.

"We're looking at the pain and war that surround oil, but still, when people say it's a war for oil, I don't think it's that simple," he reflects, "because most of these supertankers are not going from here to the States. They're going all over the world."

He's right—it's not that simple, although the armed protection of the global system of oil production, transport, and commerce had become the largely unquestioned reflex of U.S. foreign policy by the early twenty-first century. And this often undermines the principles of democracy young men and women like Gordon have pledged to defend. Also, much of this oil will in fact find its way to the United States.

In 2014, for example, the city of Richmond approved Chevron's permit application for a billion-dollar "modernization" of its refinery that will allow it to shift from "sweet," low-sulfur oil from Saudi Arabia and Alaska's North Slope to more polluting, high-sulfur petroleum from other countries including Iraq.

In June 2010, three years after the *Cosco Busan* spill, I'm flying in a small Cessna over the site of the BP blowout in the Gulf of Mexico. Below us one hundred dolphins and a humpback whale are trapped and dying in the oil that's spread from horizon to horizon. Nearby, half a dozen 1,500-foot-high columns of dark smoke rise from the surface where BP contract crews are trying to burn off some of the oil, while roaring flames shoot from one of the diversionary wells where eleven workers aboard the *Deepwater Horizon* rig were killed and dozens of ships are now positioned in the hazy smog. By the time I return in late July, on the day the wellhead is finally capped, the oil that's been released is four thousand times the amount spilled by the *Cosco Busan*.

I visit miles of fouled beaches from Louisiana to Florida; a bird-scrubbing facility, where hundreds of oiled pelicans are being cleaned; and the Atakapa Ishak Indian community of Grand Bayou near Burus, Louisiana, a small town that was kindling and rubble the last time I was there, in the wake of Hurricane Katrina. Buras wasn't much before Katrina, but it's much less now, with fewer residents, a hollowed-out strip mall where the town fire truck is parked inside the shell of a store, and no signs of recovery five years on unless you count the home-built flower boxes someone's attached to a rusting FEMA trailer. Only the heat and humidity remain unchanged.

The gravel road into Grand Bayou ends at a boat dock. The village is built along canals that wind out to Barataria Bay. There are no roads for cars, just boats to get around on. Twenty-three families used to live here, but since Katrina swept through there are nine left, though five more families are planning to return once new stilt homes are completed with help from the Mennonite Disaster Service.

We load nine people into a camouflage-painted flatboat, including Rosina Philippe, who's become an unofficial spokeswoman for the Ishak, and her brother Maurice, the boat handler. Maurice is a big, dark-skinned oysterman with a weather-beaten face, a salt-and-pepper mustache, and a camo cap with sunglasses resting on the brim. There is also Karen Phillips (different parts of the family spell their last name differently) and her grandson Brock, who's three. "His twin sister's with her mom and dad today, but we can't keep Brock away from the water," Karen explains. "He's going to be a future Bayou man."

We take off heading out the channel into the open bay. "We have seen changes in the environment here over time. We've lived here for time without number. We do not have a time in our memory of being anywhere else," Rosina tells me. She's a proud, broad-faced woman, though tired-seeming now, with a long black braid that she keeps in front of her where she can keep an eye on it.

"We're still subsistence people in the twenty-first century," she explains. "Everything we need—the animals, vegetables, medicinal plants, and herbs—we have here. But the situation with the oil and dispersants is having unknown effects on our waters."

We've crossed into open water now, and after twenty minutes Maurice slows the boat, steering us toward the edge of the marsh, where the bottom of the saw grass is stained black up to the high-tide mark, about two feet above the waterline.

"We still fish, shrimp, oyster, and trap—our men do this and we teach the little ones," Rosina says, gesturing at Brock, who's playing with the straps on his small blue life vest. "But if we can't teach shrimping to him in the next ten to twenty years—"

"It'll kill our culture," his grandmother interrupts. She's a big, light-skinned woman in a pink-and-white-striped shirt. She's been holding on to Brock as we've rocketed across the bay.

"This is Bay Batiste, and that's Bay Jimmy," Maurice points to what looks like an island where a government wildlife boat is cruising, its aluminum cabin topped by several carrier cages for oiled birds.

This stretch of the lower Mississippi wetlands has been shredded by years of oil-company canal building, making it easier for the newly released oil to get in. "When they built the canals, they became little bays, and when they build parallel canals, soon all the marsh in between becomes open water," Rosina explains.

"We're passing oyster reef. We have some seventy acres here, and I see nothing but lots of oil in grass. I see lots of death here—all the oysters gonna die!" Maurice worries.

I ask him how much he'd normally collect.

"Good day, we caught one hundred sacks by lunch. That would be six hours." Maurice was the first one to report the oil that surged into Barataria Bay in early June, and it has since become the epicenter of what's known as the Battle of Barataria, the ongoing struggle to clean and protect parts of these famously productive swamp waters west of Port Sulphur and the Mississippi River.

We push up against the blackened grasses so a C-SPAN crew riding with us can interview Rosina, but the wind is rising and dark clouds are closing in. Tarred oil boom is floating on the edge of the marsh with orange drops of oil dispersed inside and outside the snaky one-hundred-foot-long barricade.

"Oil came into this bay forty-six days after the disaster, and they didn't block it!" Rosina says bitterly. Later the Coast Guard captain in charge at the BP facility being used as the state incident command center (ICC) outside Houma will tell me the oil was so dispersed in so many separate slicks that it "infiltrated into the bay under the booms," though I have a hard time believing that.

As the waves begin lapping against our hull and the sky turns black with fat drops of rain starting to fall, we cut the interview short and run for shore. A couple of dolphins surface nearby, maybe curious to see what we're up to. Maurice jigs and jags the boat through grassy dogleg channels of a natural canal that hasn't been oiled yet, the black clouds falling off behind us, and with the freshening wind and thump of the boat, it feels good to be on the water again, even if I'm here to report on yet another apocalyptic scene of unnecessary waste and destruction.

We pull into the main channel at Grand Bayou and up to Rosina's small stilt house, where the C-SPAN crew sets up to try the interview again and a fat dachshund barks happily.

"He's a big-boned dog," I suggest.

"That's Maurice's dog. He loves that dog, but he overfeeds him." Rosina grins affectionately at her rough-hewn brother, who pretends not to hear as he ties up the boat.

Aaron, a staffer from the Gulf Restoration Network, a New

Orleans–based environmental group, reminds her that when they'd talked a year ago she was reluctant to criticize the oil companies.

"We were looking to restore our coasts collaboratively," she replies, "but this disaster shows that the oil industry doesn't care. This death in the Gulf of Mexico should not be the price of cheaper gas."

Then she starts to repeat her story about how the four-hundred-plus Atakapa Ishak were scattered after Katrina so that they're now living in Texas and Tennessee as well as southern Louisiana, and how they were starting to come back here to live together again where they have lived forever. But given their region's ongoing disasters, they may soon lose their homeland forever.

In 2014 I return to New Orleans for a conference of the Society of Environmental Journalists (SEJ). BP's vice president for communications and former Pentagon spokesman Geoff Morrell tells the gathered reporters how we've failed to cover the story of the great recovery and resiliency of the Gulf since 2010, how BP's cleanup efforts have left beaches "in better shape than they've been in years." With dead dolphins and tar balls still washing up on the coast, a BP spokesman talking about the resiliency of the Gulf strikes me as about as appropriate as a Vatican spokesman talking about the resiliency of abused children. The following day a federal judge will find BP "grossly negligent" in the *Deepwater Horizon* disaster.

Top coastal and climate scientists attending the SEJ conference, including several I've invited to participate, predict that within a few decades the coastal Indian and Cajun cultures of Louisiana will be gone along with the bayous that define them, victims of wetland loss and sea-level rise from oil-company operations and fossil fuel–fired climate change. South Florida and the Everglades are also slated to go the way of Louisiana's bayous, coastal Bangladesh, and the small island nations of the Pacific.

I'm depressed by the whole deal, not hopeful that we'll be able to cut our addiction to petroleum in time to save the ocean or much of human civilization that I also believe still has some value. The best I can do to comfort myself is recall a day I spent with the late New Jersey activist Dery Bennett, winner of Blue Frontier's 2004 Hero of the Seas Award, which later became the Peter Benchley Ocean Awards.

Bennett, an ex-navy man and journalist who died at age seventy-nine, stood six feet three, more gristle than fat, with skin like salted salmon leather, curly gray hair, and brown eyes that could turn from mournful to mirthful with the changing of the light. A longtime leader of the coastal conservation–oriented American Littoral Society, he was a mentor to many marine activists up and down the eastern seaboard.

The Highlands Historical Society asked Bennett to speak one evening I was visiting with him back in the year 2000. At the time, he was fighting federally funded beach replenishment and seawalls along the narrow strand of the north Jersey Shore, not a popular position with the local tourist industry or beachfront property owners, either before or after the lessons we were supposed to have learned from Hurricane Sandy.

"Wherever you build seawalls and other structures, the ocean curls around behind and begins to erode them," he explained. "If you want to make a beach disappear, build jetties and seawalls."

"But things are getting cleaner, aren't they?" someone in the audience asked.

"Some places yes, some no."

"So what's your feeling about the future?"

"If you're asking if I'm optimistic or pessimistic, I'd have to say it depends on what day you ask, or what time of day."

That was a perspective I could respect.

Back in 2007 I'd organized a Blue Frontier "Lessons Learned" meeting for fifty people who'd been involved in the *Cosco Busan* spill response, including port officials, International Longshore and Warehouse Union (ILWU) members, bird and wildlife rescuers, a fishermen's association, ocean activists from the Waterkeeper Alliance and the Surfrider Foundation, staff members from House Speaker (now Minority Leader) Nancy Pelosi's office and Senator Barbara Boxer's office, and others. We quickly coalesced around the need to pass a suite of conservation-oriented "spill bills" at the state and federal level.

Within the next year California passed seven new laws to speed oil-spill response and improve cleanup and volunteer support efforts. The feds are still working on theirs. It's worth also noting that the BP blowout of 2010 was the first major U.S. oil spill that led to no new laws or safety reforms being implemented by Congress.

Luckily, while my faith in Congress has been undermined by the dominance of political bribery (unlimited corporate campaign spending as endorsed by the conservative Supreme Court majority), I can find solace in places such as my home state of California. Working on my 2013 book, *The Golden Shore: California's Love Affair with the Sea*, helped restore my optimism. It's all about how the Pacific defines California's culture and how if we can support a healthy ocean ecosystem and coastal economy in the nation's most populous state (with thirty-eight million people), which is also the world's eighth-largest economy, we can do it anywhere.

California certainly has protected some of the most beautiful and healthy marine habitat in the world off its 1,100 miles of shoreline. And so here I am snorkeling through Fisherman's Cove on Catalina Island, the site of a small marine reserve, a little over twenty miles off the urban coast of Los Angeles. Under California's Marine Life Protection Act that came into effect in 2012, 16 percent of the state's waters are now protected as underwater parks, including this no-take reserve from the 1980s that's being expanded from half a square mile to three square miles. Its kelp forest is healthy and thick, swarming with large calico bass (a.k.a. kelp bass), orange Garibaldis, and shoaling baby fish. At one point I spot several five-foot bat rays flying through the water column. Closer to the beach, my buddies and I find rocky nooks and caves full of lobsters and rays hanging out on the sandy bottom. Under a pier I encounter a sizable school of white sea bass of about twenty pounds each, as indifferent to my presence as the big bull sea lion on the hunt that cruised past me earlier.

Along the cliffs on the far side of the pier the water is crystal clear, resembling the Caribbean but with kelp. Resting on the surface amid the giant brown algae, I can look up at the steep slopes covered in prickly pear cactus and Catalina live-forever plants—succulents native only to this island. Below the surface I free dive through open channels in the seaweed to play with apple-green opaleyes, caramel-spotted calico bass, and hefty orange Garibaldis. I spot suspicious antennae-waving lobsters and small bottom-cruising leopard sharks, and it feels good to be in wilderness again. I climb back onto our small rubber raft, cold, wet, salty, and grinning like a fool. At moments like this, enveloped by the wonder of the everlasting sea, it's hard, despite the best available science, not to be optimistic.

11

Blue Is the New Green

The cure for anything is salt water—sweat, tears or the sea.

ISAK DINESEN

If today we are loving our ocean to death through ignorance and short-term greed, we can stop doing that. The hope of any new frontier is that we do not have to repeat the mistakes of our past.

Of course, the ocean itself is monumentally indifferent to all our human hopes, plans, dreams, and desires.

During a big California storm surge more than a decade ago a honeymooning couple went to Lovers Point in Pacific Grove, near Monterey. The sea was as wild as their passion that day. Jennifer Stookesberry, twenty-three years old, stood with her back to the raging surf, posing for her new husband, twenty-eight-year-old Eamon Stookesberry. Suddenly, a huge sleeper wave broke, dragging her backward into the sea. Eamon dove off the cliff after her and grabbed for her hand, but the sea pulled her away. He called to her to stay afloat, not to panic as the currents took her farther out. "She got really far away and I heard her scream for help. Then there were two big waves and that was the last time I saw her." The Coast Guard rescued Eamon and pulled Jennifer out of the surf. Her eyes were open but dark. They were unable to revive her. He held her hand again at the hospital, in a special way they had, to show off their matching rings, and quietly said his good-bye. A day later he met with reporters. "If you people have anybody special, don't sweat the small stuff, make it work," he told them. "You get one chance. She was that one for me. She was my angel, my kitten."

"I really don't know why it is that all of us are so committed to the sea, except I think . . . it's because we all came from the sea," said John F. Kennedy at the 1962 America's Cup races. He was a sailor and former navy man who had survived war and his PT boat's ramming and sinking at sea, only to be felled by an assassin's bullet. His son, John Jr., died in a plane crash at sea and was buried at sea with his wife and sister-in-law. His nephew, my colleague Robert Kennedy Jr., is an environmental attorney and president of the Waterkeeper Alliance, an organization made up of hundreds of boat-based antipollution activists protecting rivers, bays, estuaries, and ocean basins, from coastal Georgia to Cook Inlet, Alaska, and beyond. Actor Ted Danson is another longtime ocean activist who founded the group American Oceans, which eventually merged with the international activist group Oceana. Singer Jimmy Buffett helped found the Save the Manatee Club in Florida, and Hawaii-based singer Jack Johnson does benefits for Surfrider and other ocean-protection groups. Australian folk singer Paul Kelly has a moving number called "Deeper Waters," about lives linked to the sea, and another, titled "From Little Things Big Things Grow," about an Aborigine who took a stand. From the little things divers, sailors, surfers, scientists, fishermen, youth activists, and artists do every day to protect our seas a new blue movement is emerging, one whose mission is nothing less than the restoration and stewardship of the greater part of our salty blue planet.

As I write this I've just returned from a quick, chilling dip in the ocean at the strand at Stinson Beach, close to where it hits the lagoon channel separating Stinson from Bolinas. Lots of harbor seals like to haul up inside the lagoon. California Academy of Sciences white shark expert Dr. John McCosker does not recommend this beach as a good place for hitting the waves. "If you want to get bitten, surf Bolinas around Labor Day," he cautions. "I won't guarantee you'll be bitten, but it's your best chance." My response: If there's not something bigger and meaner than you out there, it's not really wilderness.

While I'm on an adrenaline high, the ocean is on a bad acid trip. It's been scraped raw, emptied out, overheated, poisoned, and abused, not a good time to be ingesting dangerous chemicals. Normally carbon dioxide isn't considered a dangerous chemical compound to the sea or to us, but rather a natural part of the chemistry of life. At 225 parts per million in the atmosphere, this greenhouse gas, along with methane and water vapor, has created an exceptionally stable and temperate climate over the past ten thousand years—a period that has also seen, not coincidentally, the rise of modern civilization. But since the Industrial Revolution over 150 years ago, humans have been adding carbon dioxide to the atmosphere through the burning of fossil fuels like coal, oil, and natural gas, along with the burning and logging of forests, also adding to the carbon load. Today carbon dioxide has grown from a pre-industrial 225 to 397 parts per million in the atmosphere, and it's still climbing at .5 percent a year, a rate of change one hundred times faster than at any time over the past 650,000 years. A predicted doubling of pre-industrial carbon dioxide, as almost every reputable climate scientist warns, will have catastrophic consequences for the present mix of life on the planet. Some (inspired by author/activist Bill McKibben) are advocating a concerted campaign to actually try to roll back atmospheric carbon dioxide to 350 parts per million, though that would require the kind of technological and economic innovation and societal mobilization that hasn't been seen since World War Two. Unfortunately, we're still treating the climate crisis like the invasion of Grenada.

At the turn of the twenty-first century climatologists were having problems with their computer models even in the wake of the hottest years and decades in recorded history. Given the increased emissions of industrial carbon dioxide, it appeared the atmosphere should be heating up even more rapidly than it was. Then, around 2003 and 2004, testing confirmed that about 30 percent of human-generated carbon dioxide was being absorbed by the ocean—computer glitch solved.

The only problem is, when carbon dioxide dissolves in seawater, it forms carbonic acid, increasing the acidity of seawater and decreasing the ability of shell-forming critters—including various forms of algae, plankton, corals, oysters, clams, sea urchins, and sea stars—to pull calcium carbonate out of the water to build their homes and skeletal structures. If I've mentioned this before, it's worth repeating. Some have called this the osteoporosis of the sea. Since cold water can also hold more carbon dioxide than tropical seas can, the consequences are becoming more evident in the polar regions, where migratory gray whales spend their summers furrowing the muddy bottom of the Arctic sea, feeding on tiny shelled marine arthropods while walruses feast on nearby clam beds. Reduced calcium carbonate will likely mean less whale and walrus chow, just as melting ice means less habitat for polar bears and ringed seals. At the same time, warmer, more acidic waters hold less dissolved oxygen— bad news for fish and other wildlife in much of the global ocean.

So little is known about what's going on with ocean acidification (and research funding is still so limited) that some scientists are speculating the ocean is now supersaturated with carbon and can't absorb much more, and atmospheric heating will soon accelerate. Others believe the opposite, that acidification will continue along with ocean warming, so that by the end of the century it will look more like it did millions of years ago—an ocean full of jellies and bacterial mats with fewer bony fish, shellfish, corals, and mammals. This is what one of the world's top coral reef scientists, my friend Dr. Jeremy Jackson, calls, "the rise of the slime."

And if you're thinking this is a problem we'll have to confront in the future, consider the plight of Washington state's $270 million shellfish industry and aquaculture companies like Taylor Shellfish whose oysters are already being impacted, with their larval survival declining since 2006 as a direct result of more-acidic waters. These economic impacts inspired the governor to appoint a blue-ribbon panel to find ways to limit the effects of acidification and also to call for dramatic cuts in greenhouse gas emissions at the regional, national, and global levels. The *Seattle Times* published an award-winning, globe-spanning series on ocean acidification in 2013 titled "Sea Change"—not bad for a daily newspaper that by definition is itself an endangered species.

Still, with all these types of cascading disasters threatening the survival of our living seas, it's easy to understand why some people have just given up.

One time I asked the ranger in charge of the Crocodile Lake National Wildlife Refuge in the Florida Keys if he was involved with any ocean protection groups. "No," he said, unsmiling, "but when people ask me what environmental group they should join I say, 'Planned Parenthood.'"

While I admire that kind of bold misanthropic sentiment—and the genuine need to address human population growth—I also recognize we can't save the crocs or the sharks or the corals without also saving ourselves. People, as an expression of evolutionary nature made self-conscious, are both the problem and the solution. Twice in the twentieth century we muddled through what could have been civilization-ending problems, including the rise of Fascism that led to World War Two and the nuclear balance of terror that ended with the fall of the Soviet Union.

At a more modest scale, forty years after police attacked ten thousand of us in Chicago's Grant Park for protesting the Vietnam War, over 200,000 people jammed Grant Park to celebrate the election of Barack Obama, America's first African American president and heir to generations of civil-rights and social protests that expanded and continue to expand our freedoms. With Blue Frontier we're working to turn thousands of diverse ocean activists and ocean users into a broad-based social movement able to turn the tide of public opinion and make protection of our public seas a public policy issue that people understand is worth caring about.

In 2004, 2009, 2011, 2013, and 2015 we organized Blue Vision Summits in Washington, D.C., and launched our annual Peter Benchley Ocean Awards to acknowledge solution-oriented leaders and innovators across a broad swath of society, including science, policy, national stewardship, media, exploration, youth, and grassroots activism. We named the awards for Peter Benchley, who keynoted our 2004 summit, in part because, while many people know him as the author of *Jaws*, few know he also dedicated his life to the protection of sharks and their ocean habitat. So in 2009 I got Wendy Benchley's agreement to relaunch our summit awards in honor of her late husband and conservation and dive adventure partner. Since then we've named over fifty Benchley winners, including the heads of four nations (Costa Rica, Senegal, Kiribati, and Monaco) and three U.S. senators.

In the spring of 2009, a time of great hope and huge challenges, Blue Frontier organized our second four-day Blue Vision Summit in D.C., around the theme "Blue Is the New Green." Despite an economy diving faster than a startled seal, over four hundred blue leaders from around the nation and the world showed up to make their presence felt. They represented organizations ranging in size from a two-diver outfit working on removing abandoned fishing gear off the sea bottom in California to the National Geographic Society, New England Aquarium, and Google.

In 2011 we returned and took our vision to Capitol Hill while also celebrating artists and writers and others who connect us to the everlasting sea, such as "Her Deepness" Dr. Sylvia Earle, Philippe and Celine Cousteau, Thomas Lovejoy, the marine artist Wyland, *Sherman's Lagoon* cartoonist Jim Toomey, NBC's Anne Thompson, NPR's Richard Harris, Dr. Roger Payne, who put out the first whale song recordings, and authors Bill McKibben, Carl Safina, Juliet Eilperin, and yours truly. Ocean explorers in attendance included Don Walsh, one of the first two humans to venture to the bottom of the sea, and Blue Frontier's Roz Savage. Savage, a small, photogenic blonde with an iron will, rowed solo across the Atlantic in 2006. I met her months later through New Jersey's Margo Pellegrino, an activist mother of two small children who, inspired by *50 Ways to Save the Ocean*, had paddled a small outrigger canoe from Miami to Maine in 2007. In 2009 she paddled from Florida to New Orleans to raise awareness of coastal pollution in the Gulf of Mexico, and in 2010 she paddled from Seattle to San Diego for Blue Frontier before becoming our outreach coordinator. She said she did it for her family.

Savage, by contrast, had left her husband and job as a financial consultant in London in her midthirties after writing two obituaries for herself, the one she'd like and the one she'd have if she remained doing what she was doing. With that, she decided to carve out a more significant role and purpose in the world. She hoped through her example to inspire other people to act in ways that make a difference, "one stroke at a time." Now, she told me, she wanted to row solo across the Pacific in a twenty-three-foot rowboat to raise awareness of ocean issues and needed a nonprofit sponsor. After doing due diligence and assuring myself she knew what she was doing and had a good navigation and

safety plan, we agreed to bring her under our nonprofit wing
(fin?). We then organized a launch party for her three-part
trans-Pacific journey. Some eighty friends and a Hawaiian band
came out to wish her bon voyage in late summer 2007.

Unfortunately, when she finally got offshore she was hit by a
storm that capsized her rowboat three times and tore away her
sea anchor. My environmental project (Roz) was then rescued
by my book project, the U.S. Coast Guard (the subject of *Rescue
Warriors*), which sent out a Dolphin helicopter and rescue swimmer. After getting pulled from the water and flown ashore, she
went back out with a salvage vessel to retrieve her boat. After
she refitted it, I watched her discreetly relaunch on a midnight
tide under the Golden Gate Bridge in May 2008, and got to greet
her with a video crew and flower lei ninety-nine days later in
the waters off Honolulu.

At age forty, she'd become the first woman to row solo from
California to the Hawaiian Islands. In May 2009 she rowed from
Hawaii to the South Pacific island of Tarawa in 105 days and
then on to Papua New Guinea in 48 days. In 2011 Savage rowed
from Australia to Mauritius in 154 days, becoming the first
woman and first Brit to row the Atlantic, Pacific, and Indian
Oceans solo.

Pellegrino's next plan is to paddle from New York to New
Orleans via the Hudson River, Great Lakes, and Mississippi River
with daily stops to link up river, watershed, and coastal activists
into a more effective blue movement and seaweed rebellion.

Back home in Richmond I encountered my own seaweed
rebels, a small group of volunteers named Citizens for a Sustainable Point Molate (CFSPM). We quickly agreed to make CFSPM
a project of Blue Frontier. A friend had called Point Molate "the

most beautiful part of San Francisco Bay nobody's ever heard of." Indeed, I'd been living in Richmond for several years before a grasslands botanist took me to see it. This 422-acre headland is an example of the resiliency of nature left largely unpaved, its range managed by ospreys, owls, wild turkeys, and mule deer and including fifty acres of offshore eel grass beds, a perfect habitat for juvenile fish and hangout for harbor seals. It supports hilly native grasslands and giant Christmas berry shrubs the size of live oaks, as well as actual live oaks and eucalyptus trees. Once a historic wine port with a brick castle, it later served as a navy fuel depot till it was decommissioned in 1995. In 2003 the navy sold it to the city for one dollar. After that it was slated to become a gambling casino and resort complex, the largest west of Las Vegas. Unlike the Presidio park in San Francisco or Fort Baker in Marin just across the bay, this natural waterfront gem had been targeted because of its location in a poor community of color where the developer thought he could take ownership with promises of service jobs as maids and security guards and favors to city council members. But CFSPM, in alliance with Richmond's Green Party Mayor Gayle McLaughlin and her supporters from the Richmond Progressive Alliance, waged a successful campaign that forced the city council to take the issue to a referendum.

2010's Measure U was heavily fought over, with close to a million dollars spent, both by the developer and local card rooms that didn't want competition from a monster casino complex with four thousand slot machines. Given the choice, city residents voted 58 percent to 42 percent against the casino, most citing fear of increased traffic, crime, and gambling addiction. The three city council candidates supported by the casino developer (and also by Chevron) lost their election bids. Despite being out-spent almost two to one the mayor was reelected, as were two other progressive candidates opposed to the casino. A short time later, the council voted five to two to cancel the casino plan and reclaim Point Molate as public parkland. The developer then sued the city unsuccessfully, apparently being unclear on the concept that when you gamble, you usually lose.

In the spring of 2014, after years of cleanup and restoration work, partly funded by the *Cosco Busan* oil spill compensation fund, we reopened the quarter-mile crescent beach at Point Molate for the first time in a decade. I helped Mayor McLaughlin cut the ribbon as a Latin jazz band played by the water and dozens of citizens picnicked on the beach park's grassy bluff. While this was a historic moment for our city and its waterfront, for the kids playing along the shore it probably felt like just another day at the beach, even if for some it was their first day at a beach. A few weeks later Blue Frontier, with a small grant from a Berkeley café, brought a busload of biology students from Richmond's under-served JFK High School to Point Molate for their first field trip of the year. Getting off the bus, the girls were thrilled by the geese and fluffy goslings we saw, and later some of the boys got excited when they found a dead bird on the beach. Lech Naumovich, the grasslands botanist, hiked the students over the hills in the rain, and we showed them osprey nests through viewing scopes. By the end of the day they were planning their senior class sunset at Point Molate. And that's how we recruit new seaweed rebels.

"Our oceans face an unprecedented set of challenges from climate change, pollution, energy extraction, and more," warned seaweed rebel and U.S. Senator Sheldon Whitehouse (D-RI), the opening speaker at our fourth Blue Vision Summit in May of 2013. Married to a marine biologist who's helped stoke and inform his love of the ocean, Whitehouse went on to argue that we have the power to move from "takers to caretakers of the sea." That power was on display as hundreds of activists from twenty-one states went up on Capitol Hill to advocate for a healthy ocean during constituent meetings with their elected representatives and staff members, including direct meetings with seven senators and sixteen House members. In our meetings on the Senate side of the Hill we advocated for ratification of four international treaties targeting illegal, underreported, and unregulated (IUU) pirate fishing. Months later the Senate unanimously ratified the treaties. I wasn't sure whether to celebrate the idea that the ocean could be the last bipartisan issue or wonder if the bar has gotten so low that we feel compelled to cheer when Republicans and Democrats can agree to oppose pirates.

The fourth Blue Vision Summit opened on a Monday evening with a Celebration of the Sea in the historic Carnegie Institution, whose marble rotunda was decorated with hanging plants that resembled a kelp forest. Four hundred revelers wandered among tables full of food and spirits, admiring stunning underwater photographs.

Tuesday's keynote by Senator Whitehouse was followed by Vice Admiral Peter Neffenger of the Coast Guard, who spoke of living in a "wet world without state and coastal boundaries," and how his service now has to deal with a "new ocean" in the Arctic where melting ice from climate change is opening up blue-water trade routes and a rush for oil, minerals, fish, and other resources. Twenty-five-year-old research submersible pilot

Erika Bergman spoke of the challenges and thrills of getting it right in our old, but still largely unexplored, oceans. She talked about how she went from being a *Star Trek* fan to a young scientist diving one thousand feet below the surface of our own alien world. She described visualizing science in the "opalescent shades of sea color above" and how she's teaching young people that "science rules," both with podcasts from inside her sub and by getting them down to the shore and into the sea themselves.

Tuesday was as jam-packed as a school of sardines, with great panels and workshops such as "Disaster & Restoration" (lessons learned from BP and Sandy), "Climate as a Blue Issue," "Youth Leadership for a Blue Movement," and "Thinking Story Like a Journalist." A few highlights included an NOAA official pointing out that climate-linked, billion-dollar-plus extreme-weather disasters are on the increase, with twenty-five having occurred just in the United States between 2011 and 2012; a leader of the shipping industry surprisingly suggesting that if corporate leaders faced jail time instead of fines, there'd be fewer preventable disasters like the 2010 BP blowout; and Mike Tidwell of the Chesapeake Climate Action Network stressing the need to "build big coalitions and never, ever give up." He used as an example the coalition his group helped forge to pass the Maryland Offshore Wind Act, which should get that state's offshore wind power production up and running in the next few years. Gordon King of Taylor Shellfish, whose oysters, as stated earlier, are already being impacted by acidification, expressed his personal doubt that we'll act in time to restore the ocean to health.

There was no doubt on the youth leadership panel, however, that new ways of thinking and finding solutions can and will be realized. Organized by 2013's Benchley Youth Award winner

Sean Russell, founder of "Stow It—Don't Throw It," this panel included representatives from Teens4Oceans, 5 Gyres, EarthEcho International, Youth Service America, and the New York Harbor School with its Billion Oyster Project to restore New York Harbor. "Youth are not our leaders of the future," one panelist noted, "but today's change makers that adults need to partner with."

"Be yourself and don't be afraid to let your passion for the sea show. This is the biggest ocean Hill Day ever, and it's creating a buzz that will keep getting around," Dave Wilmot of Ocean Champions, a political action committee for ocean conservation, noted the following morning as our troops gathered at 8 A.M. in the Dirksen Senate Office Building for a long day of "walking the marble." Among the largest state delegations were thirty-four watermen and -women from California and twenty from the Boulder-based Colorado Ocean Coalition (organized by Blue Frontier board member Vicki Nichols-Goldstein), who understand that every state is a coastal state, even five thousand feet above sea level. Senator Brian Schatz of Hawaii greeted us and recalled the beginning of his calling as an ocean advocate when he couldn't go bodysurfing at Sandy Beach on Oahu at age sixteen because the water was polluted and the beach had been closed. Others who greeted us included Representatives Jared Huffman and Lois Capps of California, Chellie Pingree of Maine, and Kathy Castor of Florida. We spent the rest of the day hiking the labyrinthine hallways, basements, offices, cafeterias, and trolleys of the Capitol complex. In seemingly countless meetings (actually we counted just over one hundred) people advocated for a commonsense National Ocean Policy that the president had signed off on, thanked those senators who voted for Senator Whitehouse's National Endowment for the Ocean (to fund research and coastal restoration), and promoted a safe seafood bill as well as the treaties to counter pirate fishing.

That evening was elegant and inspiring as the Peter Benchley Ocean Awards got under way back at the Carnegie Institution. Sylvia Earle was master of ceremonies as both presenters and award recipients spoke passionately of their work to restore and protect our ocean planet. The National Stewardship winner was President Macky Sall of Senegal who, after leading the opposition to victory in a contentious but ultimately democratic election in 2012, canceled the licenses of twenty-nine foreign fishing vessels operating in his nation's waters. This resulted in dramatically increased catches for local fishermen and their families. After receiving our award, which was widely reported on in West Africa, he resisted pressure from the EU and others to reopen his waters to foreign fishing fleets and instead began working with Greenpeace to develop a sustainable domestic-fisheries program for his people.

Representative (now Senator) Ed Markey of Massachusetts was delayed and so received his Policy Award from the former winner Senator Whitehouse at the dinner party after the official ceremony; Whitehouse wryly commented about "typical House disorganization."

"You gave this award to the Ocean State [Rhode Island] last year and the Bay State [Massachusetts] this year," Markey joked, "so I see a trend. But if you want to give it to someone from the Pelican State of Louisiana next year, you'll have to change the criteria." (In fact, the 2014 policy award would go to former Pew Ocean Commission Chair and Secretary of Defense Leon Panetta.) Senator Markey, like Senators Whitehouse and Schatz, has become a fierce proponent for ocean and climate action; as a

Congressman he forced BP to release the real-time video feed of its deepwater oil gusher in 2010. So now we have three out of one hundred senators with a deep understanding of our oceans, coasts, and the communities that depend on them. It's a start.

Thursday morning Sean Cosgrove of the Conservation Law Foundation led a series of reports from our state delegations who'd been on the Hill, and most talked about how empowered they felt speaking truth to power and realizing they could have an influence. Some of their comments were telling:

"This is my first trip to D.C. since eighth grade, and we met seven people yesterday and I got to speak with my congressman."

"This is my first time doing this and I'd like to do it again."

"I talked to my representative but I don't think I convinced him, so we'll get him at home with our students, who are very active."

"I was with the California delegation, so it was sort of a love fest for us."

"I hate you Californians. I had to deal with my politicians from Alabama."

The summit's final speaker was 2009 Policy Award winner Representative Sam Farr (D-CA), a good friend of Blue Frontier, who's told me that, "In California you can get elected or lose your job depending on your positions on coastal protection and offshore oil. We have to be able to spread that around." On this occasion his message was one of encouragement: "The politics of the ocean is still fresh," he said, "and the blue revolution is still young and growing."

In 2014 Blue Frontier began organizing an "Over the Horizon" coalition of blue groups to expand our youth outreach and make sure that our public seas are a public policy issue in the 2016 presidential elections and beyond.

While nothing is ever assured in politics, I'm hopeful things may finally be flowing in favor of the ocean, with growing public awareness and better stewardship practices emerging from California to Rhode Island, Palau to Portugal, and from sea to shining sea.

Not only from sea to shining sea, of course, but also from tide to turning tide. Our planetary ocean bulges on two opposite points of the globe every moment of every day, drawing the tides behind it—one point is where the sea is closest to the moon's gravitational pull and the other is on the opposite side of the planet, where, free from the pull of the moon, it rises up, trying to escape into the vacuum of space, restrained only by Earth's gravitational field and centrifugal spin.

A few billion years ago, when the moon was closer to Earth, its tides ripped minerals from the land, turning the primordial seas into a chemical cooking pot that led to the emergence of life on earth. When the tides and continents met they also created friction that slowed the spin of the planet and lengthened the days of our lives. Now that the moon has retreated and the waters have slowed, it's hard to imagine what our early seas might have been like except in a few special places.

One night a group of us landed at the dock in St. Andrews, Canada, at 10 P.M., having sailed across the Bay of Fundy from Maine. The next morning at 8 A.M. we had to climb twenty feet down the now steeply angled dock ladder where the tide had dropped out from under our small ferryboat. Sailing back to Maine, we saw harbor porpoises feeding near big whirlpools in the bay's tidal bore, where billions of tons of water rush in and out every twenty-four hours. Talk about sea power (and potential clean energy)!

At the Columbia River Bar between Oregon and Washington I've motored across a six-knot current where the quarter-million-square-mile watershed of the river discharges a quarter million cubic feet of water per second, depositing thousands of tons of sediment and rock that, encountering the Pacific's fetch, creates massive waves that have given its tumultuous offshore waters the justified moniker "graveyard of the Pacific." Two thousand ships have foundered and gone down here over the last two centuries.

In the Southern Ocean, below the Roaring Forties and Furious Fifties but north of the Antarctic convergence, I spent several days the same gray-green color as the thirty-foot seas that broke over the bow and rolled across the deck of our research vessel like Neptune's angry fists. Forty- to fifty-foot seas, with the occasional seventy-foot rogue wave, are not considered that unusual at the bottom of the world ocean.

More recently I flew from California to Washington to ride on one of the Coast Guard's big icebreakers heading north. As I looked down at the snowcapped northern California mountain ranges, I was reminded of great white-capped ocean waves. Actually, they're not unlike waves in geological terms, bridging up across the landscape, surfing the magma where the Pacific and North American tectonic plates collide and subside beneath them. Mountains are the rippling breakers of the planet, though functioning in a time frame that makes our species seem as transitory as mayflies or molecules. Only evolutionarily hardened species of marine life such as horseshoe crabs and nautiluses have been around long enough to see mountain ranges rise up and erode away again.

While there's a sense of solidity in the mountains, the ocean is in a constant flux from winds, tides, and currents, upwellings and mixings both chemical and biological, both sensuous and predatory. It's the oxygen pump that never quits, the maker of atmosphere, rain, and fog and the buffer of chemical balances, the paddle wheel of circulating vapors that is the bouillabaisse and the crucible of life, both the soup and the pot it comes in. Some people love the mountains and some people love the sea. Some like the steady companionship of dogs and some the mercurial nature of cats.

Because these are domesticated animal species (except for the cats that choose us), they will likely survive this way-too-crowded nanosecond of planetary evolution we've created, along with our meat animals and camp followers (roaches, rats, and raccoons). But can the world's last wild creatures and places—can the reefs, sea dragons, ringed seals, and mangroves—also survive us?

I was not born for peaceful times or calm waters, nor have I seen many. We're living in the age of global markets and mass extinctions; the birth of celebrity Web sites, YouTube, and Twitter; and the death of sharks, sea turtles, and others of our planetary brethren who were already ancient when the first small mammals left their dirt-filled burrows.

While I've gone from radical activist to war reporter, private investigator, TV producer, author, and activist again, I do so with a more sober assessment than when I was young, running wild in the streets chanting "Power to the People!"—a slogan recently appropriated for a battery-powered Oral-B toothbrush ad.

Today I don't really expect a revolution in either politics or consciousness to radically alter the cascading ecological collapse of our ocean planet. I do, however, note a rising line of ecological mindfulness approaching the declining plane of biological diversity on our water world. Where that X crosses will tell us how much is left to save and restore if we can.

I'm not sure it will be enough to turn the tide. All I know for certain is that if we don't try, we lose. And this salty blue world of ours is too heart-achingly beautiful, scary, and sacred to lose. If you don't believe me, join the space program, travel out into the cosmos, and look back from the heavens. It's not God's green earth—it's God's blue marble.

Recommended Additional Reading

Benchley, Peter. *The Girl of the Sea of Cortez*. New York: Berkley, 1983.

Biel, Steven. *Down with the Old Canoe*. New York. W. W. Norton, 1996.

Brinkley, Douglas. *The Great Deluge*. New York: William Morrow, 2006.

Broad, William J. *The Universe Below*. New York: Simon & Schuster, 1997.

Callahan, Steven. *Adrift*. New York: Mariner Books, 2002.

Carson, Rachel L. *The Sea Around Us*. New York: Oxford University Press, 1951.

Casey, Susan. *The Devil's Teeth*. New York: Henry Holt, 2005.

Clarke, Arthur C. *The Deep Range*. New York: Harcourt, Brace, 1957.

Clover, Charles. *The End of the Line*. Berkeley: University of California Press, 2008.

Coleman, Stuart Holmes. *Eddie Would Go*. New York: St. Martin's Press, 2004.

Conrad, Joseph. *Lord Jim*. New York: Penguin Classics, 1998 (originally published in 1900).

Cordingly, David. *Under the Black Flag*. New York: Random House, 2006.

Cousteau, Jacques-Yves. *The Silent World*. New York: Harper, 1953.

Cramer, Deborah. *Smithsonian Ocean*. New York: Smithsonian Books, 2008.

Cronin, John, and Robert F. Kennedy Jr. *The Riverkeepers*. New York: Scribner, 1997.

Cuyvers, Luc. *Sea Power*. Annapolis: Naval Institute Press, 1993.

Dana, Richard Henry Jr. *Two Years Before the Mast*. New York: Barnes & Noble Classics, 2006 (originally published in 1840).

Davidson, Osha Gray. *Fire in the Turtle House*. New York: Public Affairs, 2001.

Dean, Cornelia. *Against the Tide*. New York: Columbia University Press, 1999.

Dennis, Jerry. *The Living Great Lakes*. New York: Thomas Dunne Books, 2003.

Diamond, Jared. *Collapse*. New York: Viking, 2005.

Dolin, Eric Jay. *Leviathan: The History of Whaling in America*. New York: W. W. Norton, 2008.

Doubilet, David. *Light in the Sea*. Charlottesville, Virginia: Thomasson-Grant, 1989.

Duane, Daniel. *Caught Inside: A Surfer's Year on the California Coast*. New York: North Point Press, 1996.

Earle, Sylvia A. *Sea Change*. New York: G. P. Putnam's Sons, 1995.

Ecott, Tim. *Neutral Buoyancy*. New York: Grove Press, 2001.

Ellis, Richard. *The Empty Ocean*. Washington D.C.: Island Press, 2003.

Franklin, H. Bruce. *The Most Important Fish in the Sea*. Washington, D.C.: Island Press, 2007.

Fujita, Rod. 2006. *Heal the Ocean*. Gabriola Island, BC: New Society, 2003.

Harrigan, Stephen. *Water and Light*. San Francisco: Sierra Club Books, 1992.

Helvarg, David. *Blue Frontier: Dispatches from America's Ocean Wilderness*. San Francisco: Sierra Club Books, 2006.

Hemingway, Ernest. *The Old Man and the Sea*. New York: Scribner, 1995 (originally published in 1952).

Hersey, John. *Blues*. New York: Vintage Books, 1988.

Hiaasen, Carl. *Stormy Weather*. New York: Alfred A. Knopf, 1995.

Higgins, Jack. *Thunder Point*. New York: Berkley, 1994.

Horwitz, Tony. *Blue Latitudes*. New York: Picador, 2003.

Junger, Sebastian. *The Perfect Storm*. New York: W. W. Norton, 1997.

Kipling, Rudyard. *Captains Courageous*. West Berlin, New Jersey: Townsend Press, 2007 (originally published in 1896).

Knecht, G. Bruce. *Hooked*. Emmaus, Pennsylvania: Rodale Books, 2007.

Kunzig, Robert. *The Restless Sea*. New York: W. W. Norton, 1999.

Kurlansky, Mark. *Cod*. New York: Penguin, 1997.

Kurson, Robert. *Shadow Divers*. New York: Ballantine Books, 2005.

Labaree, Benjamin W., et al. *America and the Sea*. Mystic, Connecticut: Mystic Seaport, 1998.

Lancek, Lena, and Gideon Bosker. *The Beach: The History of Paradise on Earth*. New York: Viking, 1998.

Langewiesche, William, *The Outlaw Sea*. New York: North Point Press, 2004.

Larson, Erik. *Isaac's Storm*. New York: Crown, 1999.

Lewan, Todd. *The Last Run*. New York: HarperCollins, 2004.

Lilly, John C. *Man and Dolphin*. New York: Doubleday, 1961.

London, Jack. *Tales of the Fish Patrol*. London: Macmillan, 1905.

Mathiessen, Peter. *Shadow Country*. New York: Modern Library, 2008.

McCullough, David. *The Path Between the Seas*. New York: Simon & Schuster, 1977.

McPhee, John. *Looking for a Ship*. New York: Farrar, Straus and Giroux, 1990.

Merle, Robert. *The Day of the Dolphin*. New York: Fawcett, 1977.

Melville, Herman. *Moby-Dick, or The Whale*. New York: Penguin Classics, 1992 (originally published in 1851).

Motavalli, Jim, ed. *Feeling the Heat*. New York: Routledge, 2004.

Mowat, Farley. *Sea of Slaughter*. Mechanicsburg, Pennsylvania: Stackpole Books, 2004 (originally published in 1984).

Nunn, Kem. *The Dogs of Winter*. New York: Scribner, 1997.

Philbrick, Nathaniel. *In the Heart of the Sea*. New York. Penguin, 2001.

Ricketts, Edward, Jack Calvin, and Joel W. Hedgpeth. Revised by David W. Phillips. *Between Pacific Tides*. Stanford, California: Stanford University Press, 1985 (fifth edition).

Roberts, Callum. *The Unnatural History of the Sea*. Washington, D.C.: Shearwater Books, 2007.

Safina, Carl. *Song for the Blue Ocean*. New York: Henry Holt, 1998.

Shubin, Neil. *Your Inner Fish*. New York: Vintage Books, 2009.

Smith, Martin Cruz. *Polar Star*. New York: Ballantine Books, 2007.

Sobel, Dava. *Longitude*. New York: Walker, 1995.

Sontag, Sherry, and Christopher Drew. *Blind Man's Bluff*. New York: Public Affairs, 1998.

Steinbeck, John. *Cannery Row*. New York: Penguin, 1992 (originally published in 1945).

Stewart, Frank, ed. *A World Between Waves*. Washington D.C.: Island Press, 1992.

Stone, Robert. *Outerbridge Reach*. New York: Ticknor & Fields, 1992.

Sullivan, Robert. *The Meadowlands*. New York: Scribner, 1998.

Theroux, Paul. *The Happy Isles of Oceana*. New York. Mariner Books, 2006.

Troll, Ray, and Brad Matsen. *Ray Troll's Shocking Fish Tales*. Anchorage, Alaska: Northwest Books, 1991.

Verne, Jules. *20,000 Leagues Under the Sea*. West Berlin, New Jersey: Townsend Press, 2007 (originally published in 1870).

Warner, William. *Beautiful Swimmers*. Boston: Little, Brown, 1976.

Woodard, Colin. *Ocean's End*. New York: Basic Books, 2000.

About the Author

David Helvarg is the executive director of Blue Frontier, an ocean conservation group, and the author of *Blue Frontier*, *The War Against the Greens*, *50 Ways to Save the Ocean*, *Rescue Warriors*, and *The Golden Shore*. He is the editor of *The Ocean and Coastal Conservation Guide*, organizer of Blue Vision Summits for ocean activists and the Peter Benchley Ocean Awards (cohosted with Wendy Benchley), and winner of *Coastal Living* magazine's 2005 Leadership Award and the 2007 Herman Melville Literary Prize. Helvarg has worked as a war correspondent in Northern Ireland and Central America, covered a range of issues from military science to the AIDS epidemic, and reported from every continent, including Antarctica. An award-winning journalist, he has produced more than forty broadcast documentaries for PBS, the Discovery Channel, and other organizations. His print work has appeared in the *New York Times*, the *Los Angeles Times*, *Smithsonian*, *National Geographic*, *Popular Science*, *Sierra*, and *Parade*. He has done radio work for Marketplace, AP radio, and Pacifica and led workshops for journalists in Poland, Turkey, Tunisia, Slovakia, and Washington, DC. He is a bodysurfer, scuba diver, and licensed private investigator.

www.bluefront.org